Nomad Girl

With very best wishes

Niema Ash

Keep on dancing

By the same author
Touching Tibet
Travels with My Daughter
Travels With Loreena McKennitt
Connecting Dors

Nomad Girl

My adventures with Bob Dylan,
Leonard Cohen, John Lee Hooker,
the Dalai Lama and more

Niema Ash

Matador
9 Priory Business Park,
Wistow Road, Kibworth Beauchamp,
Leicestershire. LE8 0RX
Tel: 0116 279 2299
Email: books@troubador.co.uk
Web: www.troubador.co.uk/matador
Twitter: @matadorbooks

ISBN 978 1838594 046

British Library Cataloguing in Publication Data.
A catalogue record for this book is available from the British Library.

Printed and bound in Great Britain by 4edge Limited
Typeset in 11pt Minion Pro by Troubador Publishing Ltd, Leicester, UK

Matador is an imprint of Troubador Publishing Ltd

For Shimon Ash
and
Ronit Corry

Contents

Part One
The Finjan

———

I

The Party

———————

M Y PHONE SAID 3.15 a.m. Everyone had left and I was putting the finishing touches to the clearing up. I hate waking to a mess – wine stains, sticky plates, soggy napkins. Better to clean up while still in the glow of party mode than in the harsh light of sobriety. Not that I had been drinking much. Actually, I had hardly been drinking at all, but I felt intoxicated – delightfully light-headed from all the laughing.

It had been one of those special nights when laughter just happens and becomes infectious. The party had been in its mellow moments. The wine bottles were almost empty. Only a few carrot and celery sticks remained from the bowls of crudités, the Japanese hot and cold delicacies were no more, the small pots of crème brulee were licked clean and the candles were burning low. We were laying back among the cushions in aftermath content when Irina, who had been sprawled on the living room floor, suddenly stood up, turned off the music and began enacting her latest adventure. With Russian passion enhanced by vignettes of mime, the exuberant fling of waist-length hair and the odd pelvic thrust, she began demonstrating how she had been belly-dancing on a table in Ramsgate's Belgian Bar, in protest at the substandard belly-dancing being performed on stage. She would show those excuse-for-belly-dancers what belly dancing was all about. But the excuse-for-belly-dancers were in no mood to be upstaged by a belly-dancer fundamentalist, and called the manager. The manager asked her to get off the table. When she refused, he called the police. By now we were hanging on every word.

The police made no pretence at niceties. One of the officers grabbed Irina's arm, not only pulling her off the table but gruffly escorting her out the door. Irina was scandalized. She was accustomed to only the most respectful, even adoring treatment from the male sex. Struggling to free herself and in a voice riddled with scorn she said, 'Sure, go ahead, push me around. That's what guys with small dicks do.'

The police were not amused. And, in the line of duty, had hardened their hearts, if not any other organ, undersized or otherwise, against the effects of chestnut hair with red gold flecks and astonishing sapphire eyes. Irina was handcuffed, bundled into a police van and taken to the nearest jail. There, she was locked into a police cell and handed over to a female officer to be strip-searched.

'Down to your underwear,' the officer instructed, handing Irina a prison uniform.

But Irina wasn't wearing underwear. And no way was she going to put on prison clothes.

She refused to undress. The officer, realizing she was no match for a Russian refusnick called for help. All hell broke loose as two policewomen wrestled Irina to the ground while a third forcibly removed her red gypsy dress and embroidered boots. Irina became a caged tigress. She kicked, she screamed, she cursed, she shouted obscenities. She created such havoc that several male officers rushed to the scene to prevent meltdown. As they burst into the cell, Irina jumped up, stark naked. Flushed with struggle, her hair wild, her eyes blazing, she raised her arms, spread her legs and thrust her hips forward: 'There, have a good look!'

We were all spellbound. That is, all except Mark, known intimately as Marky-Mark. Marky-Mark had been around the Irina block one time too many. She could no longer do anything that would faze him. His long-time exposure had created immunity. He was buried in his phone, seriously immersed in cyber space – not a laugh, not a giggle. He was deaf to the suspense, to the humour; blind to Irina's fascinating rendition. Then, suddenly, he interrupted the story, just like that – no apology, no by-your-leave – and in deadpan tones, said: 'Did anyone know that the female kangaroo has three vaginas and the male has a two-pronged penis to accommodate her?'

That gem of information was so dazzling and the juxtaposition so off the wall that even Irina, who was in the throes of resisting arrest, abandoned her story – police brutality being unable to compete with three vaginas and a two-pronged penis. Comments from left field followed.

Tamar: 'A two-pronged penis? Does that mean one vagina gets left out?'

Peter: 'Perhaps there's a rotation system, a vagina-in-waiting list.'

Claire: 'I could do with two vaginas, it would give one a bit of recovery time.'

My stomach ached from laughing.

I was on automatic with the washing-up, conjuring up remnants of the hilarious banter, knowing it wouldn't be that funny next day.

I jumped when I heard the phone ring putting both Irina's insurgency and the kangaroo's sexual prowess on hold. It was after 3 am. Who could be calling at that hour?

It was Ronit. My heart sank. She was aware how late it was in England, eight hours ahead of Santa Barbara. I braced myself for the bad news.

'Don't worry, Mum, nothing's wrong.' She knew my anxieties. 'I'm so excited, I just had to tell you even if it meant waking you up. You'll love this.'

'Tell me what?' Curiosity replaced anxiety. What could be so important that it couldn't wait until morning, I wondered.

'Dad just phoned. There's a new CD out called *Bob Dylan at the Finjan Club*. He said it's the hottest bootleg around.'

'Bob Dylan at the Finjan Club!' The words were like gold. I forgot the party. I forgot the clearing up. I even forgot the kangaroos. Ronit knew what information couldn't wait until morning.

I was too excited to sleep, and before the sun was up I had ordered a copy of the CD. A few days later, before I was fully awake, the doorbell rang. I opened the door just a crack. 'Delivery!' I swung the door open, suddenly entirely awake. Although I instantly knew what it was, I turned the package over and over again, inspecting the label, examining the postage, lingering over the return address. I was holding in my hands a small miracle packaged in brown wrapping paper and ink stained tape, the opportunity to relive a treasured experience resurrected from the distant past. I needed time to be ready for it. And there it was. BOB DYLAN FINJAN CLUB, a recording of that night when Dylan had performed at the Finjan. I listened to it over and over, remembering every detail; how Dylan had looked, how he had played, how the audience had disappointed him, and especially remembering what happened after his performance. For the memory of that night was the kind of memory that shines through a lifetime.

Then I read the liner notes. There was something about the Finjan, a little about my former partner Shimon, even a mention of me. However, it was obvious that whoever wrote the notes had never been to the Finjan. And it suddenly occurred to me: I had not only been there, the Finjan was a fundamental part of my coming of age, even part of my DNA. Finjan memories were so indelibly inscribed on my psyche I conjured them up even when I didn't try. They had no regard for space or time because they lived within me and were as vivid now in London, as they were all those years ago in Montreal. And, after all, I was a writer. Why didn't I write about the Finjan days, about the musicians, about my experiences with them? And so it was.

2

In the Beginning

———————

I T ALL BEGAN IN the sixties, 'the decade that wanted to change the world' – and it did: a time of exuberant happenings, of overflowing optimism; a time when the dams of convention were beginning to open and the changing times flooding in, defiant, liberating, a time when bras were discarded and draft cards burned; when girls wore flowers in their hair and, with sweet smiles, offered them to soldiers to adorn their guns; a time of overt sensuality, when males had hair you could run your fingers through; when clothes were unconstrained, with tiny waists and tight skirts giving way to long flowing dresses, collars and ties to colourful scarves; a time when women proudly displayed their pregnant bellies and men were allowed to cry; a time when 'swords were beaten into ploughshares and spears into pruning hooks,' when peace was the question and love the answer; when songs proclaimed: 'We ain't going to study war no more' and 'Love is all you ever need.'

It was my time.

It was in the cradle of this time that the Finjan was born. It happened almost by chance. I had just returned to Montreal with my partner Shimon, because I was seriously pregnant – another chance happening – and we needed somewhere to have the baby. We had met in Israel and embarked on a hitchhiking adventure through east Africa to South Africa, Shimon's birthplace, a prelude to launching ourselves into the wonder of travelling the world, which had been my driving passion for as long as I could remember.

The question 'what do you want to be when you grow up?' troubled my childhood. I had no answer. The suggestions on offer – nurse, teacher, hairdresser – were firmly ruled out. They lit no spark in an imagination nourished on the excitement of the yellow brick road and the adventures of Peter Pan.

Then, when I was about eight, I read a story about a nomad boy who lived in the desert. He lived in a place called an oasis and had many wonderful adventures. His life was filled with adventure and magic, because he didn't have to stay in just the one oasis but moved from oasis to oasis. Each oasis was different and exciting and when he got tired of one, he just moved on to another and made new friends and had new adventures. Discovering that nomad boy, that story, was like finding the pot of gold at the end of the rainbow. Suddenly I had the answer. I would be a nomad girl. I would stay in one place until the adventure ran out and then go to a new place where another adventure would begin.

I began to dream about being a nomad girl. I knew there were many requirements that were unavailable to me, like a desert and an oasis, but that didn't deter me. Over time the story faded but the dream remained and acquired more definition, as I grew older. By the time I was a teenager, I had worked out the perplexing knots in my dream. The world would be my desert. I would travel the world and wherever I stayed would be my oasis. And suddenly the dream unfolded like a map, laying out before me a vision of my life. And so it was.

**

Since early adolescence maps had been my pin-ups. Maps of the world papered my walls: they were an endless fascination, a magnet for my fantasies. I wanted to know the world. Whereas my friends were intrigued by names like Elvis Presley, James Dean, Marlon Brando, I was intrigued by names like Tanganyika, Kalahari, Botswana, Swaziland, Mozambique; names I caressed on a large global lamp that glowed in the dark, adding to their seductive power. I knew that one day I would see with my eyes the places I had touched with my fingers. And when that day finally arrived, I was ready for it.

Actually, by then several appetizers had already whetted my appetite for travel. When I was fifteen I travelled from Montreal, where I was born and grew up, to New York with a friend and had a wonderfully exciting time. And, at sixteen two friends and I bussed and hitchhiked across the US into Mexico, a difficult journey at times, but one filled with adventure.

In Mexico we had one of those travel experiences that make it all worthwhile. Through cheekiness and outrageous fabrication, we got to meet the famous Mexican artist Diego Rivera. Diego Rivera was not only one of my favourite artists, but I admired the revolutionary principals he stood for. I had read 'I Paint What I See', the poem about Rivera written by E. W. White, and become a devotee. Seeing a Diego Rivera mural was one of my main Mexican ambitions.

When we finally got to Mexico City, the first thing I did was to locate one of his most famous murals and we trudged through the streets of the city, frequently losing our way, to see it. However, to my fierce disappointment, the building housing the mural was closed because the master himself was repairing it. It was not only closed, it was cordoned off, with guards standing at the entrance to prevent the people gathered outside from entering. But I was determined to see the mural, and knowing that Diego Rivera was within reach, even more determined to see him.

My father's motto was, 'always be prepared for the best' and he had instilled in me the idea that if you want something enough, just go for it. And I went for it. Having read somewhere that Diego Rivera was a friend of Henry Ford and had painted a mural for him in Detroit, I wrote a note addressed to the artist, saying I was from Detroit and knew Mr Ford, and that Henry had told me so much about this particular mural that I had made a special trip to see it.

I dispatched the note with a reluctant guard who was loath to disturb the master and required both threats and cajoling to do so. My friends stuck by me although not entirely happy with my tactics. Meanwhile a group of people had gathered around us, curious about this somewhat dishevelled trio, dressed in flamboyant colours, and even more curious about my rather lively discussion with the guards, and we waited nervously, dreading imminent public humiliation. However, instead of exposing us as frauds, Diego Rivera stopped work on the mural and invited us in. The doors to heaven had opened.

Rivera made us feel instantly at ease with his good humour and easy laughter. When we confessed our deception, instead of being annoyed, he laughed a large, belly laugh, slapping his thigh in delight, as though in praise of our ploy. I remember feeling so comfortable with him that I cheekily asked how an ardent communist like himself got to be friends with an arch capitalist like Henry Ford.

'It's for insurance,' he shrugged. 'When the revolution comes he wants to have a friend on our side, in case we win. And in case we lose, it's good to have a friend on the other side. No?' His ample face crumpled into smiles.

'Yes,' I agreed.

Usually not one for good sense, I somehow had the good sense to leave while we were ahead, even though I longed to stay, and he had offered tea. He hugged us goodbye with kisses on both cheeks.

That incredible experience with Diego Rivera fortified my nomad aspirations, and the travel plan I later made with Shimon cemented it.

***

The plan which I had enthusiastically conceived about three years after the Mexican adventure, had been to begin our African journey by flying from Tel Aviv to Nairobi, where we would visit his sister and her family before hitchhiking to Johannesburg. From there we would travel the world, from oasis to oasis, working whenever we ran out of money, basking in adventure and moving on when the adventure ran out. Shimon was far less enthusiastic about the long-term aspect of the plan, but if he was able bring his guitar he could live with it

This plan had significant advantages. We would not only be able to spend time with Shimon's family – he had six older sisters: two in Nairobi, four in Johannesburg – but earn money to fund onward travels. Shimon's parents had come from Eastern Europe early in the 20th century, to escape the horrors of growing anti-Semitism. Hoping to go to the US, they had somehow ended up in a god forsaken part of South Africa, a semi desert called the Karoo, more hospitable to sheep than to people, in a small town called Willomore, populated by Afrikaner sheep farmers, descendants of the original Dutch settlers. Because they were not English, whom the Afrikaners hated, they were welcomed into the community, learned Afrikaans and became sheep farmers. They had six daughters and two sons, Shimon being the youngest, (he said he had seven mothers) all brought up speaking only Afrikaans. Although the work was hard, and their backgrounds, culture, and religion vastly different, the family enjoyed life with no discrimination, with respect, and even with a modicum of popularity. Shimon's father who had been a cantor, had a golden voice, and became a soloist in the town's choir. However, when the daughters were reaching marriageable age, his father moved the family to Johannesburg to enable the girls to learn English and find husbands who were more culturally suitable. Shimon spoke no English until he was eleven years old.

For me, hitchhiking through east Africa would be a major blessing. It would unlock the mystery of places I had only been able to imagine and allow me, however briefly, to enter their domain. However, unlocking the mystery was to result in a series of surprising events, one of which was to change my life.

The fact that there were no roads in most of east Africa – only dirt tracks riddled with potholes – or, for days on end, nowhere to buy food or find a bed, was not something we had taken into consideration. It was not surprising, therefore, that several weeks later, when we reached the civilization of Dodoma, Tanganyika, now Tanzania, we splurged on the luxuries of Hotel Dodoma. These included a bedroom with a four-poster bed, silk sheets and a mosquito net. The contrast with nights cramped in vehicles, on the floor of wooden shacks, under trees or in ditches and gullies, was so intoxicating that I became pregnant. However, that fact did not reveal itself until we reached Johannesburg, six weeks later.

For me, having a baby was an alien concept. Going to Mars was more of a consideration. I wanted only to travel, to experience the universe, to be that nomad girl I had dreamed about for so long. I had begun travelling at age fourteen and by eighteen was already a veteran. Music and dance were the threads that held my life together and travel was its embroidered tapestry. I wanted to be the ultimate wild child, the adventurous nomad girl – happy, young. And a baby meant old.

Travel was my high. I was not interested in drugs or alcohol. Drugs were not in my vocabulary and neither Shimon nor I was into alcohol. Much later when we were in Spain, on the rare occasion we went to a restaurant for dinner, we would leave the bottle of wine that accompanied the meal untouched, even though it was free. This had nothing to do with being pregnant, a condition I was intent on disregarding.

I had never developed a taste for alcohol, which had been a great disappointment to my father. Since the age of 10, he had been preparing me for adulthood by giving me small quantities of hard liquor. 'So you'll know how to take a drink when you're out with a man. You won't be a sissy,' he'd say. 'I want you to know how to handle your liquor.' My father was known as Pistol Pete, to his friends, although not to my mother, who disliked the name. She called him Jack, the name on his birth certificate, as did close family members. For even though he had cultivated a tough guy image, the family knew him as a gentle loving man. However, years later, shortly after he had passed away, I did find a pistol, with a beautiful pearl handle among his belongings. I adored Pistol Pete but, his world was something I knew little about, except that it didn't tolerate sissies. I had forced the drink down like taking medicine, because I loved my father and wanted to please him. However, his good intentions had worked in mysterious ways. As an adult I disliked even the smell of anything alcoholic. I hardly ever drank. Unwittingly, I was doing something right for the helpless foetus, thanks to Pistol Pete.

But, like it or not, after the Tanganyika indulgence, I was forced to stay pregnant. Only witch doctors performed abortions in Johannesburg. This meant either abandoning our travel plans, which was akin to killing the thing I loved, the thing I had nurtured since childhood, or ignoring the pregnancy, secretly hoping it would go away so we could carry on. I convinced a reluctant Shimon to adopt the latter option.

In the end, we spent three months in Johannesburg, a longish-stay oasis, working, visiting innumerable relatives and hating apartheid. That is, I was working. I had found a job stuffing envelopes and filing papers, which paid good money but which I couldn't wait to leave. I could deal with the boredom of the work because I knew it was temporary. But I couldn't deal with the constant grumble of the other female employees, who spent most of the time complaining about their 'schwarzes', their black servants, because that was not temporary. It was too close a brush with apartheid and I loathed it.

While I was working, Shimon was perfecting his guitar playing and learning new songs, which I listened to with increasing admiration. He not only had a beautiful voice – rich and plaintive, inherited from his cantor father – but his guitar playing had escalated from amateur strumming to sophisticated picking and plucking. He had even bought one of those metal things professionals wore on their fingers and also something which looked like a lady's garter, called a 'capo'. All very impressive.

However, after three months the oasis had dried up. I could not only hear the road calling, I could hear it howling. By now we had saved enough money, eaten enough dinners and attended enough celebrations. It was time to move on. I had grown fond of Shimon's family and they of me. Although they considered me somewhat of a weirdo who spoke a foreign language –English, but with a Canadian accent so unlike their Afrikaans twang – and who not only ate the unthinkable – Chinese food – but who did the unthinkable – walked the streets after dark and pursued

African music and dance – they forgave me all eccentricities. Word had escaped I was pregnant and everyone knew pregnant women had strange cravings that had to be indulged. I was especially sorry to leave Florrie, the sister we had been staying with, who had been kind and gracious and who didn't burst out laughing every time I said 'banana', or 'eh?', but I wasn't sorry to be leaving Johannesburg and delighted to be heading for the road.

We hitchhiked from Johannesburg to Cape Town. Although the trip was less than a thousand miles, it took us five days. Shimon had wanted to visit his birthplace, Willowmore, in the desolate depths of the Karoo, where hitch hikers were a foreign specie, not to be trusted, and certainly not to be given rides. Although we ended up walking for miles, we found ourselves in the same forbidding landscape. Even the few lifts we got dropped us in the middle of nothing and nowhere.

Although it was summer in most civilized parts of the world, it was winter in the Karoo. We spent several nights sleeping in gullies under bridges to shelter from the bitter wind, sharing the space with tramps who accepted us as one of their own. This wasn't surprising as we looked like one of their own, only more dishevelled and unkempt, and with strange swellings, the result of wearing all the clothing we possessed to keep from freezing. Our only consolation was that our knapsacks were easier to carry. Willowmore was a great disappointment to Shimon. It was much smaller than he remembered, and much colder. A highway now ran through the town and its few streets were cluttered with antique shops, coffee shops, rooms to let, and tourist paraphernalia. He wanted to leave almost as soon as we arrived so that he could preserve the happy memories of the past without having them destroyed by the reality of the present.

Cape Town somewhat redeemed South Africa. It was a soft city. Not only was it stunning looking but gentler than Johannesburg, which had been riddled with anger, prejudice, hostility and heartless behaviour. Apartheid seemed less entrenched in Cape Town, 'Whites Only' signs less evident. Johannesburg had seemed like an ingrown toenail, digging deeper and deeper into itself: self-obsessed, introverted, and shut off from the world. It was not a destination for visitors. Cape Town, on the other hand, being surrounded by the sea, looked out into the world. Ships coming and going brought a variety of visitors, a variety of influences. Besides, Cape Town was warmer.

From Cape Town, we sailed to the Canary Islands because I wanted to hear Flamenco music and see volcanoes. Both Shimon and I were delighted to see the back of South Africa. Apartheid had not been an easy thing to live with. It had spoiled anything good we had experienced. Besides we were booked on a luxury liner, a gift from his family, a wonderful contrast to the rough times on the road and the uncertainty of everything. Even though I loved the adventure of that roughness and uncertainty, I was not averse to a spot of luxury and a dollop of security. A luxury liner was just the ticket.

After several weeks in the Canaries that included an abundance of Flamenco but a dearth of volcanoes, we bought third-class tickets on a small elderly ship going to Malaga. Up to that point I had forgotten I was pregnant. My body had always been a good friend and pregnancy seemed to enhance the friendship. There was nothing to remind me: not sleeping rough, not walking for miles, not eating mainly bread and cheese to save money. However, being confined to the hold of a ship, shared with bedbugs, garlic sausages and crying babies refreshed my memory. That memory became etched in blood when the ship began tearing itself apart in a sudden violent storm.

Everyone was sick. The smell of diesel fumes combined with vomit was brutal. I had to force myself to breathe and then not to breathe. Shimon carried me to the tiny, first-class wooden deck, which was forbidden to third-class passengers, to keep me alive. After depositing me on the floor with nothing but a beer can filled with water and a few hippie shawls, he slipped away surreptitiously in case he was ordered to dispose of me somewhere else. However, he made furtive visits under cover of night to see if I was still alive. Fortunately, no one else braved that postage-sized excuse for a deck and I was allowed to suffer without interruption.

Although terminally nauseous and unable to eat, I couldn't stop the violent retching. My guts were tearing themselves apart. Shimon had searched for a doctor or a nurse, fearing the worst. He had been unable to find so much as a first aid kit or anyone who spoke English. I thought I was dying and didn't much care. But somehow, mercifully, miraculously, both mother and foetus survived. And even more mercifully, more miraculously, I was completely recovered only hours after setting foot on dry land. Life has a way of asserting its presence.

Spain was a treasure chest of Flamenco music and dance. Besides it was cheap, a huge bonus. I loved Spain, the Alhambra, the gypsies, the old part of Seville, the wide tree-lined avenues, the unfamiliarity with everything: architecture, people, language, tapas for breakfast, dinner at ten at night, all of them together. It was a great adventure, the very stuff of my nomad dreams, a perfect oasis. Shimon had to drag me away with stark reminders that time wasn't on the side of unlimited travel.

After a month, we took to the road again, hitchhiking through Spain, to France and then to England. We stopped wherever we chose, we stayed however long we liked; me basking in the wonder of travel, the joy of waking each morning to new possibilities; Shimon, getting a bit frayed around the edges, with creeping signs of wear and tear, which I did my best to ignore. I thought the plan was working beautifully. Although the pregnancy didn't go away, it was hardly noticeable and no hindrance to the adventure. I gave it no heed. That is, until the persistent kicking and sudden belly expansion forced me to acknowledge that not only was I actually going to have a baby, but that the event was imminent.

There was no longer an option. The plan had to be abandoned. I was bereft, but Shimon was not-so-secretly relieved. Whereas travelling filled me with energy, excitement, exhilaration and a thousand miraculous moments, he was fed up with sleeping rough, eating only grapes two days a week to conserve funds and standing on the road sometimes for hours waiting for a lift. It had been far easier hitchhiking in east Africa where we were considered explorers, in the tradition of Livingstone, instead of bums, even beggars. Sometimes, while waiting for a lift, Shimon would practise some difficult chords on the guitar – he was always refining his playing – and people would fling a few coins our way with expressions of pity. Once someone offered us hardboiled eggs. It wasn't exactly dignified.

Abandoning the plan gave rise to a new dilemma: we had to find somewhere to go, somewhere to have this baby, a baby-friendly oasis. It's not that I hadn't considered this possibility before, but I had brushed it aside in favour of more immediate concerns, like finding some place to spend the night with access to a decent loo, the smell of which didn't make me retch – I had developed an acute sensitivity to smell after the ship incident. Since we had no fixed address – the idea of 'settling down' had filled me with horror – there was no choice but to opt for Montreal, where I was from. At least I had parents in Montreal who, by the way, were delighted that their wayward daughter was coming home – and not only with a partner but with a soon-to-be baby. I could almost feel Pistol Pete's elation and my mother's ecstasy. Besides, I had to admit, it would be wonderful to see them. I consoled myself by thinking Montreal would be a temporary oasis. We would stay just long enough to spend time with my parents, visit friends, replenish resources, and then move on.

***

My older brother, Arthur, had always been closer to my mother, Rose. (There were only the two of us, a third sibling having died when he was nine months.) I didn't mind because they were into first-class everything – clothes, travel, food, cars, appearance, everything – and I wasn't. I was Pistol Pete's girl. He didn't care that I refused to wear lipstick or how long my hair was. I loved long hair whereas Rose hated it. Besides, my father supported whatever I wanted to do, whereas she preferred the occasional boundary.

Both my parents were exceedingly open-minded and liberal, allowing me freedoms that were an anathema to my friend's parents. My parents, unlike theirs, shunned the Protestant ethic of hard work and limited pleasures. They thrived on pleasure and encouraged my brother and myself to enjoy life, rather than endure it. They were certainly not remiss about our wellbeing, on the contrary, our emotional and physical health, was of paramount concern. And, most important, they wanted us to know that their support was something we could always rely on. When I was fifteen, I remember my mother saying to me, 'I know you have enough sense not to let this happen, but if you ever became pregnant, don't do anything foolish, just come to us and we'll take care of it.' This was in Catholic Quebec, where abortion was not only a heinous sin, but a criminal offence.

Before I was sixteen, I had taken a bus to New York with a friend to visit an unknown pen pal, an all-night journey, not only didn't my parents disapprove, my father took us to the bus station to accommodate our journey. And, as we mounted the bus, I saw him slip the driver some money and heard him say, 'That's my girl, take good care of her and her friend.' Pistol Pete was a big tipper. Not only was he dedicated to tipping, but to tipping in advance of the actual service. We often went to restaurants for dinner and as soon as we had occupied our table, he tipped the waiter. Even as a pre-teen I was aware that the waiter's radiant smile reflected the size of the tip. 'You get better service that way,' he said, and we did. Returning home to Pistol Pete and Rose grew more enticing the more I considered it. There were, after all, many advantages, the major one being the assurance of love.

Rose and Pistol Pete not only loved us, they loved each other. Outwardly, Pistol Pet was a man's man, not especially tall, but all muscle, lean, hard, tough. But he had a loving heart and exuded affection. And oh how he loved his Rosie. 'My Rose', he called her. And although she was often spikey and impatient with him, being more driven than he was; he had unlimited patience with her. His reply when she was angrily complaining about something or other, was to say, 'Oh My Rose, never mind about that, it's not worth fretting over,' and take her in his arms. Rose melted into his love and the anger was quelled. When he died in his early sixties, she was still in her fifties, attractive, vibrant. Men were drawn to her, but she was quick to rebuff any suitor. She wanted only Pistol Pete. 'One life, one man,' she would say. But for me it was obvious, no man could match Pistol Pete. He was a one off.

***

Nevertheless, the decision to end our travels at this point, even briefly, left me inconsolable, hopeless, visualizing a life of sameness and routine. It would mean the death of adventure, the death of the nomad girl. However, it left Shimon with renewed vitality and unlimited hope. While my dream of travelling the world was temporarily in tatters, Shimon's dream of carving out a bit of stability, a small space in the universe where he could play his guitar, where one day he might even become a performer, was approaching reality. My sky had fallen. But a tiny diamond shone in Shimon's sky.

We spent our last money on the cheapest transportation available – third-class passage on a ship to Montreal. We were an implausible couple walking the gangplank – a tall, lean guitar-playing folk singer, longing for somewhere to stay, and a small, very pregnant, quasi dancer, longing for somewhere to go; a penniless duo with no home, no money, and about to become parents. But we had one thing in common, one very special thing; one thing that would fulfil our disparate needs, our disparate desires and which was about to change our lives: the Finjan.

3

The Birth

A s soon as we set foot in Montreal, I found myself
the leading lady in a theatrical production called
'Childbirth', a blockbuster epic with a cast of thousands. I
became stricken with anxiety. Not only hadn't I rehearsed my
lines, I hadn't even read the script. I was suddenly engulfed
in a full-time production, with a troupe of relatives – aunts,
nieces, cousins and, of course, my mother – who felt it their
duty to get me up to speed for the imminent performance,
with an arsenal of reprimands, advice, must-do's, tales of
woe, laying on of guilt and chilling warnings. Reviews were
held concerning my body. My skin was a bit dry; my ankles
were a bit swollen; my hips were a bit narrow; my belly bulge
was either a bit too high or a bit too low – no agreement on
that score. It seemed to me my body was being dissected and
I wasn't even dead.

All this interest in my 'condition' came as no surprise. I came from a large, close, intense family. It had been wonderful growing up in its folds. Every summer, we all went to a sort-of communal farm, owned by all of us and managed by one of my aunts. Each family had its own living quarters, but we kids treated all of them as our own. The farm had chickens and cows and even a goat. It also had a 'haunted house', a grand old relic hidden by neglected shrubbery and allowed to deteriorate undisturbed. It had once been owned by a wealthy farmer and still held remnants of its former glory: broken chandeliers, cracked hand-painted tiles, carved bedposts. We invented scary stories about its secret passageways and dank cellars, and loved to shiver with delicious fright as we dared each other to explore its inner sanctums, curtained by spider webs and teeming with creepy crawlies.

But, best of all, the farm was on a river in which my cousins and I wanted to spend the rest of our lives. We had to be dragged out of the water to be force-fed and only agreed to come out voluntarily when we were turning blue. The river was our playground: we swam; threw balls, hoops and Frisbees; we did backward summersaults; and we played tricks on people. Our main prop was an old rowboat and one of our favourite tricks was toppling the boat and diving under it, treading water and surviving secretly in the air space under the boat, while people on shore panicked.

We never tired of waiting for some poor unsuspecting soul to come to the river for a swim. We would then shout: 'Watch this!' Pretending to perform some spectacular water act, we would hold hands and bow, like in the circus, then dive into the water and disappear. The victim's hair would turn grey with anxiety, fearing we had drowned, while we thrilled with excitement in our secret hideaway, emerging just as the innocent bystander was desperately trying to recall life-saving techniques.

We spent hours under the boat, exchanging secrets; practising skills, like holding our breath until our lungs caved in; and planning the rest of our lives. My favourite cousin, Hershey, and I exchanged marriage vows under the boat, deciding where we would live and how many dogs we would have. I was just getting into the global map phase and thought Mozambique sounded promising, but he voted for Montreal. Somewhat disappointing. We also planned our careers. He would be a bandleader – he could already play *Come back to Sorrento* on the harmonica – and I would be a dancer, as soon as my mother bought me pink ballet slippers. Although I wasn't into girly things, I made an exception for pink ballet slippers.

I didn't return to the farm until Ronit was about eight. I had told her so much about it that she was eager to see it. By this time my aunt who had run the farm had died and the farm had been sold. Like Shimon, when he had revisited Willowmore, the experience was hugely disappointing. What had seemed so vast and exciting in my childhood, now seemed cramped and shabby. Everything was suffering from neglect; faded, cracked, withering; and, worst of all, the haunted house was no more. Vanished. Like Shimon, I couldn't wait to leave, anxious to blot out the 'now' in order to preserve the 'then'.

But back in those halcyon days, we had lots of mothers, lots of homes, lots of fun and, most important, lots of love. And I had the bonus of Pistol Pete, who thought I could do no wrong and I rode on his shoulders, like an adored princess, the envy of my universe. However, what we didn't have, and which became increasingly important as we grew older, was lots of privacy. Our business was everyone's business and could be approved, criticized or even condemned. It was this other side of the coin that I was struggling with now, on my return from the recklessness of the road.

The overwhelming vote in my pregnancy case was condemnation, albeit tinged with a modicum of forgiveness on account of ignorance and inexperience, championed by my father and, less enthusiastically, seconded by my mother. What had been a warm embrace in childhood became a bear hug in adolescence. And now, as an adult, I was squirming for release, but for the sake of all that past affection, I had to submit. I put myself in the hands of 'those who knew best' – an all-female consortium. Although my father and brother were eager to offer me support, this was exclusively female territory in which they didn't dare set even a toe. Even Pistol Pete, knew not to mess with the dark mysteries of the 'female condition'. I was abandoned to the experts.

The first obligatory prerequisite for my new role was an urgent appointment with an obstetrician. After my initial visit to the doctor back in South Africa, when my pregnancy was confirmed, I hadn't consulted the medical profession even once. When I admitted this to the coven of concerned females, the admission was greeted with shock and awe. The red alarm blared. There was an immediate swinging-into-action. An obstetrician had to be selected immediately, if not sooner. This necessitated references, phone calls, recommendations, private consultations – it seemed more complicated than selecting the Pope but, then again, he wasn't pregnant. I had no involvement in this part of the drama. As a matter of fact, little of this pregnancy had anything to do with me. It was obvious I couldn't be trusted with my own body; my record so far had been one of dismal incompetence. I did insist, however, that I visit the doctor accompanied only by Shimon. Even this minor concession created such fallout that several people abandoned the ship. But they were mostly second cousins and third aunts and not part of the hard core.

Shimon was not allowed into the examination room; he was confined to the waiting room. I had been warned to expect well-deserved castigation from the doctor because of my reckless behaviour. Stepping into his surgery felt like entering a battle zone without a single ally and with no ammunition. When I confessed to the obstetrician that I had been without medical attention or advice throughout my pregnancy, I could feel the axe poised above my head.

He drew his eyebrows tight, sucked in his lower lip and with utter lack of comprehension, as though I had informed him that I had just come from a walk on the moon, he said, 'You're telling me you haven't had regular check-ups, you haven't taken any vitamins or supplements and you haven't attended a single pre-natal class?'

The axe was about to fall.

'You see, I was travelling,' I said weakly, apologetically, 'and going from country to country.'

'Going from country to country...' he repeated slowly, making an effort to understand, as though I was speaking a foreign language, and although he understood the words, he was unable to grasp their meaning. He remained silent for a moment, while the axe grazed the back of my neck. Then, mercifully, almost kindly, he pronounced the verdict: 'Well then, let's assess the damage.'

Actually I *had* made one concession to pregnancy while in South Africa, but I didn't dare admit this to him, it seemed so paltry, so insignificant when weighed against my transgressions. Besides, I didn't dare evoke his displeasure in case he disapproved. I had bought a book on natural childbirth by Dr Grantly Dick-Read, a British doctor, who had lived in South Africa. Natural childbirth was considered primitive, even uncivilized, at the time. The main facts I had gleaned from Dr Dick-Read was, one, that having a baby didn't hurt if you did it right – after all, women did it all by themselves in the middle of fields – and two, that grapes were good for pregnant women. Promising myself that I would *do it right* – although I was doubtful about the fields – and eat lots of grapes, I had put the entire matter out of my head and gone on to enjoy myself, which now seemed like the mother of all abominations.

After an extensive examination, where I feared the worst as retribution for my outrageous ways, the doctor said, almost in disbelief: 'Well, you and the baby seem to be fine, no problems at all.' I had a sneaking suspicion he was a little disappointed, but just a little. Mainly, he was baffled but intrigued. After all, the entire medical profession could be on trial. He shrugged his shoulders in a 'there's-no-accounting-for-providence' sort of way. Then he shook my hand and gave me a fatherly pat on the back, in a congratulatory sort of way. I almost got on my knees and kissed his feet, but the weight of my protruding belly dissuaded me. I had escaped without even a crumb of condemnation. I couldn't wait to tell that to the coven!

Summoning Shimon into his office, he said: 'You have both been very fortunate, but don't press your luck.' And addressing Shimon, he added: 'Make sure she takes care of herself; giving birth is a serious business and needs serious attention.' Shimon nodded in agreement, relieved that he was not being accused of aiding and abetting. I was then handed about 25 pamphlets and a long list of things to swallow, things to drink, things to eat, exercises to perform and a long list of things not to drink, things not to eat, exercises not to perform and booked for another appointment only days away. We were now in the final stretch and I wasn't ahead.

Grateful that the visit had ended without tears, I left the doctor's office with new confidence and new affirmations. I would take more control over what was to happen and read everything I could lay my hands on. I would attend pre-natal classes every single day to make up for lost time. I even made a secret vow: I would redeem myself to myself, to the doctor, to everyone concerned, especially my parents, and most important, to the unborn baby, by following the doctor's orders to the letter.

I would honour the pregnancy and the birth. And, hardest of all, I would put my nomad aspirations on hold.

In accordance with this vow, I was determined to have natural childbirth, the major tenet Dr Dick-Read championed in his book. I would not harm the baby with drugs and medications, which he warned against. I would also breast feed to give the baby the best start in life, another one of Dr Dick-Read's main doctrines. Both practices, if not exactly frowned upon, were not the prevailing fashion and sure to cause dispute – bottle-feeding and numbing injections being much in vogue. But I would hold my ground.

**

Three weeks later, in a strategically-placed mirror hanging somewhere above the operating table I was lying on, legs forced apart by metal stirrups, I watched my baby being born. Shimon wasn't allowed in the delivery room and I felt abandoned and alone. Ironically, although I was the centre of attention, I was virtually ignored by the hospital staff, who were busy with more important concerns. I could hear their crisp, one-word utterances: 'dilation', 'uterus', 'diaphragm', 'placenta'. But it was as though none of these were related to me.

It was disorientating having to look up toward the mirror to see something happening down inside myself, while glaring lights distorted my vision and brutal, spasmodic thrusts contorted my womb. The pain was especially cruel because I hadn't anticipated its intensity. But the only time I cried out was in protest to doctor Dick-Read. 'Damn Doctor Read,' I wailed, 'He betrayed us. This hurts!'

Engrossed in mastering a body in chaos, I was suddenly aware of a gentle, cajoling voice nuzzling my ear and a hand soothing my forehead. I looked up into the pained eyes of a young intern bending over me, coaxing me into accepting whiffs of gas to ease the pain. I pressed my hand into his with the intensity of a new lover, but refused the gas – losing consciousness was even more frightening than giving birth. Besides, although Dr Dick-Read had been disloyal to me, I would not be disloyal to him. No gas.

Heaving and panting, I strained to eject the foreign presence trapped in my womb, while a disembodied voice I recognized as the doctor's urged me to 'keep pushing' and the intern's fingers gripped mine, offering the only comfort.

'Can you see the head?' the voice asked, interrupting the 'keep pushing' mantra.

'No...' my voice scratched through an arid mouth.

'It's right here.' A finger flashed into view in the mirror and disappeared.

'I can't see it,' I moaned, my muddled brain straining to comprehend the fragmented images in the mirror, through a haze of pain and excitement.

'What do you mean you can't see it – the head is out, can't you see the hair?'

But, in my confusion, I had mistaken the dark patch of fluff for my own pubic hair, forgetting I had been shaved.

'Keep pushing, it won't be long.'

'I see it now," I said with exhilaration and relief as a small dark fuzzy orb appeared in the mirror, balancing in space.

'Push hard. It's almost over...'

Then suddenly through the searing pain, a large fleshy lump, raw and bloody, slid into view.

Minutes later, the doctor gently placed it on my belly, umbilical cord still uncut. But it was no longer an amorphous lump. It had become a glistening, beautifully formed baby, like a rubber doll I had as a child, with succulently curved arms and legs. Except, instead of pink, it was entirely purple. Suddenly, I felt like the leading lady in a gala performance that had been

handed a beautiful bouquet of flowers after the final curtain call.
'It's a girl,' the doctor said. I hadn't thought to ask.
'Congratulations!'

'But you told me I was going to have a boy,' I said confused.

'Never believe what I say,' he laughed.

I put my hand on my baby's head and ran my fingers over her body. Then I smiled and closed my eyes against the wonder, the dire exhaustion and the intense satisfaction. I now had a baby. The mystery was overwhelming.

***

I was astonished to see how lovely Ronit was when the nurse brought her for her first feed. She was a true joy (Ronit, being an Israeli name, the feminine of Ron, which means joy). Although I had promised myself to love her anyway, I thought she would be bald and wrinkled. Through some magical metamorphosis, the shapeless lump in the mirror had changed into a beautiful baby. She had a full head of black hair, creamy white skin and large dark eyes. I gazed at her with the same wonder I had watched nasty-looking eggs, splattered with muck, turn into fluffy yellow chicks, back in the farm days. Next day, the young nurse on duty tied Ronit's hair with a red ribbon and asked if she could show the baby to her boyfriend.

'Just to prod him a little,' she explained. She planned on enticing him with a state-of-the-art product.

Each time Ronit was brought for her feeding, the nurse closed the curtain surrounding my bed so as not to offend the other mothers, none of whom were breast-feeding.

'The sight might be a little repulsive to them,' she explained. 'Mind you, I think it's a good thing,' she added quickly, dodging the daggers darting from my eyes. 'Cow's milk is for calves, mother's milk is for babies. But then, they don't see it like that.'

'Well I do!' I said with my newfound assurance. And that was that.

The adventure of the birth was over, but the next big adventure would soon begin...

4

Motherhood

SOMETIMES, WHEN WE THINK the worst possible thing has
occurred and life is no longer worth living, circumstances
do some unpredictable manoeuvring and suddenly that which
was conceived as the end to all happiness, turns out to be the
ultimate happiness scenario. In my case, although there were a
few twists and turns along the way, and a few hurdles to jump,
that is exactly what happened. Although I felt as if I had been
forced to abandon the universe, the universe hadn't abandoned
me.

When we had returned to Montreal, Pistol Pete – although
not at the height of his good fortune – was able to offer modest
assistance. Whereas in the past I had refused any help from
him in a bid for independence, this time I could not afford that
luxury. After staying with my parents for the first few months,
we accepted a small loan that made it possible to rent a little

one-bedroom apartment close to them. Ronit had the bedroom, Shimon and I slept in the living room on a pull-out sofa donated by an aunt. Although it was a vast improvement over the ditches and gullies of our travels, I longed for the latter.

Shimon, among his various talents, was a skilled sign-writer and we had hardly finished accumulating the essential bits of furnishing – all donations – before he got a sign-writing job. Shortly after that he began performing, firstly at private events but soon after at more public venues. I found work teaching dance in a young adult institute and, with some of my pupils, formed a performing dance group. There were twelve of us, including me – six males and six females. With setting up the apartment, teaching, dancing, caring for a new baby and entertaining relatives and friends who insisted on frequent baby visits, which I suspected were to check on Ronit's welfare, distrusting my competence, any restless impulses were temporarily quelled. Although this oasis was not of my choosing, it provided sustenance. I became caught in the flow of survival, too busy to know where that flow was taking me.

And very soon I became even busier. Montreal television channels, broadcasting in both French and English, were in the market for entertainment that could appeal to both factions. Dance was perfect as it didn't depend on language. One of the dancers in the group had part-time work in television production and it didn't take long before we were invited to perform on a television show, which led to more television appearances.

I was delighted. Although I had little experience as a choreographer, I had been dancing since childhood – folk dancing, modern dancing, ballet, jazz, tango, you name it. If anything had a dance label, I was there. I had even studied in New York with Martha Graham, the mother of modern dance, one summer. Dance was in my blood. Now, hardly out of my teens, I had no difficulty creating easy-to-look-at, light-hearted dance performances.

Our dance skills were, on the whole, minimal. But what we lacked in technical proficiency we made up for in enthusiasm. To lively recorded folk music, like Italian Tarantellas and Russian Cossack dances, we would swoop onto the stage in single file, holding hands, with smiles that could ignite the universe, skirts swirling, sashes flying, bursting with vitality. Then with hops, skips, jumps, twirls and stamps, the line would become a circle, and the circle would become whirling couples dancing into smaller circles and, voila, two lines facing each other. As if by magic the patterns and shapes would weave in and out of each other.

We were full of bounce, jumping, leaping, twirling, filled with the joy of movement – of being young and alive. There was no angst, no unrequited love, no dying swans. We were the dance equivalent of the song 'How Much is that Doggy in the Window', unadulterated feel-good. How could anyone not love us?

For a while I became so engrossed in the excitement and the glory of performing on television and in all the work this involved, I forgot about fretting over my lost travels, my lost passion. My not-so-loved oasis even qualified for a place on the adventure scale, although just barely. But the fly in the ointment was the stickiness of motherhood. I had almost forgiven motherhood for disrupting my travels but soon it began to interfere with my dance ambitions.

It hadn't take me long to become dissatisfied with my candy-floss choreography. It began to feel like I was writing limericks when I wanted to write poetry. And the repetitiveness of my creations, the limitations of my dance technique, which had become rusty, became all too obvious. I wanted to develop real choreographic skills instead of improvised ones. I wanted to become a fully-fledged dancer and choreographer, instead of a half-assed one. I wanted to create something more significant, something with soul. I *wanted* the angst, the unrequited love, the dying swan. I wanted and wanted and wanted. But my wanting had nowhere to go.

Before I could contemplate choreography with more depth, more meaning (and even if I had the talent to do so, which was questionable), I had to develop a versatile dance vocabulary, and my dancers had to develop more than rudimental dancing skills. This involved serious commitment and hard work, with hours and hours of training and rehearsing. However, even if my dancers had been willing to commit to such a regime, which they weren't, I could not. Although I received a great deal of help, the main burden of motherhood fell squarely on my shoulders. I hadn't the time or the freedom for my dancing to become my passion.

Ronit was not only beautiful, but alert and responsive. In my good motherhood moments, I couldn't help admiring her, even adoring her. I certainly loved her. She was mine in a way that nothing else had ever been mine. My parents considered her a joy beyond joys, and delighted in caring for her in their limited free time. But for me the joy was tempered by an on-going frustration, not only because of the dancing–motherhood conflict and my thwarted dance ambitions, but because of the haunting fact that this baby would never go away. For the rest of my life I would be saddled with the responsibility of caring for her. The young and free and alive would be sapped from my soul. It was like contemplating a small death.

It was very different for Shimon. Despite his full-time sign-writing work and devotion to his music, he took to parenthood as though he was born to it. He didn't plague himself with questions about fatherhood. He just did it. If he was happy with his guitar and his painting, he was delighted with Ronit.

Fatherhood rested lightly on his shoulders. He always woke up singing.

Shimon was surrounded by his loves – music and art – which were now augmented by becoming a father. He didn't need anything else or anyone else. Most importantly, he had himself. I remembered that on the ship from South Africa, he spent so much time on his own, playing music and painting, that I had to make an agreement with him to spend at least two hours a day with me. He did so willingly; it's just that the idea hadn't occurred to him.

But I was a slow learner when it came to motherhood and needed more than a little nudging. I was finding it hard to grow up, 'to put away childish things', to become an adult, a mother.

My heart wasn't in it. Actually I had never wanted to grow older, even as a child. While my friends couldn't wait to wear lipstick and high heels, I wore neither. I brought my skipping rope to school when they were playing spin the bottle. The only time I remember Pistol Pete being angry with me is when my mother wanted me to wear lipstick for a high school graduation photo and I refused. Lipstick was for being older.

Although I never neglected the essentials like breast-feeding, I was resentful of the never-ending demands, the endless routine of motherhood. At times I longed to say: 'I did that beautifully. I had natural childbirth, I'm breast-feeding, I'm reading all the books. But now the job is over, finished.' But the job was never over, never finished. There wasn't even an end in sight. It came as an unwelcome revelation that motherhood was not only a full-time job; it was a lifetime commitment. It would never go away.

If I needed a little nudging into motherhood, a honing of my instincts, a renewal of my vows, an incident occurred while we were still living with my parents that gave me a violent thrust forward.

When Ronit was less than six weeks old, Shimon and I were invited to a New Year's Eve party. I was determined to go. My parents were unable to babysit so we decided to take Ronit with us. My mother protested, raising objections of the cold – it was many degrees below zero – of noise, of cigarette smoke, but nothing could dissuade me. I needed a reprieve from motherhood, even if only temporary. I needed to participate in conversations that excluded the baby word. I needed to dance. I needed a party. We didn't have a carrier cot but, undeterred, I wrapped Ronit in blankets and placed her in a cardboard carton with holes in the lid for air, and Shimon carried the carton to the party.

Once there, I put the carton in an unused room, out of harm's way. But soon afterwards when I went to check on Ronit, I couldn't find the carton. I searched the other rooms frantically but it was nowhere to be seen.

Petrified, I rushed to tell Shimon. Not suspecting its contents, someone had moved the carton to the cloakroom, where Shimon found it under a pile of coats. Terrified that Ronit had suffocated under the heavy winter garments, I panicked. I leapt at the carton and, unable to breathe in symbiotic empathy, pulled my baby out, gasping to fill my lungs, fighting a thick barrier like a plastic wedge jammed into my throat, preventing air reaching my lungs.

Ronit was breathing quietly, fast asleep. As I rocked her in my arms with tears streaming down my cheeks, I made a silent vow to be a better mother in future. After all, if I hadn't asked for her to be born, neither had she. Only Shimon ever knew of the near calamity. He shared the blame and spared me the full guilt.

But despite that traumatic incident, despite the vows, despite the guilt, despite the effort I made to pluck enjoyment from the jaws of motherhood, I became increasingly restless, even dispirited. If my wings had been clipped and I could no longer fly, at least my soul needed engaging. But my soul was withering. There was a gnawing ache growing inside me which I could not soothe, a longing I could not name, a bare, empty space which travel had filled – the excitement of the road, the unpredictability of each day, the thrill of the adventure. Dance did not fill it, Shimon did not fill it, motherhood did not fill it. My oasis was not only dry; it was parched. I needed something, some nameless something.

5

The Finjan – the Long-Stay Oasis

S OMETIMES, IT'S AS THOUGH life is a jigsaw whose pieces lie scattered in limbo, in need of a subliminal force to fit them together to complete the picture. And, sometimes, such life-changing opportunities have humble beginnings. This one presented itself in the form of a casual chat.

One evening Shimon and I were sitting in our living room with two close friends, Cecil, a down-to-earth accountant and Hi, an all-over-the-place drummer. Shimon was bemoaning the fact that there were so few places in Montreal where he could perform the music he wanted to play.

'I'm getting fed up with entertaining musical virgins at sweet sixteen parties and pregnant ladies at baby showers. And I'm fed up with hosting sing-alongs. How many times can I sing

"Michael Row the Boat Ashore" and get everyone clapping? I want a serious stage, somewhere I can play the songs I want to play, but there's no decent folk music club in Montreal.'

'That's true,' I said. 'There're so many music clubs and coffeehouses in the US, especially in New York,' I said, remembering Rhoda and I dashing from club to club, not wanting to miss anything. 'And, in Canada, Toronto has The Purple Onion and The Riverboat; Ottawa has L'Hibou; there're several coffeehouses in Vancouver. But Montreal has only a few Calypso clubs in Old Montreal and no coffeehouses with live music.'

'Then why don't you open one?' Hi said, simply.

And just like that, the Finjan was conceived.

'My own club?' Shimon said, in a way that didn't preclude possibility.

'Why not?' I said, feeling an instant rush of excitement. The same kind of excitement I had once felt when I was about to embark on a journey. 'Then you can sing whatever you like, whenever you like. It's a brilliant idea. Hi, you're a genius.'

Suddenly it all seemed so obvious, so right.

Things mushroomed after that. The more we talked about it, the more excited we became and the more apparent it was that we had to make it happen.

'Shimon, you can be the house singer and we can have different guest singers,' I said, again invoking those magical times in New York – and the overwhelming joy I had experienced when I met one of my favourite singers.

***

Although Rhoda and I were both teenagers, I was already a folk music devotee. If maps of the world papered the walls of my room, they competed with photos of folk and blues musicians like Pete Seeger, Lead Belly and, of course, Woody Guthrie, 'The father of American folk music'. He combined both my loves – music and travel. I had read his book *Bound for Glory*, and it became my inspiration. He had given up fame and fortune to travel the US and sing about its people, especially its working people, and memorialize their struggle in song. The road called to him in the same way it called to me. Woody Guthrie was my star pin-up.

This was my first trip to New York and I was smitten by its unlimited possibilities; theatre, dance, music, yellow taxi cabs, bargain basements, sidewalk dramas; a giant billboard man in Times Square smoking Camel cigarettes with real smoke, the air electric with excitement. Rhoda and I were exploring Greenwich Village, visiting places we had read about and eating pizza for the first time, feeling like characters in an adventure story, when we saw a poster saying Woody Guthrie was giving a benefit performance that very afternoon. I was thrilled. Wood Guthrie, my idol – and I actually had the possibility of hearing him sing, of seeing him in the flesh. Phenomenal. It was as though I could witness Jesus walking on the water. I had to go.

But alas, when we got to the hall where he would be performing, we didn't have enough money to buy tickets. As we retreated down the street, bitterly disappointed, I couldn't believe my eyes. There was Woody Guthrie himself walking toward us. I recognized him from the posters, although he was shorter than I had imagined. We walked right past him, struck dumb, unable to do or say anything. Then, on an impulse, we turned around and followed him. He went up the back staircase of the hall and disappeared behind the stage door. I stood there dissolved in bliss. I had actually seen Woody Guthrie and now he was only feet away. I couldn't bring myself to leave.

Rhoda and I sat on the metal fire-escape steps, hoping for a miracle. About half an hour later Woody came on to the landing to smoke a cigarette. I held my breath. Suddenly he looked down and saw us.

'What're you girls doing down there? Come on up here and say hello,' he said, with a twinkle. Feeling like we were climbing the stairway to paradise, we clattered up the steps. I explained that we didn't have enough money to buy tickets. 'I'll fix that,' he said. 'You just come with me.'

He led us through the door and, to our amazement, right onto the stage. He got two chairs and put them in a corner. 'You girls sit right here,' he said. 'I gotta lubricate my tonsils, won't be long.' And with that he disappeared. We sat stone still, not a murmur, not a twitch. We were paralyzed with ecstasy. He could have been gone a minute or an hour, or a day. His presence had eradicated time.

When he returned, he put an arm around each of us and led us to the centre of the stage. The curtain went up. The hall was packed. In a loud, playful voice he announced, 'Presenting Woody Guthrie and his Bobby Sox Brigade.' Everyone clapped. We had become part of the act. We even bowed and the clapping grew louder. I don't know how I survived the joy. We sat on the stage with him right through his performance, feeling profoundly blessed. The miracle I had wished for had happened.

After the show, he took us for 'eats' in a little working man's café close to the hall. 'Gotta keep my Brigade in eats,' he said. He ordered chilli for all of us, said it was the house speciality. Although it blasted my taste buds, I made no protest and finished every drop. Woody introduced us to the café owner as 'my Canadian girls.' I was sure I had died and gone to heaven.

**

There was almost a 'meant-to-be' element to our living room discussion with Cecil and Hi that evening. It's not as though a seed had been planted. It was as though the seed had already been there and just needed some recognition, some nurturing, to blossom. Because Shimon was a folk singer who needed a place to sing and because I was a devotee, a kind of born-again groupie, even before the term became fashionable, who needed an adventure to replace the one denied me, opening a folk music coffeehouse was just the ticket. It ticked all the empty spaces.

Within minutes of our discussion, what had been a random suggestion became a significant possibility, then a substantial likelihood and, finally, a resounding YES. It became that special dream that would make the difference, a dream we didn't even know we had, but that needed only the kiss of life to become a reality.

Everything about the coffeehouse fell into place so smoothly, so easily, it was as if arranged by that mysterious subliminal force. The very next day we began looking for a venue. The property rental market was buoyant. With no difficulty, we located a one-bedroom apartment with a decent-sized kitchen close to where we lived. It was on 5650 Victoria Avenue, a main shopping street, above a bakery and beside a pharmacy. An apartment was perfect as we wouldn't have to pay commercial rent and a kitchen was ideal as it would give us the possibility of serving food, or at least drinks. The apartment was located in a non-residential area, busy with shops and shoppers, not too good for sober living but perfect for our purposes. There would be no complaints about noise from neighbours, because there were no neighbours. The landlord seemed eager to let the property and liked the idea of a coffeehouse with music. He agreed to allow us to demolish the bedroom wall, giving us one large room, plus the kitchen. In addition we were offered a month's free rent. It couldn't have been more perfect.

Shimon and I took to the project as though it was part of our destiny: for me, it was like planning a journey. I had always loved the planning stage almost as much as the travel itself.

Everything was exciting: even the most trivial details took on a special satisfaction because they made the plan a reality.

Now that we had a potential venue for our coffeehouse, we needed to name it. It was Hi's idea to call it 'The Finjan'. Hi had been in close contact with Arabic cultures from where the name originated, with a finjan being a coffee pot around which people gathered to meet friends, drink coffee and be entertained; it was a focal point where storytellers and musicians could tell their stories and sing their songs. The name was a winner. It had all the right ingredients – even a touch of the enigmatic. And so the Finjan drew its first breath.

Within hours of signing the rental agreement, the manual work began: the breaking, the building, the painting, the organizing. Friends helped. Even the landlord, who seemed almost as enthusiastic as us, helped. In the evenings we spent hours deciding what we wanted the Finjan to be and what we would do to make that happen. The idea that we could make of it anything we liked was exhilarating. It was like conceiving the perfect offspring. The Finjan became our life. We dreamed Finjan, we talked Finjan, we ate Finjan. We had heated discussions, we made cool calculations – but, finally, we decided on some fundamentals we were all agreed upon and hammered out the rudiments of a coffeehouse we were all excited about.

One thing we decided right from the start was that we wanted our coffeehouse to be unique. It was to be not only a place to listen to music but an informal, welcoming place; a place where one could not only meet friends but also meet the performers. There would be no back stage for musicians to retreat to, to separate themselves from the audience. We would create an intimate atmosphere, with a Middle Eastern flavour to complement the name; not overwhelmingly exotic but interesting, comfortable, different: Moroccan lanterns, wall hangings – I had a lovely woven one I would donate – tablecloths, candles and a small stage. Shimon would paint murals of Middle Eastern scenes – mosques, minarets, arched gateways, cobble stone alleyways – to enhance the atmosphere. To begin with, we would open only at weekends until we found our feet. Then, if things went well, we would open every day except Monday.

The question of whether to serve food took a lot of discussion, but in the end we agreed to have food. I was all for food – eating made for wellbeing, especially if the food was good. We would have a simple but original menu. Arabic cuisine was virtually unknown in Montreal and would be ideal. I liked cooking and learning to prepare Arabic food would be fun. Just a few dishes: falafel, humus, t'china, pita bread and Arabic coffee. No alcohol. We were adamant about that. In our coffeehouse, people would listen to the music and there would be no rowdy drunken brawls.

In our enthusiasm for planning the ideal coffeehouse, we had neglected one thing: financing it. But that issue inevitably reared its unwelcomed head. For a while we were stumped. None of us had any money. But nothing could deter us. Cecil, who was the only one with a proper job, decided to take a bank loan to get things started. We didn't need much. We would do all the work ourselves, buy second-hand tables and chairs and beg, borrow and steal the rest. Our enthusiasm trumped money concerns.

After the financial blip was sorted, the question of the music was next. We decided to focus on acoustic music. As agreed, Shimon would be the in-house performer to begin with and, later on, when we could afford it, we would hire guest performers, with Shimon as the opening act. This would give him the opportunity to gain performing experience and would give me the opportunity to meet the musicians. From an early age, I was not only obsessed with folk music but with folk musicians and the possibility of meeting them in the flesh was like having one's pin-ups walk into your living room.

At the time, folk music had expanded to include less traditional songs, and it now embraced other forms of music like blues, jazz and country. But most important for me, it embraced a new type of musician. In fifties' coffeehouses, performers sang mainly politically-orientated, contemporary songs with lyrics like 'My father was a miner and I'm a miner's son and I'll stick to the union 'til every battle's won'; and traditional ballads, like *Green Sleeves* and *The Lady of Shallotte,* as well as spirituals and gospel songs, like *Joshua Fought the Battle of Jericho.* But sixties' coffeehouse music was beginning to include not only a new genre of music but a new genre of performer: the singer-songwriter. These musicians, such as Pete Seeger, Carole King, James Taylor and Cat Stevens, to name only a few, wrote their own songs emanating from personal experiences, often with lyrics that were more like poetry. Some musicians, like my hero, Woodie Guthrie, straddled all genres: traditional songs, political songs and songs he had written himself. These singer-song writers bared their hearts in songs that were profoundly moving; songs that spoke directly to me, that often moved me to tears, songs like the poems and novels I lived in.

Writers, musicians and poets had always fascinated me. Actually, it was more than a fascination. I considered them to be magicians who had special powers, special insights, who could understand me better than I could understand myself. The idea that I might actually be able to meet these special beings would be the ultimate adventure.

6

Opening Night

———

T HE FINJAN WAS AN immediate success. Even before the doors were open, people came off the street to check out the mysterious happenings above the bakery, to see for themselves what was going on there. Shimon had devised a way to spark public interest. After the initial breaking of walls and the beginning of the decorating, he made a striking 'Opening Soon' sign. It had an almost three-dimensional painting of an exquisitely etched brass Arabic coffee pot alongside the beautifully-lettered name, The Finjan. There was no other wording, except 'Opening Soon'. He placed the sign on the street outside our door in such a way that people walking in either direction couldn't fail to notice it. The sign was intriguing. The name was strange. It was evocative, but of what? What was opening soon?

We purposely left the street door open so people could venture up the stairs to find out. Shimon was always present, first painting the walls and then the murals. I was often there, prevailing upon my mother, my aunts, my cousins, anyone, to baby-sit, while I unpacked donations and created a more or less functioning kitchen. We welcomed everyone who crossed the threshold, sharing our plans and ideas, and asking for theirs. We tried to include anyone who showed the least bit of interest in our venture. It was great publicity. Almost every person we spoke to loved the idea of a coffeehouse as a musical venue. They not only assured us of their patronage but promised to spread the word.

Opening night was a gala affair. Everything looked lovely, almost magical. Besides decorating the walls, Shimon had draped the ceiling with waves of fish net to create an intimate setting. Moroccan lanterns with coloured lights hung between the waves, twinkling like stars. The room glowed with candlelight. It was like entering an Aladdin's cave, mysterious but cosy, hinting at exciting things to come.

The room was crowded. The audience had no identifiable age range: it included a few grandparents, even several children. There was an air of anticipation, a sense of something good about to happen; a something that everyone wanted to be part of. Shimon and I were smothered in good wishes. There were telegrams of congratulations, good luck cards, bouquets of flowers. I found it really moving that, right from the start, people seemed willing to adopt the Finjan as their own and give it their blessing.

The kitchen was busy to near panic. My only helper was Pistol Pete, who spent the night washing dishes as we hadn't nearly enough of anything. He even had to run home to get more sugar and milk and to report to my mother, who was babysitting.

I had prepared an 'opening night' menu. Since I hadn't yet perfected the Arabic dishes, it consisted mainly of drinks, two special desserts and promises of original offerings to come. The desserts were baklava and Turkish delight, which I considered suitably exotic. The mother of a Turkish friend had made the baklava. It was delicious with paper-thin filo pastry made with rose water and a honey-nut filling. The Turkish delight was studded with almonds and pistachios, equally delicious. There were also several drinks I had devised, 'Finjan Specials' consisting of exotic fruit juices, like mango and lychee, elderflower cordial, fresh mint and sparkling water – and, of course, free coffee and tea.

That evening, Shimon sang his heart out. He did two long sets that exhausted all the songs he had rehearsed, and was then coaxed, with shouts of 'encore' and 'more', into doing a third set of songs he had not rehearsed and which were missing not only words but entire stanzas. But he could have sung 'God Save The Queen' and the applause would have been equally enthusiastic. The mood was that of love overflowing.

No one minded anything that night; not being squashed together and sharing tables; not having to repeat orders three times and then not getting the right one; not even being splashed with coffee by our inexperienced waitresses; and certainly not missing stanzas. Shimon was a great success. He got the audience clapping out rhythms and singing choruses. Everyone loved him. The atmosphere of good will, of pure enjoyment, of a desire to launch the Finjan into an orbit of triumph, prevailed over all else.

Just for opening night, we made our one and only alcohol concession. At the stroke of midnight we served champagne, insisted upon and provided by Pistol Pete. When the drinks were poured and the paper cups raised to toast the Finjan, something strange happen. Someone spontaneously began to sing Auld Lang Syne and everyone joined in. Somehow it seemed appropriate. Although it wasn't the beginning of a new year, it seemed to signify another new beginning. I couldn't help the tears.

That night, I went to bed with a tingling sense of aliveness I hadn't felt in a long while. A new adventure had begun. And I was more than ready for it.

7

Phase Two

B Y OPENING NIGHT, BOTH Hi and Cecil were no longer involved in the Finjan. Cecil had been interested in the concept but too busy to involve himself in implementing it, and Hi was off on a drumming tour. However, Cecil had provided most of the money to set it up and repaying him was a major concern. Although Pistol Pete had loaned us some money, it wasn't enough to repay Cecil and cover the mounting expenses. Shimon decided to take a bank loan and Pistol Pete offered to be the guarantor. That bank loan caused us more consternation than the entire setting up of the Finjan. Our previous bank dealings had consisted of changing currency for foreign travel. Now we had to get our heads around concepts like 'interest', 'capital', 'liquidity', 'cash flow', 'liability' and, most importantly, 'guarantor'.

Neither of us had ever owed money before. We were suddenly plunged into the real world of financial dealings, and we didn't like it. It dawned on me that the Finjan was not a hobby or a lovely vision, but a serious risk. It wasn't as though I was averse to risk taking, but it had always been at my expense, not at someone else's and it had involved things such as travelling in dodgy vehicles along the edge of cliffs, or hitchhiking on lonely roads; repaying money had never been involved. That bank debt was an ever-present chill.

Before we had opened the Finjan, we spent hours mulling over finances, struggling with figures, intentions, plans, until we had finally hammered out a strategy we could start with and then modify when we began hiring musicians. Opening the Finjan only on weekend nights would give us the opportunity to see what problems occurred and allow us the time to fix them. Entrance would be free. We would only charge once we began hiring musicians. Before that, food and drink would be our only income. And that income would largely depend on me, since food was my department. I accepted the responsibility with the kind of light-heartedness that only a novice with a total lack of business experience could have done.

The first few weeks were fraught. The pots, mainly donated, were the wrong size; I couldn't find places to get the special ingredients I needed; the recipes I followed were for intimate dining, not for mass consumption. First I prepared too little, then too much. There were non-kitchen problems as well. The chairs we had managed to acquire as donations were uncomfortable and the ones we had ordered turned out to be too expensive and had to be returned; the tables wobbled; our lovely ceramic candle holders were easily chipped and the toilet rebelled from all the flushing.

Expenses kept mounting and our income did not cover them. Things weren't working out. We had to devise a formula that would make it possible to sustain our vision. In order to implement our objective of the Finjan being a unique place to socialize with friends, listen to music, meet musicians and eat delicious food, we had to make sure it was financially viable. And, most essential, before we began hiring musicians, we had to know we could afford them.

Neither of us had business experience and we were at a loss as how to rectify the situation. Some nights I would wake up in a cold sweat because I dreamed the police were evicting us for non-payment of rent. In one police nightmare, all the customers were filing out the door, while Shimon stood on the stage playing his guitar until everyone was gone and the Finjan was empty and forlorn. We had no choice but to borrow more money, but we knew the reprieve would only be temporary.

However, it wasn't all worry. We were too inexperienced, too naive and too enthusiastic for that. The plusses were manifold. Shimon loved performing and learning new songs. It was great having our very own club. We could invite friends for free coffee or to play chess – Shimon was a keen chess player – or just to hang out. I was more inclined towards the hanging out. On some nights when the Finjan was closed, we would pile up the tables and chairs and dance. I loved that. It was party time and we were the hosts. The worry and the glory were intricately entwined and the glory was ahead, if only marginally.

Eventually, we hit on an idea to increase our income, an idea which should have been obvious right from the start, had we been more business savvy. As selling food was our only means of making money, we decided to increase the opening hours, so people could come for afternoon snacks or for dinner and not necessarily for the music.

I spent hours perfecting the Arabic dishes. Through sheer persistence, I finally got it not only right, but very right. Our humus got rave reviews and our falafel was the best in town, probably the only in town. People would come just for the food. I expanded the menu to include a special dinner plate and more

Arabic sweets. I didn't mind the hard work; I even enjoyed it. Besides, we had lots of support. Pistol Pete spent hours grinding soaked chickpeas, friends helped, and my mother curtailed her social activity so she could baby-sit. Slowly, finances began to improve.

During those initial settling-in months, Shimon was the only singer although various local musicians would drop in for informal jamming sessions. Sometimes, Shimon would bring one of them on stage for a guest set. There was always a musical ambiance, an informal environment with musical surprises. This worked beautifully for the first two months. But then people began to ask what musicians we were bringing in, when that would happen and how much we would be charging. It was reassuring to know that people had no objection to paying an entrance fee as long as it was reasonable and the musician was good. But it was somewhat scary to know this was expected sooner than we had anticipated.

After the first few months, things began to fall into place. We had a group of 'regulars' who treated the Finjan as their local, as well as a constant stream of visitors, some of whom became regulars. Food and drink sales improved significantly. To our surprise, we began making a small profit. The moment had come for the big gamble. Although people loved listening to Shimon and, by now, could join him in the chorus of many songs, we knew it was time for a change, time for Shimon to step down, or at least move over, while he was still ahead.

Shimon was not only a singer but a superb entertainer. He had the unique ability to draw an audience together and make them his. He could make his audience laugh – he could be very funny – as well as sing, clap and hang on every word in rapt silence when he sang a melancholy ballad. People came to hear him over and over and over again. But over and over again had its limitations. We knew it was time to expand the musical repertoire, to move to phase two: the hiring of guest musicians. We still didn't know if we could afford this but we had to take the risk. After all, this was what the Finjan was supposed to be all about. For me, this was the most exciting part of the venture. It's what I had been waiting for.

Inviting guest musicians was a whole other endeavour and required many decisions, some of which were very scary – especially as they involved even more serious risk taking. To begin with, we had to initiate the entrance fee, which would vary depending on how much we paid the musician. We weren't sure how our customers would react when it came to actually buying a ticket; they had become accustomed to free entrance that enabled them to drop by even for just an hour or so. An entrance fee was a commitment, a more formal arrangement. It meant wanting to hear that specific musician and usually spending an entire evening. We hoped it would not deter people. But our very existence was on the line.

Another risky decision was the question of accommodation. When calculating financial viability, we decided that the musicians would stay with us. This was a necessity as hotel prices were very high in the area. The problem was, we didn't have an extra room. We dealt with this difficulty by getting an extra bed and putting it into Ronit's room. Ronit was too young to object but we didn't know if the musicians would go for it. What if they didn't? After all, the least he or she would expect was a bit of privacy. But we had no alternative.

We began phase two by printing a roll of entrance tickets and hiring Roz, a regular Finjan goer, to sell them at the door. Roz was delighted. Not only wouldn't she have to pay to listen to music, she would be paid for doing so. We also hired someone to help in the kitchen. We had no trouble finding employees. There was a list of people, mainly female, keen to work at the Finjan. Although we paid them, they would have been prepared to work just for the opportunity to meet the musicians and, probably, would have been willing to pay us. Together with our two waitresses, we now had a staff of four females who fashioned themselves into what was to become a self-styled 'Welcoming Committee'. This was to form the basis of a phenomenon that became a Finjan speciality and which played an important role in Finjan history.

We had all the changes in place. Now it was time for our first guest musician.

8

Sonny Terry and Brownie McGhee

S HIMON BEGAN THE NEW Finjan music venture with a bang. 'If you're taking a risk, make it a big one,' he said. 'That way, there's more chance of success.' I didn't know if he was right but he was the boss in music matters. He hired Sonny Terry and Brownie McGhee, two legendary blues musicians – top of our Blues Musicians list, and 'the most recognized duo in blues history'. It was a real coup. It seemed to me remarkable that they would play in a small club like ours. After all, they had recorded numerous albums, both together and separately; performed in concerts, festivals, in Broadway productions – even in major venues like Carnegie Hall, with such icons as Pete Seeger, Josh White and Woody Guthrie, to name only a few. They had inspired white musicians to play black blues and were fundamental to that major musical phenomenon. They were headline attractions; veritable stars. Wouldn't a small coffeehouse be a comedown?

When, much later, I asked Brownie how come they had agreed to perform at the Finjan, he said: 'Small clubs gave us our chance, I don't forget that, the big joints jumped in way down the line. I want to see the colour of the eyes of the people who come to see us. And Sonny, he agrees, he don't see, but he can feel them.'

Shimon had been able to negotiate a special deal with their agent. They would get a small fee but a major percentage of the ticket sales. That way, we wouldn't have to front a large sum of money that we couldn't afford and there was no advance payment. We would hire them for two weeks instead of one; they would perform every night but Monday; two performances a night, with two separate audiences. We would provide hotel accommodation. We could hardly expect them to stay in Ronit's room. I couldn't believe our good luck.

When we got to know them better, Brownie elaborated on why they had accepted the Finjan engagement. He explained how they liked performing in small clubs; it brought them in touch with ordinary people they could relate to, instead of agents, producers, directors: 'Folks too busy to give a man the time of day, or too rich to save a man from drowning,' he said. They never got into media hype, celebrity indulgence. Their roots were with working folks, farmers, labourers, street cleaners – people who struggled for a living; people on the edge; musicians who sang on street corners, like they had done. They never abandoned those roots.

I had seen photographs of Sonny and Brownie, and had heard them play on various recordings, but I wasn't prepared for the impact that meeting them and hearing them play live would have on me. They were a striking duo, in their late forties to early fifties. Sonny was almost blind, he could only see large shapes and could tell the difference between night and day, but no more, and Brownie was lame, with a paralyzed leg. Brownie's lameness was a result of having polio as a child; Sonny's blindness a result of two accidents – one as a child, the other as a teenager. Sonny was a big, bulky man; slow-moving, 'black as the ace of spades' he said of himself; with a wide, quiet smile, startling white teeth, soft dark eyes and a big belly laugh. He had massive hands with surprisingly elegant fingers that flashed with gold rings. A large gold chain around his neck made it look thicker and blacker. He dressed immaculately, with a glistening white shirt, bright blue tie, black jacket, black trousers and always polished boots. He radiated ease, good will, and a love of sparkle and shine. He spoke with a black, Southern accent that was so heavy I had difficulty understanding what he was saying, especially at first.

Brownie limped badly, pulling his crippled leg behind him as though it didn't belong to him. He was taller and leaner than Sonny. His skin was much lighter than Sonny's – a mid-brown. His eyes shone with the energy that his entire body radiated. Had he not been lame, I could imagine him with spice in his step. He smiled easily. He dressed casually in tan-coloured slacks, a loose shirt open at the neck, no jacket or tie and special orthopaedic shoes. Although from the Deep South like Sonny – Brownie came from Tennessee and Sonny from Georgia and North Carolina – his speech was vibrant with imagery and dismissive of grammatical correctness, but not difficult for me to understand. He was far more articulate than Sonny. They were so easy, so unassuming and so larger-than-life that I took to them immediately. Although we were miles apart in all things discernible, I was exceedingly comfortable with them. They were like favourite uncles, only black.

Shimon was more than right. They were a sensation. For two weeks, there were queues down the street. Everyone loved them. Not only was their music stunning but, visually, they were unforgettable. They would approach the stage, walking slowly, blind Sonny behind lame Brownie, with his hand on Brownie's shoulder for guidance, while Brownie would be limping, dragging his crippled leg. At first it was painful watching that torturous walk to the stage, then it became beautiful.

Shimon would help them up the ramp to the stage, Sonny feeling his way on to a chair and Brownie arranging himself on the high stool beside him. But when they began to play, the blindness, the lameness disappeared as though it had never happened. Any pity for their physical impairment was swallowed up by the overwhelming power of their performance. That initial burst of music, the whooping and wailing of Sonny's harmonica, combined with his raucous hollering, sharp falsetto cries and foot-stomping – together with Brownie's strident guitar playing, and the power of his voice – was so stunning, so explosive, so exhilarating, it brought instant jubilation. It made people want to raise their arms and shout, 'Halleluiah!'

Sonny played his harmonica like a lover: stroking it, cradling it, coaxing out the wails and whoops and howls with caresses; wooing it with his fingers, his lips, in an exuberant, impassioned duet of voice and music. He sang to the harmonica; a fragment of song, a riff of Brownie's guitar; a word, a shout, a wail, a hoot; faster, wilder, until he raised the harmonica to the heavens with a jubilant cry, his love triumphant.

Brownie was a wonder with the guitar. Seeing him up close bore no resemblance to hearing him on tape. His fingers had a life of their own. They flew over the strings; picking, plucking, strumming, making the guitar talk, laugh, cry, as though it were a living being. It twanged, it moaned, it quivered; it pounded like a troubled heart; it raced like a speeding train; it wept with the poignancy of a lament; it smiled at his outrageous nuances. His lyrics ran the gamut of living. They were sad, tender, humorous, angry, raunchy; all of them together. Brownie was spectacular. Together they were magic.

They always finished their sets with their song 'Walk On', written by Brownie, the audience joining in the chorus. Towards the end of their performance, Brownie would slowly get off his high stool and help Sonny rise from his chair, both still playing and singing 'Walk On'. Sonny would place his hand on Brownie's shoulder and Brownie would lead him off the stage, Sonny playing the harmonica and Brownie singing, while the audience joined in the chorus, chanting its refrain about walking on back home.

'Come on Sonny,' Brownie chanted, 'Let's walk on.'

By this point, the audience would be so wild with singing, with shouting, with applause, that the final stanzas could hardly be heard.

The song 'Walk On' was so much part of their trademark that the number plate on Brownie's car read 'Walk On'.

***

Sonny and Brownie returned to the Finjan many times, they were always a sensation and a great financial plus. They became more than friends. They became family. We even developed family rituals. Sonny's favourite meal was baked ham, followed by pineapple pie. I never failed to welcome them with a dinner of baked ham, studded with cloves and glazed with maple syrup... and pineapple pie. We always had a party for them on the Monday between their two-week engagements and invited their most ardent fans and any other musicians who were in town. We made sure to have an adequate supply of whisky and milk for party times as Brownie liked to drink milk before a whisky session. 'It lines my stomach,' he explained, 'so I don't get drunk.' Whether it was true or not, I never saw either Sonny or Brownie drunk.

Pistol Pete took to Sonny in a big way unlike Rose, who kept her distance. Although he could hardly understand Sonny's heavy accent, he was comfortable with him, enjoyed his company. They communicated with nods and smiles and much laughter. One day Pistol Pete took Sonny to a delicatessen for a smokemeat sandwich, a special delicacy available only in Montreal. Sonny was so profuse in his gestures of appreciation, that before he left Montreal, Pistol Pete presented him with an entire smokemeat brisket, weighing at least ten pounds.

Brownie always insisted on cooking facilities in his accommodation and would cook us a Southern meal: pork and black beans with grits or Southern-fried chicken with corn fritters. Delicious. He was more proud of his cooking than of his guitar playing. A compliment for a meal meant far more to him than a compliment for a performance.

Several times Shimon drove them to New York, when we went there to find musicians. Once, on the way there, we had a hilarious experience. Brownie wanted to buy some painkillers that could not be bought in the US. They were called 'two-twenty-twos' – 222s. Before we crossed the border into the US, we stopped at a pharmacy so Brownie could make the purchase. However, when he later opened the package, he discovered he had been given a packet of condoms. It turned out he had asked for 'triple douces' – a douce being American slang for the number two and 222s being triple douces. The Canadian attendant, whose job description did not include a knowledge of American slang, assumed it was a code word for some unmentionable, like condoms; after all, what else could have such a furtive name? We all found the incident funny, but Sonny found it uproarious and was still laughing days later.

Sonny loved to laugh. He would burst into a belly laugh at the least provocation, even if it was at his expense. Like the day Shimon walked into a restaurant that Sonny frequented when performing at the Finjan. And there was Sonny deeply engrossed, tucking into a plate of food. Shimon approached his table and, pretending to be the manager, said in his most formal voice: 'Is everything alright sir?'

Sonny replied: 'Yes. Thank you, everything is good.'

'Do you have any complaints?'

'No sir, no complaints, it's all very good.'

'Can I do anything for you?' Shimon persisted. But Sonny still didn't recognize his voice and Shimon finally said: 'Sonny, it's Shimon.'

'Shimon!' Sonny said in surprise and then burst out laughing. 'You fooled me. Shimon, you fooled me.' He could hardly talk for laughing. He found the fact that Shimon had tricked him, had taken advantage of his blindness to play a joke on him, hysterically funny. He related the incident over and over again, each time laughing his infectious belly laugh.

Both Sonny and Brownie had performed in Broadway theatres, both in *Finian's Rainbow* and in the original production of Tennessee Williams's *Cat on a Hot Tin Roof*. Sonny told me that when he was first approached to perform in the production back in 1955, he had refused.

'They told me I had to play the same thing in the same way night after night,' he said. 'I can't do that. I'm used to playing free. I can't play the same thing in the same way night after night. Then they told me how much they were paying and I said: "Sure 'nuf man, I can play the same thing in the same way night after night."' He laughed and added: 'And that's what I did. I played the same thing in the same way for over five hundred nights. That's what money does to a man.'

I only discussed Sonny's blindness with him one time. He told me the second accident occurred when a nephew, who had been playing with a stick, inadvertently hit him in his one good eye and blinded him. He said he didn't much care for living after that and it was only his harmonica that kept him going. 'My harmonica was my best friend. It didn't give a damn if I could see or not. It stood by me, it wanted me to stay living.' He told me he had recently been offered an operation that might restore his eyesight and that he was considering it. 'Me,' he said, 'I ain't all blind like Ray [Ray Charles], I see a little. He don't see nothing.' Sonny could distinguish night from day, and identify large shapes. He was afraid the surgery would cause him to lose the precious little sight he had left. In the end, he refused the operation.

Both Sonny and Brownie adored Ronit. They were accustomed to relating to children. Brownie had several of his own, including a baby daughter Ronit's age. Sonny treated Ronit to special harmonica effects, making his harmonica talk to her. Her favourite utterance was 'I want my mama'. She would sit on the floor looking up at him, her eyes wide, her legs tucked under her, waiting for 'I want my mama', with the avid expectation she'd wait for Sleeping Beauty to spring to life. And Sonny, smiling down on her, his big boot thumping beside her, his gold rings flashing, enticed whoops and hoots and howls from his harmonica until it finally wailed, 'I want my mama'. Each time he played it, her face lit up in wonder and he would laugh his great belly laugh, slapping his thighs in delight.

Brownie always referred to Ronit as 'the baby'. Even years later when I came to see Sonny and Brownie at a London performance, when Ronit was a teenager and we had moved to London, Brownie asked: 'How's the baby?'

***

The relationship between Sonny and Brownie was an extremely complex one. Their names were inextricably linked together, as were their careers, their livelihoods, their very lives. Although they performed on their own or with other people, they were at their best together and that's how the public wanted them. In many ways they became like brothers, only closer. They called each other 'River'. When I asked Brownie why, he said, 'Because a river is long and deep and forever.' 'River' was their expression of deep-felt love. Yet, despite their closeness, or perhaps because of it, this undying love, as real as it was, could be riddled with hostility, bitter arguments and severe falling-outs. Sometimes it seemed they could hardly bear to be with each other and the tension between them was so blistering it could burn a hole in the heavens.

Once they became famous, long before they played at the Finjan, agents, producers and record companies, wanted to capitalize on their successes. Success translated as more dollars. More dollars translated as enforced coupling. They travelled together, performed together, recorded together, were in each other's company day and night. Whereas in the early days, before they became celebrities, they could play together, but lead separate lives and walk away from each other. Success was a kind of bondage. In many ways they were like caged animals, which, frustrated by being trapped, began to turn on each other.

Yet I never saw this acrimony reflected in their performances and only their close friends were aware of its intensity. On stage, they allowed each other solo opportunities, supported each other musically. They sang together, called to each other, enhanced each other's playing with great sensitivity. They were far too professional to allow anything to come between them and their music.

I stayed in contact with Sonny and Brownie until their deaths, Sonny's in 1986, Brownie's in 1996. Over the years they became increasingly dear to me. Even though life took us in different directions, we made special efforts to be together. I visited Brownie in his home in Oakland, California, met his children, and stayed over several times. Sonny made sure to introduce me to his new girlfriend, Emma, and when he eventually married her, I came to New York so we could celebrate together. I spent time with them whenever they performed in England. I even made them baked ham and pineapple pie. Brownie never missed getting me back-stage passes and we partied together, laughed together, reminisced together in many green rooms. They were an important part of my life, my history. And, as I write this, I still feel the pain of their loss, but also the joy of having known them.

9

The Musicians

ONCE WE BEGAN HIRING musicians, I became a very busy girl indeed. I not only ran the Finjan kitchen, ran our own kitchen, squeezed in some university courses in English Literature and cared for Ronit, but now I had the musicians to look after as well.

Actually, caring for Ronit was hugely assisted by my parents, especially by Pistol Pete and by assorted babysitters. My mother sometimes asked the pointed question, 'Who is it bringing up Ronit, me or you?' But that was only sometimes. And, as for Pistol Pete, if I had been his Golden Girl, Ronit was his Princess. He adored her just as he had adored me, only more so.

My very first memories were not of my mother, but of Pistol Pete. Even as a small child he loved taking me along on his 'business' ventures. I would sit on his knee in lawyers' offices, in judges' chambers, in courtrooms, even as guests of the chief of police. He seemed to know everyone. I never knew exactly what he did to have such eminent friends, whom he dismissed as 'business associates', with a hand gesture that indicated no further information was forthcoming. And, as for how he made his money, if I went anywhere near that question, he would shake his finger at me and say, 'You agreed that you and me never talk business.' Although I had made no such agreement, it seems Pistol Pete had made it for me.

Pistol Pete was my personal superman. Although he was only about five foot ten inches tall, his strength and endurance were legendary. His body was like steel, but his brown eyes were tender and his lips were soft. Once, at a family get together when I was about seven, two of my teenaged male cousins, almost as tall as Pistol Pete, were boasting about their boxing ability. 'Show me,' Pistol Pete had said. 'Punch me as hard as you can,' and he indicated his belly. I held my breath, terrified, as they punched him hard, again and again. But I needn't have been concerned. They walked away nursing bruised knuckles.

Once, when Pistol Pete was tormented by a toothache, he took a pair of pliers from his tool kit and pulled the tooth out, rinsed his mouth and said, 'If the bugger gives you trouble, take the bugger out – don't wait or he'll give you more trouble.' But, despite his tough exterior he could be kind and gentle and was a bit of a ladies' man. My mother's friends loved him and he loved them, calling them pet names, noticing their new hair dos, sympathizing with their woes and giving them lots of cuddles. Like me, , they adored Pistol Pete.

I learned the ways of the world from Pistol Pete, many of which I had to forget, or at least adapt. As a child I believed that when the police stopped you for a speeding violation or anything else, you simply slipped some dollars under your driving licence. I had to learn the hard way that this tactic only worked for Pistol Pete. And years later, as a pre-teen, I remember visiting him in prison in a rather grand office. He received my mother and me, seated in a swivel chair, in front of a huge leather-topped desk, dressed immaculately. I thought he owned the prison, he seemed to own everything else. It was only years later that I discovered he was an inmate – a very privileged inmate, but nevertheless, an inmate. I knew better than ever to ask him about that one. There were just some things I had to forget, others I didn't want to know and still others I didn't understand.

I never understood why at age eight I was accompanied by a policeman when I went to the skating rink, or to a public event like the Santa Claus parade, if Pistol Pete was unable to take me. I distinctly remember my age, because the policeman and I always walked hand in hand and once we met a friend of his, who playfully said, 'I see your girlfriends are getting younger and younger,' and he replied, 'Well, if I can't get one at sixteen, I get two at eight.' I remember being resentful of that other eight-year-old girl, whoever she was. I wanted that handsome policeman all to myself.

But as I grew older I sensed there was something not quite right in my world and it centred on how Pistol Pete made his money. When the usual questions arose concerning my father's profession, I was told to say, he was a business man, but on the rare occasion when I was asked, 'what business is he in?' I had no answer. Then when I was about ten, I went through a brief religious period. I said a prayer each night before I went to bed. And the words of that prayer haunt me to this day. 'Dear God, please help my father make a good living in a legitimate way.' But if I had any doubts or unanswered questions they were buried in a love that had no doubts and asked no questions.

As a teenager I made many attempts to emancipate myself from Pistol Pete's indulgences. One summer I decided to earn my own money and become financially independent. Pistol Pete got me a waitress job in a delicatessen frequented mainly by men, as their wives and children had gone off to the mountains and lakes to escape the sweltering Montreal summer. I was the only female employee. I once overheard a customer saying, 'That's Pistol Pete's daughter, she's working her way through college. Give her a big tip.' I had wanted to shed Pistol Pete's influence like a snake sheds an old skin. But it was impossible then and it is still impossible now.

***

With Ronit being attended to with so much loving care, supplemented by adoring paid care – it was difficult not to adore her – I was free to devote myself to the musicians without guilt or recrimination. And I took to my obligations with a zest far beyond the call of duty and with a payback that far exceeded expectations. I not only took them on sight-seeing tours, on shopping expeditions, fed them and listened to their stories, but was a sounding board for their songs and their troubles. And they responded with a fondness that was palatable and a sweetness that warmed my soul.

It was the time when coffeehouses and clubs where musicians performed were much in vogue. They not only provided a platform for those who were not yet famous to gain experience, but for the new breed of singer-songwriters to test their material. Some musicians, now household names like Bob Dylan, cut their teeth in these venues. The coffeehouse trend became so popular that it spread to many US cities and overflowed into Canada. And in Canada, the Finjan was one of the first to welcome that trend. Tucked away in Montreal, how else would I have met so many musicians?

It all began in Greenwich Village in New York City. Greenwich Village was the hub of the folk music scene. It was where young and not so young aspiring folk musicians came to find each other, to breathe the atmosphere, to meet their heroes, to play music and to learn from the experts. It was their university, their church. They came from all over the US and their first encounter with the vibrant music scene was usually in Washington Square, in the heart of the Village.

Little did Rhoda and I know, when we came to New York at age fifteen and discovered Greenwich Village, that the very places we visited hosted a turning point in the history of folk music – the advent of the singer-songwriter. The very first Sunday we were in New York – that same visit when we met Woody Guthrie– we somehow found our way to Washington Square. We hurried past the chess and checkers players, and the kids throwing Frisbees, eager to get to the special area by the fountain, where on Sundays musicians played. There were young musicians, old musicians, white musicians, black musicians; they played old songs, new songs and music without lyrics. They played blues, folk, country, gospel, ballads, work songs, love songs, and they played their own songs, singing of their own sorrows, their own loves, their own betrayals. And, for us, it was all magical.

That area, by the fountain in Washington Square, was a musical melting pot with its own unspoken traditions. Tourists, new comers and passers-by sat in the back area, regulars in the front. Musicians who were known to the discerning part of the audience and especially to the other musicians, sang on their own; unknowns often accompanied them while hoping for the chance to sing a song, or maybe even two. There were jamming sessions that never ended; someone popular taking the lead, then someone else equally popular taking over, then everyone playing together before someone, not so popular, began to play. There seemed to be an unwritten protocol that worked beautifully. I later discovered that musicians like Pete Seeger, Woody Guthrie, Lead Belly, Harry Belafonte and even my own

Brownie McGhee had played there at one time. Rhoda and I had unknowingly been part of a celebrated tradition, a part of folk music history.

From the park we followed some of the musicians into the coffeehouses. There was a wide variety of coffeehouses and clubs to choose from. In one street alone there were two coffeehouses only doors apart. Artists, writers, poets and musicians – a kind of avant-garde creative community that supported each other frequented them. Some people were into singing and playing music, some were into poetry, some into dance, some into alcohol and drugs and some into sexual assignations – everyone was into a little of something, and everything was tolerated, even celebrated. The booming folk scene was born in these coffeehouses, especially the ones that had hootenanny nights, nights when anyone could take the stage and perform several songs. A circuit of coffeehouses developed, with New York as the epicentre. Musicians went from one to the next, referred by other musicians.

The Finjan became part of that circuit, part of the booming folk music scene, the singer song-writer phenomenon, the debut of the new bards. Shimon and I would go to Greenwich Village every few months and frequent the hootenannies to find musicians for the Finjan. We were meeting the very musicians at the heart of that phenomenon and booking them for a week's Finjan performance. I loved it.

For me, meeting a new performer every week was, in a way, like travelling, each musician a new adventure, a new landscape to explore, a magic carpet, a small oasis. I didn't have to court the exceptional, as every traveller does; the exceptional courted me. I learned to tread softly as though entering a new land, feeling my way into the experience, discovering its possibilities.

Performing at the Finjan could be a difficult, lonely experience. Without the benefit of electronic assistance, of extravagant lighting, of a distanced stage, the performer had no technical support. He was alone, impaled by a red-amber spotlight, caged by expectant faces, with just his guitar and his voice. Yet he created sounds and images that went directly to the centre of feeling, enhanced by the intense sensuality he projected.

Most of the performers were male. Women seemed to find the bitter solitude of anonymous cities, strung together by vast stretches of highway, with only a guitar for comfort, too difficult to repeat and rarely returned. Unless they first became popular in their home towns, like Joan Baez, and could afford more secure travel, they were reluctant to take to the road. It was mainly their vulnerability that deterred them. One female musician who played at the Finjan told me she had to change her seat in the bus coming to Montreal because the guy seated beside her kept putting his hand up her skirt. And I remember one of my female friend musicians who began her career by singing in a bar where drunk guys would grab at her and follow her home. She hated it. That's just the way things were then, female musicians had a rough time. There was no 'Me Too' movement to give women the confidence to complain. They just had to endure or stay home. If the situation was difficult for white female singers, it was impossible for black female singers. They had the additional problem of racial prejudice to contend with. Black women were not even on the circuit. We never had a black woman singer perform at the Finjan.

At the time, racism, although legally dead, was very much alive and kicking. Jackie Washington, a black musician who played at the Finjan, told me he had once entered a cafe in New York arm in arm with a white female friend, and was told to leave because the owner was 'against mixed race marriages'. Jackie wasn't that surprised. 'Black will never become white' he said. When I asked him what he meant, he said prejudice against black people is fed to us with our mother's milk. That from the time we are born we are taught to fear black and to trust white. Black is associated with evil, with death, with darkness. It is the colour of funerals, of the devil, of corruption, of badness, 'black death' 'blackmail' 'black heart'. White is purity, innocence, wedding dresses, light, everything good. Not surprising there was a deep cultural bias against being black.

At the time the music scene, like everything else was heavily male dominated and my Finjan experiences were mainly with white male musicians. They intrigued me, these determined males, these gypsy bards. I was fascinated not only by their talent and by their need to make music, but by the way they lived – on the edge, exposed and vulnerable, singing of protest and love, their lives in their song. I admired their courage, their resilience, their strength.

For me, the musicians were like the images in their songs, like the sound of their music – tender, powerful, haunting, troubled. They were like outlaws with anti-establishment lyrics as their firepower and music as their weapons. They embodied romance, mystery, rebellion but, most of all, promise. I looked into their eyes, inhaled their music and longed for the unknown, for things yet to be.

***

By now we had a well-trained kitchen staff and I was free to enjoy the music and the musicians. Part of each night I would sit in the audience, alone and hidden from view so I could better lose myself in the experience. The musician sat on the tall stool, the guitar cradled in his thighs, the fingers of one hand fingering the slender neck, while the other hand beat a driving rhythm. When he lowered his head into the curves of the guitar, I could feel the perfect oneness of guitar and man. And when he threw back his head, drawing the guitar to his breast and closing his eyes, I shivered with the embrace. He held up his soul like a mirror and I saw myself in it. Sometimes I knew I could love him because of his song. I too was the wanderer and the rebel, but as I was temporarily anchored, I was able to provide an anchor for him, a brief respite.

Because the musicians were always on the road, not in one place long enough to make friends, they responded to my care with enthusiasm and affection. In one way, they had the effect children were supposed to have: they inspired mothering, love. But, unlike children, they never overstayed their welcome; their last song left me wanting more. And they gave me more.

After the Finjan evening ended, the three of us, Shimon, me and the musician, would return home, usually around midnight. I would make tea and we would talk, mostly about music, musicians, other clubs – shop talk. Then Shimon, exhausted, would go to bed. The musician would be full of performance adrenalin, too hyped-up to sleep. I was never exhausted, and he and I would remain talking. We would spend the rest of the night ensconced in my wonderful kitchen, its wall-to-wall windows opening to the stars and the sky. The talking would become more personal, more intimate and then he would sing for me, play me songs he was composing. And in the glow of candlelight holding us in a soft embrace, I would listen to his music in rapt silence, participating in his vision, immersed in his poetry, caught in his spell.

With the first signs of light, I'd slip away, not allowing the mundane shapes of morning to dispel the poetry of the night. In what remained of the day, I would cook for the musician, ascend Mount Royal in the heart of the city to dream under the weeping willows by the lake, attend to Ronit, glance over my university work, see to Finjan preparations and wait for the night. Of course, this sort of experience didn't happen with all the musicians who played at the Finjan, but with enough of them to fulfil the adventure.

They were very important to me, those nights. The musicians not only evoked a tangle of feelings and emotions, but were an education, an inspiration. They dared to point to a new horizon over which the changing times were taking shape, and I, along with my generation, tuned into their vision, sharing their sense of triumph in breaking new ground. Armed with flowers in our hair, coils of beads around our necks and lines from their songs, we embraced the changing times.

I became very close to some of them; a few became lifelong friends, a few became lovers, and a few went on to become famous. Bob Dylan was one of the latter.

10

Bob Dylan

BOB DYLAN EPITOMIZED MANY of the characteristics that drew me to the musicians, but it was some time before I discovered this. I first heard him play in the early sixties in New York at Gerde's Folk City, one of the Greenwich Village clubs popular with folk singers. Every Monday night, Gerde's had a hootenanny and, when Shimon and I went to New York to find musicians for the Finjan, that was our main stop. The standard was high and many now well-known musicians used Gerde's as a showcase, not only to perfect their skills, but to be discovered. Agents, journalists, club owners were known to frequent Gerde's hootenannies in search of new talent and there was always the hope of a mention by some journalist, or even an engagement by some club owner.

I remember that evening well because it troubled me. When the M.C., Brother John Sellers, called Bob Dylan's name, Bob looked uncomfortable and kind of limped on to the stage, whereas the other performers leapt on to it. He looked so thin; I could see his shoulder blades jutting through his shirt. His face was strained and pale, his jaunty cap making it look even paler and his clothes had a limp scarecrow quality. I later discovered the audience didn't know him and, it seemed, didn't want to know him. He had recently come to New York mainly to meet his hero, Woody Guthrie, and to try his hand at performing. That night was one of his first public performances.

I remember him fiddling with his guitar and harmonica before he began playing and someone yelling, 'Get on with it, we didn't come here to sleep.' And before he had used up his allotted performance time, there were shouts for him to get off the stage. He tried to continue singing through the shouts, but the shouts just got louder and more enthusiastic. Finally, he slunk off the stage looking like he'd been fatally wounded. The New York music scene aficionados were not known for their indulgence or benevolence. They took no prisoners.

I was one of the few people who clapped, not only because of empathy – coming from the polite provinces, the dismissive, impatient, New York audience appalled me – but because I had bothered to listen and I was moved. His voice had a rent, rasping, wailing quality, as though it had been caught on barbed wire. It tore deeper and wailed louder as it meshed with his lyrics, giving them a raw, painful edge. It was as though I felt what he was singing, rather than heard it or understood it. I can't remember exactly what he sang that night, except that there was a lot about injustice, but whatever it was went straight to my heart.

As it turned out I wasn't the only one smitten by Dylan. The *New York Times* journalist Robert Sheldon also heard him play at Gerde's and wrote an article about him. The headline read, '*20-YEAR-OLD SINGER IS BRIGHT NEW FACE.*' It was this article that placed Dylan firmly on the road to stardom.

When Dylan came to perform in Montreal less than a year later, I went to meet him at a bar where the airport bus terminated. I had got to know him during my New York visits. During one such visit, he told me he had been hired for a two-week gig in Montreal at a club that had recently opened. He asked if I could suggest somewhere inexpensive for him to stay. Coincidently there was no one staying with us that month as we were having a month of local performers, including 'A Night With Shimon'. 'Why don't you stay with us?' I volunteered. 'I'll even pick you up at the airport bus terminal.' I didn't have to ask him twice. That's how come I was now waiting for him at the terminal.

He was very late arriving and I was just about to leave without him when he appeared, flustered and dishevelled. As soon as he saw me, without so much as a handshake – even before I had time to notice he had gained not only weight but inches – he launched into one of those sad, funny, monologues I was to become so fond of, explaining why he was delayed.

He told me that upon arriving at the Montreal airport, the French custom officials had put him through some intensive questioning – probably because he looked like an unruly hippy and spoke with a heavy cowboy drawl. The custom authorities were not keen on hippies and cowboy hippies were especially disconcerting, requiring additional scrutiny. This came as a shock to him. 'Hey, man,' he had responded to one question, 'that ain't none of your business.' His behaviour must have seemed so erratic, so surly, that the officers decided to search him. 'Can you believe those mother fuckers?' he said to me. 'They started poking into my things, my personal things.'

When the officer had the audacity to open his bag, he pulled it away, outraged by the intrusion into his privacy. 'You can't do that, them's my personal belongings,' he protested. He flashed me a look of indignation, took a long pull on his cigarette, and said: 'I hate that kind of stuff.' Apparently he had no idea they could do exactly that kind of stuff. He became increasingly incensed as the officials not only probed his belongings, but began searching his person. Offering the officer one of his harmonicas, in mock compliance, he smiled sardonically and said: 'Hey man, if it's the dope you want, I got it hid right here in my harmonica.' He couldn't believe what happened next.

'D'ye know what those mother fuckers did? They unscrewed every screw in my harmonicas looking for the dope. Those dumb-assed coppers thought I was going to tell them where I stash the shit. Those creeps couldn't even speak English.' By the time the search was over, he had missed the airport bus into town and had to wait over an hour for the next one, giving him time to dwell on the injustices and to fuel his fury.

'When I got into town, I went into the first bar I saw for a drink, y'know to cool my head – it needed cooling real bad. I ordered my drink and gave the barman a ten-dollar bill. That dude took my good US money and gave me monopoly money for change, y'know that phony-coloured money. He even gave me a two-dollar bill.' I remembered that US currency had no two-dollar bills and was all one colour, whereas Canadian money had a different colour for each denomination.

Dylan took a drag on his cigarette and shook his head in disbelief. 'Hey man,' I said, 'what do you take me for? I ain't no fool. I ain't taking none of your funny money. You some kind of crook or what? He started hollerin' and screamin' and I stared hollerin' and screamin' even louder and he said he was callin' the po-leece. That dude was sure fucking with my head. And all those streets were headin' down the hill into the river and I just knew that if I didn't sit tight, I'd roll right down into the river and drown.' He looked at me with a look of total incomprehension. 'What kind of a place is this anyway? I sure could use some salvation.' Totally spent after his tirade, he remained silent, puffing on his cigarette.

I tried to look sympathetic but said nothing, not that he expected me to say anything, and not that there was anything to say. But I couldn't help wondering if it was possible he knew nothing about border crossings, custom officials, countries with different languages or different currencies. Could it be that this was his first time out of the US? I never knew if that traumatic entry into Canada was entirely real, partly imagined, or a bit of both, but I loved the story whichever it was.

I later discovered he had left the bus before the terminal because he had spotted a bar from the window. Then, trying to find the terminus where we had arranged to meet, he wandered downhill along the side streets, and found himself by the river, Montreal being an island surrounded by the St. Lawrence River. He must have been surprised to encounter the river, hence his 'river drowning' fiction.

When I got to know him better, I understood that the impression of baffled innocence and inability to fathom the ways of the world was cultivated as part of his persona. In fact, he was astute, knowledgeable, even disciplined. It was his way of keeping people off balance; of controlling the situation by not letting on if what he was saying was fact or fantasy. I came to accept this and to enjoy whichever it was.

That attitude of incredible naivety when dealing with the practicalities of life, like he had just stepped into the present century, was in evidence during many of the subsequent times I saw him in New York. Once Dylan and I were visiting John Lee Hooker, who was staying at the Chelsea Hotel. Dylan often played with John, having been his opening act at the very beginning of Dylan's career, and they had become good friends. By this time John had played at the Finjan and had stayed with us, and he had extended an open invitation to visit him whenever Shimon and I were in New York. I, in turn, had invited my Israeli friend, Rivka, to join us. Rivka, who was temporarily living in New York, was eager to visit the legendary Chelsea Hotel.

The Chelsea was a unique New York landmark. It was the home of creativity edged with eccentricity, wild indulgences and hell-raising. It was the home of artists, writers, musicians, actors, assorted crazies, and waifs and strays. It was an 'anything goes' place. Arthur Miller, who lived there for six years after his split from Marilyn Monroe, wrote: 'There are no vacuum cleaners, no rules and no shame.'

The Chelsea had no amenities like television or room service, but there was a high level of creativity engendered by the intense energy of its residents, who, like magnets, drew more creativity, more inventiveness, more works of art into its fold. Allen Ginsberg wrote *On The Road* at the Chelsea; Arthur C Clarke wrote *A Space Odyssey* on the premises; Freda Kahlo painted there; Leonard Cohen wrote the song *Chelsea Hotel* about a night he spent there with Janis Joplin; and in Bob Dylan's song *Sad Eyed Lady Of The Lowlands*, written for his new wife, Sara, he wrote about staying up for long hours at the Chelsea Hotel, writing the song for her.

I had stayed at the Chelsea Hotel several times and had given it rave reviews. So who could blame my friend Rivka for wanting to imbibe the Chelsea atmosphere?

Bob and Rivka hit it off immediately. He seemed very taken with her and said, suggestively, that he'd never eaten Israeli food and would love to try it. And she, eagerly responding to the undisguised hint, invited him to dinner. He was delighted by the invitation, visibly excited, and was in the process of noting her address. 'Eighty-eighth street,' she told him. He stopped writing, returned the pencil and paper to his pocket and smiled apologetically.

'I can't come.'

'Why?' she asked, confused. Things had been going so well.

'I don't go above forty-second street.' He paused, then as if in explanation, added, 'There's some real weird people up there.'

'There's some real weird people down here,' John said, frowning at Dylan.

But Dylan was undeterred. 'Forty-second Street, that's as far as I go.'

And that was that.

Another time, inspired by my passion for travel, and probably by the memory of Rivka, he said, 'Yeah, I'd like to travel...I'd like to see Israel...what d'ye have to do to get there?'

'Well, first you have to get a passport,' I said, remembering that he hadn't needed a passport when he came to Montreal, as a driver's licence was adequate at that time for an American to enter Canada.

'How d'ye do that?'

I couldn't tell if he really didn't know, but I went along for the ride. 'You write to the passport office for a form, fill it, take some photos, pay some money and send it all back to the passport office and then you wait. Eventually the passport arrives.'

He looked disheartened. 'Ye' gotta do all that?'

'It's no big deal.'

'I ain't going nowhere if I gotta do all that.'

Both Israel and Rivka were off the agenda.

But all that was much later. When he came to Montreal on that first visit, his fortunes had significantly improved from the time I had seen him in Gerde's and the improvement was reflected in his bearing. He seemed to have lengthened and widened. Instead of being a complete unknown, he now had a small but devoted following, mainly other musicians who thought he was brilliant. Most importantly, he had recently recorded his first album, *Bob Dylan*. And although most of the songs on it were well known folk songs in the style of Woody

Guthrie, with only two originals, 'Talkin' New York' and 'Songs for Woody', and although sales were no great shakes, it did much to boost his confidence. He seemed more assured, more assertive. That orphaned look was almost gone. And, by the time we got home, I was meeting a vastly different Bob Dylan from the one I had encountered at Gerde's, only a year earlier.

For the two weeks Dylan was in Montreal, he stayed with us and shared Ronit's room. He was great as a house guest but somewhat questionable as a performer.

Shimon asked him to do a guest set the night he was free. He even paid him twelve Canadian dollars. The night was pretty much a disaster. He was the only musician we ever had who people walked out on. His rough, gravelly voice with its nasal twang didn't appeal to Finjan audiences. He seemed unprofessional, muttering between songs, stopping and starting over, and fidgeting with his guitar, uncomfortable on the high stool. Not knowing what to make of him or of his songs, some people walked out.

But unlike the time at Gerde's, when the weight of audience disapproval seemed to crush him, this time he pretended indifference. As people left, he stopped his playing and with a slight bow, affecting the tone of a gracious host said, 'Good night. I hope you enjoyed yourself. Thank you for coming, see you next time,' and resumed playing. Normally people not only stayed to the very last song, but insisted on encores. Aware of the depleted audience, Dylan said, 'Nearly all the people have gone, I might as well just stay up here,' and he continued playing to an almost empty room. Actually, for me, this was the best part of the evening; intimate, casual – more like a private, impromptu jamming session.

Later that night, he said to me, 'At least I played for you guys,' in an attempt to rescue at least part of the evening. And I replied, 'And us guys loved it.'

Ironically, only a few months later, Dylan had become such an icon that young musicians, like Toronto's Murray McLaughan, who was to become well known himself, vied to sleep in the bed Bob Dylan had slept in. And the people who had walked out on him wore their affront as a badge of honour. Imagine the kudos, the mileage, one accumulates by having walked out on Bob Dylan.

It turned out that Jack Nissenson, a regular at the Finjan, had recorded Bob Dylan that very night. He had asked Dylan's permission and Dylan had graciously given it, probably flattered by the request. Apparently Jack had excellent recording equipment and that recording became the CD Ronit referred to years later, when she phoned to tell me that *Bob Dylan at the Finjan* was the hottest bootleg CD. And it was that phone call and that CD which inspired this book.

But on that memorable Finjan night, provoked by the lack of appreciation, Dylan said to Shimon, 'This has gotta be the last time I do clubs, from now on I only do concerts. I'm going to play Carnegie Hall. I'm going to make it big.' Shimon laughed inwardly at the absurdity of the idea. 'Yeah, you and who else?' he thought. Shimon wasn't particularly impressed by Dylan's non-melodic songs, and by his often-off-key voice. And, was guilty of the mother of all regrets, for which he is no doubt still repenting: he refused Bob Dylan a return engagement.

But I was mesmerized right from the start. For me, that disgruntled monotone voice with its sudden wail, which people objected to that night, was a third instrument interwoven into his guitar and harmonica playing, and counterpointing, complementing, adding a new dimension to his haunting, poignant, lyrics. I loved his imagination, his poetry, and I loved what he was singing about, his challenge to authority, to injustice, to 'the masters of war', as well as his celebration of the young, the powerless, the outcasts. But also the personal agony, the grief, the anxiety, as well as the joy, involved in being alive.

That night, when people had walked out on him and he pretended it didn't matter, turned out to be one of the most special nights of my life; the kind of night that grows in significance with time; the kind of night whose memory is the jewel in the treasure chest.

Bob and I had remained talking long after Shimon had gone to bed. It was obvious he was affected by the audience reaction more than he cared to let on. The evening had taken its toll. He confessed that he was feeling down – achy, depleted. 'I'm all twisted up. I need to unwind real bad,' he said, grimacing as he rubbed the back of his neck.

'I have just the ticket,' I said, jumping in at the deep end. 'Would you like a massage? I'm really good at massage,' I added, just in case he needed convincing. He didn't.

'Is the Pope Catholic?' he replied.

Massage was not part of the Finjan contract but extras were always welcome, and massage was an extra with bows and ribbons. Although I was very much into massage – besides being wonderfully healing, it afforded a unique pretext for sensual contact without sexual complications – Dylan was the only musician to whom I had ever made the offer. But as soon as I made it, the bravado diminished. I lost confidence and retreated into formality.

Ronit was with my parents, so her bedroom was the obvious choice. Leaving the secure kitchen for the uncertain bedroom was scary. But it was too late. Bob was already there. To conceal the fact that I didn't know where I was going, I adopted the manner of a health professional; busy, efficient, capable, in a kind of 'no hanky-panky' message, although my heart was missing a few beats. I didn't even trust myself to speak. In a sort of no-nonsense fashion, in order to flesh out my professional status, I signalled for him to push both beds together and to strip to his underwear. But I didn't remove the sleeveless, knee-length summer dress I was wearing. To prevent my hair becoming intrusive, I twisted it into a knot and pinned it back. Then I washed my hands, got the almond oil from the bathroom, poured some into a dish and covered the sheets with towels to absorb any drips. Lastly, I lit a candle although this was definitely not in the script. Switching off the light, I pointed to the bed.

Dylan flopped down, melting into the bed, instantly at ease. He had obviously been there before. He abandoned himself to that massage with the intensity he devoted to his song writing – every nuance counted. I began in professional mode, attempting to hide my apprehension. But as soon as my hands made contact I was reassured. I really was good at massage, having completed most of a massage course, and I swung into automatic. As my thumbs circled and coaxed the small knots and ridges imbedded in his flesh and my palms pressed and kneaded his pale, buttery skin, my fingers reaching into the tension, I could feel his body sigh as it surrendered to my hands. He made small purring noises and at one point it seemed as though he was humming a tune. I felt good, accomplished, in a way exonerated from myself, and began to relax.

When I paused to refill the oil, Dylan said, almost in a whimper: 'Don't stop. I need this to level my head.' It was as though I was violating a wonderful reverie. Actually, I hadn't considered stopping, but the acknowledgement of my proficiency was so satisfying, it made the very idea an impossibility. I continued with an even more absolute focus. Soon nothing else existed, nothing else mattered.

Then something strange happened. I should have anticipated it as I could feel him disappearing into the massage. He began to mumble words and phrases that went nowhere, connected with nothing; lines like poetry, a fragment of dream, a snatch of story, bits of a song; sad, funny, poignant, beautiful, frightening images – all of them together. They were like bright flashes etched in the darkness; sudden leaps from sense to no sense, a kind of trance-like scribbling, visible for only a moment before disappearing into the dark. And although they moved in and out of my comprehension, they made some kind of subliminal sense. The unpredictable twists and spirals engulfed me, swallowed me. I could feel myself entering some kind of mesmerizing universe.

As I listened, my mind absorbing the flow of words turning into pictures and back again to words, the massage acquired a new dimension. It no longer bore any reference to a sensual encounter. Dylan's mind had become a collage of images in which lucidity and incongruity entwined, some kind of subconscious tapestry, a montage of overlapping weaves, colours and textures. The bed had become a small island adrift in a surreal sea of words. But it was as though I wasn't there physically. The knot of my hair had long ago become undone, but I no longer brushed it aside and was unaware where it fell. Only my hands were there. I was inside his head and I understood that which was not understandable. It was astonishing, strange, exceptional. It was where I had never been.

And just as he couldn't stop talking – it was more than talking, impressions seemed to be pouring out of him – I couldn't stop massaging. It was more than massaging; energy seemed to be flowing from my hands, which had become powerful entities, shaping, creating, releasing wild images trapped in his head. I had the sense I was no longer entirely me; I was just hands and if my hands didn't expel those images, they would explode and it was my hands that were maintaining stability, balance, even sanity. I was compelled to go on and on. I continued the massage until morning came and he was asleep and I was exhausted but exhilarated.

That massage remained a mystery to me. And, although I wanted the mystery to remain intact, I couldn't help wondering about it. Where had I been? Where had he been? What had happened? Many years later, I read something Dylan said in an interview with the music journalist, Paul Zollo, which shed just enough light to put the mystery within my grasp, while still retaining its magic: 'It's nice to be able to put yourself in an environment where you can completely accept the unconscious stuff that comes to you from your inner workings of your mind.' Perhaps that night had been such a time.

Later, Dylan told me if he ever got rich the first thing he would do is get a fulltime massage person. Although I didn't apply for the job, that massage cemented our friendship. I saw him whenever I went to New York, and I went fairly often to see friends I had made the summer I spent there studying dance, as well as going to the theatre and to hear music, and just to imbibe the vibes of a city I loved. Our times together were a treat. He had an unexpected side to him that I adored. He liked being the jester, being silly, leaping into capsules of off-beat acting out, improvising tiny performances which plunged in and out of other realities. He often shared these fantasy morsels with Rambling Jack Elliott, his musician friend who greatly influenced his music, his style, even his behaviour – both of them Woody Guthrie devotees. They were very funny together, breaking into incongruous scenarios of whatever took their fancy.

One summer night when I was in New York, the three of us were tripping through the streets, feeling on top of the world. Both Bob and Jack looked like a pair of transposed cowboys, in cowboy hats, boots, worn jeans, guitars and dark glasses. It was unseemly for cowboys to wear glasses but 'shades' were acceptable. I was the purple cowgirl sidekick, with my own cowgirl hat. They were at their playful, fun-loving best; laughing, joking, bouncing off each other. Suddenly we came to a wide square with an illuminated fountain in its centre, the water rising and falling in bursts of colour. The setting was irresistible – an ideal backdrop crying out for improvised theatre. Bob and Jack climbed the fountain wall and pulled me up after them.

We sat on the wall, our legs dangling over the side, the fountain at our backs, looking down at the passers-by, playing 'king of the castle'. Bob raised his guitar to toast the occasion and began strumming and picking, country style. Jack joined him. A crowd gathered beneath us.

Bob looked down on the raised faces and burst into Shakespeare. 'I'm Ham-let,' he drawled, in fluent cowboy, accompanied by twangs and licks on the guitar, 'and this here is Or-feel-ye-ah.' He pointed the guitar at Jack, who nodded and tipped his hat to accompanying strums and riffs. 'Far out!' someone yelled. And, with this crumb of approval they launched into a personal rendition of Hamlet, narrated by two laid-back cowboys sitting around a campfire and supplemented by Country and Western guitar picking. It was hilarious. The play on the words 'to be or not to be' had me laughing so hard I almost fell off the wall. Later, we found the ground strewn with coins.

Another time I was with Dylan, walking along a Greenwich Village street when I heard giggling behind us. I turned to see two teeny-boppers and was sure they were following us; that is, following Bob. It was his first experience with that kind of recognition and it was hard to convince him that the girls were actually following him. 'No way,' he said, and stopped abruptly to see if they too would stop. They did, shyly and at a safe distance. He was ecstatic. 'I'm being followed,' he whooped. 'Can you believe it, I'm being followed!' I believed it.

The incident inspired a confession. 'It's not that unusual. I once followed Woody Guthrie when I was a teenager, right here in the Village,' I said, aware I was unleashing a boomerang.

'Y'mean you followed Woody Guthrie, *the* Woody Guthrie?' He was as stunned as if I had just revealed that I was really the Virgin Mary. Woody Guthrie was his hero, his guru, the formative influence in his life, in his music. One of the first songs he wrote was 'A Song to Woody'. He talked like Woody, sang like him, even wrote talking blues like him. His main reason for coming to New York had been to meet Woody and hopefully to play with him. Unfortunately, by the time he came to New York, Woody was very ill and in hospital. Dylan often visited him there and played for him. Woody was especially pleased with Dylan's 'Song for Woody'.

I had never told him about that following Woody experience and he insisted on hearing every detail. The story was a winner. I think it was after hearing the story that he offered me the key to flat 3, his apartment in the Village, on West 4th street, in case I wanted a place to rest when I was visiting New York. Anyone who had such an amazing experience with Woody deserved at least a place to rest. The apartment was a luxury for him as until that point he had been sleeping in Izzy Young's bookstore, 'The Folk Center', curled around the free-standing wood stove, which he pointed out to me one day. Although small and cramped, the apartment was definitely an upgrade.

I was with Bob in that very apartment when he wrote 'Tomorrow is Such a Long Time', the song about his girlfriend, Suze Rotolo. Suze is the girl pictured on the cover of his second album, *The Freewheelin' Bob Dylan*, huddled into Bob for protection against the cold as they hurry down a windy Village street, covered in snow. When he wrote the song, Suze had torn herself away from Bob, seduced by a trip to Italy to study art. He was bereft. That day, in his apartment, he composed the lyrics, just like that. No hand wringing, no endless re-writes. The emotions were so raw, so all-consuming, so much an expression of 'that unconscious stuff that comes from the inner workings of the mind', that writing it seemed natural, easy. I was gripped by the heartbreak imagery he was able to create seemingly without effort. I found the song achingly moving, an anthem to lost love. I can still hardly hear the song without feeling the anguish, the grieving, feel the imagery of a broken man – blind, deaf and mute with pain.

The last time I saw Dylan in New York was at Gerde's Folk City, where I had first seen him in the early sixties. Only a few years after that first meeting, our lives had irrevocably diverged. He had suddenly become a super star, touring Canada, Europe and Australia, recording six albums by 1965 and marrying in the same year. He was no longer in New York, no longer on the same planet.

At that last encounter, Shimon and I had been at Gerde's to check out performers for the Finjan as usual. The word quickly circulated that someone was booking for a club. Dylan was talking to us when several musicians approached Shimon, eager to have a word with him. Shimon excused himself, saying, 'Business is business,' and retreated to a more secluded corner, followed by the musicians.

'Your husband sure is famous,' Dylan said, impressed.

II

Cedric Smith and Lucy in the Sky

I F BOB DYLAN WAS one of the musicians who became famous, Cedric Smith was one of the musicians who became a lifelong friend. It happened the moment he walked through the door. I'm not sure how, but sometimes energies mesh so beautifully that although there is no physical coming together, there is an even more profound coming together which just *is*.

No doubt Shimon had a lot to do with it. Surprisingly, he and Cedric became instant buddies. On the whole, Shimon was somewhat detached from the musicians. They kept an unspoken distance from him and he from them. After all, he was the boss. Not that he was in the least bit boss-like. On the contrary, he respected the musicians too much to want any power over them. But want it or not, it came with the territory. It was he who made all the technical and financial determinations; the hiring, the signing of contracts, the decision on return engagements, all of which he found uncomfortable and which helped create a more formal relationship between him and them. Also, the musicians had to impress him if they were to be invited back, which added to the formality and increased the awkwardness.

Besides, Shimon had always kept himself pretty much to himself. He liked doing his own thing and it often didn't include anyone else, not even me. Then too he was very busy. Aside from all the Finjan work, he was still performing, and could hardly keep up with the accolades, like the one from the Association of Young Women, when he played for them one night, '... it was one of the most satisfying programs we've had this year – and the people are still taking about it and you.' He was learning new songs, practising guitar, painting and spending time with Ronit. He was happy to participate in anything I organized: dinners, jamming sessions, country drives. But it was up to me to do the organizing. He was more than content to have me do the socializing, to have me stay up nights talking to the musicians, addressing their needs, entertaining them, having them entertain me. Keeping the musicians happy was my department. And for me that department was the icing on the cake, the adventure in the oasis. The arrangement, although unspoken and unregulated, suited both of us.

But with Cedric it was different. Shimon took to Cedric in a way he hadn't taken to any other musician. They had much in common, not only musically but politically, and relished their political discussions. Shimon enjoyed Cedric's company and sought him out. But then, who wouldn't enjoy Cedric's company? Cedric, besides being amazingly talented and funny, was knowledgeable, interesting and interested in everyone and everything. Shimon and Cedric had long chats about a wide variety of subjects. With most of the other musicians, the communication was limited to music and musicians.

Cedric also made me laugh more than anyone I had ever known, and that alone merited lifelong affection. He could speak in a variety of accents, breaking into spontaneous mini skits, instantaneously creating both characters and plot, speaking several parts, both male and female, turning an ordinary situation into a hilarious one. He once did a one-man show called 'Billy Bishop Goes to War', where he played sixteen parts, including an airplane and a French prostitute. He was both an accomplished actor, playing major Shakespeare roles in Stratford Ontario's Festival Theatre, and a talented musician and songwriter, who had recorded several albums and who ran The Black Swan, a popular after-hours club in Stratford, where he was also the star attraction. Most importantly, Cedric communicated easily with Shimon, whereas most of the musicians left the communicating to me.

Despite a long list of accomplishments, one of Cedric's most endearing qualities was an inherent modesty. He shunned celebrity status and had no prima donna affectations. Although he was often the star of a production, he was helpful and attentive to actors and musicians who were new to the stage. He was known as 'a treat to work with'. Despite being the same age as the other musicians, he had a lot more experience on and off the stage, which gave him a certain confidence, making communication effortless. Shimon found him easy to relate to and respected him, not only as a musician but as a human being.

As for me, aside from admiring his accomplishments, I was also in awe of his principles, his ethics and morals. When he was hardly out of his teens, his band, the Perth County Conspiracy, recorded an album for the high-profile Columbia record company. This meant being showered with all the sought-after celebrity trappings that accompanied becoming a Columbia recording artist. These included a first-class promotional trip to England; chauffeured limos at his disposal; fine wining and dining, five-star hotels and access to a superior selection of groupies and smokes.

But Cedric was more concerned that Columbia was ripping off the public by overcharging for the album, than flattered by his star-status treatment. He was concerned to the point of advising Columbia he would break his contract if they refused to lower the price of the album. They refused, secure in the knowledge that no aspiring musician would dare break a lusted-after Columbia contract. But, despite receiving threats and warnings, that's exactly what Cedric did. He broke the contract, unheard of among ambitious young musicians.

Cedric had been born in England and emigrated to Canada with his parents when still a child. He came from a working-class background and never allowed the glow of celebrity to tarnish his working-class sympathies. The people he most respected were single working mothers, who faced the burden of raising a family on meagre wages, and the man he respected most was his father, who worked as a window cleaner but who was always singing. One of his major distastes was big, wealthy companies exploiting hard-pressed working people. Breaking the contract was his personal form of protest.

The album *The Perth County Conspiracy* (Perth County being his home county) and the concerts which accompanied it were so influential that many young people began coming to Perth County, arriving at his door to join the mythical 'conspiracy'. He then had to produce a second album called *The Perth County Conspiracy Does Not Exist*, in an effort to dissuade them.

The Perth County Conspiracy had started life as a quasi-band founded by Cedric and Richard Keelan, an American musician, and it had expanded to include a host of other talented musicians, as well as an assortment of artistically inclined friends. However, Cedric and Richard remained its backbone, especially Cedric. Actually it was more than a band, it was a way of life, a kind of hippie commune with music as its focus. Performances included girls in long dresses dancing and offering homemade baked delicacies to the audience, a stage decorated with flowers and colourful patchwork backdrops, and original folk rock music with inserts of mine, dance, poetry and Shakespearian dialogue. Cedric's aim was to integrate theatre, poetry, satire and commentary with music, a kind of multi-media event. The heavy female involvement created a special vibe, which set the band apart from its male counterparts. Women dancing with sparklers often stole the show and fuelled fantasies to do with communes, free love, and other radical concepts prevalent at the time. The message was peace, love and justice, and the concerts were so joyful, so unconventional and so provocative that it was little wonder young people saw The Conspiracy as an alternative lifestyle, while the media perceived it as being an 'original phenomenon' worthy of their attention.

Although Cedric played in clubs all over the US and was offered many opportunities to live there, earn mega bucks and become mega famous, the seductive New York and California music and film scenes were unable to persuade him to leave Canada. He hated US hype and preferred living in low-profile, less materialistic Canada.

Cedric and I became close, intimate friends, even closer because our relationship was devoid of sexual complications. We got that issue done and dusted early on. Somehow, in some unconscious part of my being that keeps me safe, I was aware that that aspect of things would deplete our relationship rather than enhance it. Also, I became friends with his lady friends and especially with his main lady, the gentle and beautiful Dorit. Dorit had the amazing ability to make everything she touched beautiful, something I was in awe of. I would never have wanted to cause her even a morsel of grief.

It wasn't that I found Cedric undesirable. On the contrary. He was drop dead gorgeous – 'alarmingly sexy', as one of his female admirers put it. But I was aware that if I pursued an undeniable attraction, it could become a fatal one. Things weren't meant to happen that way. The test came when I first visited him.

Cedric was always inviting Shimon and me to visit him in Stratford, to attend a theatre production and to hear him play at The Black Swan. One day I took him up on the offer, although Shimon was unable to join me.

Cedric had other visitors that night and it turned out that he and I had to share a room. It was late by the time we got back from The Black Swan and we stayed awake, talking, making it even later. We were both giddy with tiredness and flopped onto the bed. Cedric was hilariously funny and I laughed until my sides ached. In the midst of the laughter, sort of arising from it, Cedric made a half-hearted sexual advance. He probably felt it was the only polite thing to do. I knew he had several ladies on the go and not including me in the mix would have seemed churlish. However, my reaction was just to continue laughing.

I'm not sure why the idea of sexual contact seemed funny; it just seemed to blend in with the rest of the hilarity. But, in retrospect, I realize it was an instinctive protection from something that was not a good idea. For a brief moment he looked a little hurt, but then he joined me and we both laughed. Cedric was not offended – on the contrary, I think he was relieved – and the boundaries were set.

Once we got over that hurdle, the path was cleared for an affectionate, intensely close relationship, with embraces that were free from jealousy and its accomplices: bitterness, vindictiveness and tears. It was, and still is, a relationship the likes of which I've never had with any other male, or any other female for that matter.

***

Cedric was a regular performer at the Finjan. He was extremely popular and, like Sonny and Brownie, the audience couldn't get enough of him. Neither could I. It was always fun when Cedric was the guest singer. Besides, he introduced us to musicians he had performed with in US clubs. Some, like Ramblin' Jack Elliot, became friends. And he introduced us to much else.

I visited Cedric regularly in Stratford, Ontarios and he visited me in England long after the Finjan was no more. He joined me in Morocco where we travelled together. We had wonderful adventures in Ireland, in Italy, in Scotland. I adored Cedric. Anyone who could always make me laugh deserved my undying adoration. Cedric was one of the most precious gifts the Finjan gave me.

Shimon, too, developed an enduring relationship with Cedric. The easy communication between them mushroomed into a lifelong, close friendship. And I suspect Cedric's frequent Finjan engagements were partially inspired by Shimon's desire to spend more time with him.

The 'much else' that Cedric introduced us to had a lasting effect both on my life and on Shimon's, even though some may challenge its life-enhancing value. Each time Cedric performed at the Finjan, he raved about the wonders of listening to music with a head full of marijuana.

'You don't know what you're missing. Just try listening to the Beatles and you'll know what I mean. You'll see those diamonds in the sky,' he enthused. And each time he played at the Finjan, his enthusiasm grew more vociferous: 'What kind of club owners don't smoke grass?' he complained. 'It's practically illegal. You'll lose all club cred.' He felt it was his personal mission to address this unheard-of failing.

Both Shimon and I had never smoked anything; not tobacco, not marijuana, not anything. We were often teased, even reprimanded for this serious inadequacy. I remember telling one of the performers about our trip to east Africa.

'How was the ganja in Africa?' he asked.

'Ganja?' I pondered. 'I don't know. We didn't smoke anything.'

'Then why did you go?' he said, genuinely bewildered.

However, Cedric finally cracked our resistance with his incessant rave reviews exalting the glory of the weed. Late one Saturday evening, in a celebratory mood after an especially brilliant and lucrative performance, we decided to take the plunge. Cedric was delighted and, as soon as we gave him the word, began preparing a coming-of-age ritual. Everything had to be just right for the initiation: the right music, the right lighting, the right incense, the right rolling paper and, most important, the best weed available, which fortunately he happened to have with him.

The preparation of the 'joint' was a ceremony unto itself, almost as important and enjoyable as the finished product, for it heralded untold wonders. And on this occasion the ceremony took on a special initiation significance. Cedric wanted to create the perfect joint to enable us to have the perfect experience. I had watched this ritual many times before, but this was the first time I would be a participant and I was somewhat apprehensive. I disliked the idea of losing control and hadn't even taken a mild anaesthetic to relieve the agony when I was giving birth. But putting aside any misgivings, I gave myself up to the possibility of experiencing new dimensions of being.

Cedric took the first draw; long and slow and professional. He held the smoke tight in his lungs as he passed the joint to me. I inhaled in tiny, suspicious draws, with a caution I was not known for, but ended up coughing and sputtering despite the precaution, my throat aflame. Shimon inhaled as though drawing his last breath, exhaling enough smoke to power a small locomotive and gasping for breath.

'Good toke,' Cedric applauded, 'you've got the hang of it,' giving Shimon full marks, something I didn't merit.

'You just need a little more practice,' he said, passing the joint back to Shimon for instant 'more practice'.

Another round followed; Cedric a professional, me a sissy novice, Shimon inhaling as though his life depended on it, encouraged by Cedric's praise. After another two rounds, or perhaps it was three, we lay on the floor, sinking into the cushions Cedric had arranged close to the speakers, for maximum effect. With eyes closed, we listened to 'Lucy in the Sky with Diamonds', the volume raised to a decimal short of unbearable. I squeezed my eyes shut, intent on discovering new insights, new revelations, my body disappearing into the cushions, my head filled with good vibrations. Yes, I was beginning to get the point.

The first diamond was twinkling in Lucy's sky when I felt a restless shuffling beside me. It was Shimon trying to get to his feet, then struggling to get to the loo, staggering so badly he had to cling to the walls. By the time he staggered back, the diamonds had retreated into the sky and the mellow abandonment I had experienced was replaced by an indefinable stone-cold-sober anxiety. Shimon was hunched over, clutching his guts and, even in the dim light, I could see his face was several shades lighter than normal and tinged with a greenish hue. 'I'm very sick, I can hardly breathe,' he groaned, his eyes bulging with increasing alarm. He was in a really bad way.

Cedric jumped up to address the situation. With wisdom born of experience, he knew exactly what to do. 'Sit down and breathe slowly,' he said, guiding Shimon to an armchair while asking me if we had any vitamin C. 'In and out, in and out, deep slow breaths,' he instructed, as I got the vitamins and a glass of water. But instead of calming down, Shimon was becoming more agitated.

'Don't worry, it's okay, it will pass. Just stay calm. It will pass – just breathe in and out, slowly, in and out,' Cedric repeated, like a mantra.

But it did not pass and Shimon did not stay calm and instead threw up the vitamin C. I tried massaging his shoulders but he was beyond massage; he was hardly aware of my presence.

In full-blown panic, he said: 'I need to get to the hospital, I need to see a doctor. I'm sick, man, I'm really sick.'

However, it was the era when doctors had to report anyone who had smoked marijuana to the police and the penalty was severe.

'We can't go to the hospital, you'll end up in jail if we go,' Cedric said, almost apologetically.

'Listen man, I want to go to the hospital. Jail is better than dying,' Shimon moaned.

'You're not dying,' Cedric consoled him. 'This sometimes happens. It's normal. All you have to do is wait it out.'

But Shimon didn't want to wait it out.

'I've never felt this sick before,' he said, attempting another run to the loo, but almost collapsing en route.

I was becoming panicky as well. I had never seen Shimon looking so ill. I knew he hated hospitals and if he was begging to be taken to the hospital, things were dire. I thought he was about to have a heart attack or worse. I too begged Cedric to take him to the hospital.

'But he'll get arrested,' Cedric protested.

Shimon moaned a long pitiful moan, his head between his knees his armpits stained with sweat.

'I don't care. I'm too sick to care. I need a doctor.'

Even though the hospital was very close, Shimon looked as though he might not make it. His hands were trembling so bad that he couldn't hold the glass of water I had given him. And his legs had turned to jelly; they kept bucking under him. Although not the most reliable crutch, Cedric reluctantly agreed to escort a dying Shimon around the corner to the emergency unit.

I woke my father and asked him to babysit so I could meet them there. By the time I got to the hospital, I found Shimon semi collapsed in the front row, his eyes closed, his head on his chest, clutching his guts. Cedric was at the counter in another part of the room, trying to get the attention of someone, anyone – the place was packed but no one seemed to be in attendance. Shimon opened his eyes when I put my arms around him. Until that point, neither of us had taken a good look around. Shimon was too engrossed in misery and I was too much in a hurry to locate him. But all of a sudden we found ourselves in Dante's Inferno.

The room was full of people in various stages of disintegration. One man was holding a blood-soaked towel to his nose, blood dripping onto the floor; another had a gash in his arm so deep you could see into the sinews; a young girl was staggering through the door, her dress torn, her face so bruised, one eye had emerged from its socket. Another girl was throwing up into her boyfriend's hat; an elderly tramp was having a seizure on the floor; a baby lay limp in its mother's arms, its head dangling like a broken bird, the mother too intoxicated to support it. Yet, aside from the intermittent cries of the baby, there was a grave-like silence, a surreal, long-suffering despondency, which was especially unnerving.

I surveyed the scene and was about to faint. Shimon surveyed the scene and was suddenly fully recovered. 'Let's get out of here,' he said.

I hurried Cedric away from reception before he could condemn Shimon to a prison term. We left the hospital in an almost jubilant mood and returned home to Pistol Pete, who hadn't even had time to doze by the television. No doctor; no treatment; no police; no jail. Just the emergency hospital ward on a very busy Saturday night.

Later, recalling the scene in all its gory details, Shimon said: 'And I thought I was sick...' After several hugs and a cup of coffee, he had been ready to try the experiment again. Cedric, not fully recovered from the brush with catastrophe, agreed: 'But not right away.'

**

12

Casey Anderson

I F B O B D Y L A N W A S one of the musicians who became
famous and Cedric Smith one of the musicians who became
a lifelong friend, Casey Anderson was one of the musicians who
became a lover.

Right from the start, Casey Anderson was in a category of
his own. Whereas most of the musicians were hired through
our New York procurement trips or by word of mouth, Casey
Anderson had an agent. And the agent, keen to promote Casey,
contacted Shimon. Playing clubs was ideal for perfecting new
material before concert or recording engagements, and by now
the Finjan had an excellent reputation as a showcase for new
material. The terms and conditions of Casey's contract were not
arranged with him, as was the case with the majority of musicians,
but with his agent. And, whereas most of the musicians had a
one-week engagement, Casey's agent insisted on two weeks,

twisting Shimon's arm until he relented. But Casey Anderson did not have to involve himself in the negotiations; he left the quibbling, the compromises, the dialogue, the hype to his agent. He did not concern himself with details. Casey Anderson was 'A Musician', full stop.

Most of the musicians who played at the Finjan travelled by bus, arriving from other clubs in Canada, usually exhausted after a long, tiring journey, which followed an especially late farewell performance at the previous venue. Casey arrived in a sleek white convertible direct from New York, daisy fresh, having rested overnight in some select accommodation – big, black and alarmingly attractive. And Casey Anderson had an acute awareness of that attractiveness.

Also, Casey was older than most of the other musicians. He was in his late twenties, whereas they were in their early twenties. Those extra years gave him a definite advantage. His career was more advanced than theirs and he was more confident, more experienced both with handling the music world and with handling life, especially female life. He was an expert in that sphere, with an instinctive knowledge and awareness of things feminine.

When he first leapt out of his convertible – the white beauty he called Maggie, himself a perfect complement to its seductive power, wearing a rough, hand-knitted, off-white sweater pushed up at the elbows, black jeans tucked into leather boots stitched with silver, and a leather belt with a snake-like silver buckle – my blood screamed a resounding YES, while all my solid bits crumbled.

He was well over six feet and he moved like a panther, lean and hard and beautiful. Casey Anderson was irresistible and I knew, at that very first moment, I would be unable to resist, just as he knew he was more than able to resist. Resistance was his speciality, his trump card. I also knew that Casey Anderson would be the prize among prizes for the 'Welcoming Committee' (that particular Finjan phenomenon having grown from several keen staff into an unofficial coalition of enthusiastic females). And the challenge among challenges for Amora.

Amora was the leading lady of the Welcoming Committee, a name we had given to that self-styled coven which took it upon itself to welcome the musicians in a way I was unable to, being the wife of the club owner. She was a dark-haired, dark-eyed beauty in her mid-twenties, buzzing with ungrounded energy, with eyes that ate and fingers that clutched. She reminded me of a hawk, beautiful in flight, but, in the end, fatal. She wasn't my favourite person.

I had met Amora well before the Finjan days, when she had attended several of my dance classes and had made a concerted effort to become my friend. She invited me to her home in the most desirable suburb of Montreal, where she introduced me to her husband and her twin greyhounds. I admired her home, shook hands with her husband, patted her dogs and listened to her story. But I never really took to her. Although there was something about her that intrigued me, that kept me coming, there was something even more powerful that kept me away.

Amora had taken me into her confidence, insisting that I know intimate details of her life that I had rather not know. She was married to a prominent member of the community who was engrossed in both business dealings and church matters and saddled with a religious intent that kept him staid, self-satisfied and incredibly dull. He even looked incredibly dull, with the beginnings of a protruding belly, a bald spot he attempted to conceal and eyes of an indeterminate colour that lacked curiosity. He was of no use to Amora, who was keenly alive, burning with a passion for living, a craving for experience and an artistic compulsion frustrated by a lack of artistic endeavour or, possibly, ability. She told me she had wanted to become an actress and had attended acting school in New York, but because she had become pregnant when still in her teens after a brief fling, she had missed her calling. Instead, she had married a wealthy older man who had put an end to any acting possibilities, if not an end to her prima donna aspirations.

I never knew what Amora did; that is, if she did anything. She didn't work; money seemed of no concern, her wallet was always bulging; her young son was away at a private school; and she refused to engage in her husband's world, which involved attending events often hosted by him, and which necessitated listening to uninspiring speeches and meeting uninspiring people. From what I could see she remained at home, smouldering with dissatisfaction, tinkering with the empty hours and bored to distraction. That is, until she discovered the Finjan.

Our initial encounter had been brief and uninspiring. Sometime before the opening of the Finjan she had slipped from my life without a twinge of regret. I hadn't had contact with Amora for several years when Shimon happened to be the guest singer at a prestigious black-tie dinner. According to him, it was a snobbish, stuffy affair. He was the token 'hippy artiste', hired to demonstrate the ability of the rich to be tolerant and egalitarian – even 'with it' – while making it obvious he was 'not one of us'. He told me how much he hated that performance, how he had found it demeaning. The audience was unresponsive, having expected more cultured entertainment like a piano recital or violin sonata, music that would reflect their sophistication. After each song they clapped tiny, stiff, indifferent claps, as though their fingers ached. Shimon couldn't wait to get off the stage.

Apparently, the one redeeming feature had been meeting a lovely lady who approached him after the performance to say she normally avoided such pretentious events, and the only reason she was there was because of him. She had heard about him and was delighted to have the opportunity to hear him sing and especially delighted to meet him. 'She saved the day,' he said. That lady was Amora.

Of course, he invited her to the Finjan as his guest. Amora had no idea I was connected to Shimon or to the Finjan and was delighted to find me, embarking on a soliloquy about how much she had missed me and how wonderful it was we could be together again. In her version, our lukewarm relationship suddenly metamorphosed into a sterling friendship and I into her best friend. From the moment she walked through the door, I knew she would become inseparable from the Finjan, from Shimon, from me and especially from the musicians. And that's exactly what happened. She not only became a Finjan regular, she became a Welcoming Committee devotee and soon its star member.

The Welcoming Committee was more than a glorified collection of groupies. It was more refined and more subtle, although the agenda was not dissimilar. By now it numbered several young pretty girls who were at loose ends, shunning the nine-to-five tedium of the job choices on offer, and seeking an alternative, an adventure with the unconventional, and with the wild excitement of the sixties, which they could relive when they were no longer young and pretty.

The girls came to the Finjan night after night and, because they were not only willing but eager to lend a hand, and because they added a certain spark to the atmosphere, they enjoyed free admission and special status. The Finjan became their second home, if not their first home. And, if they were seriously interested in the music, they were passionately interested in the musicians. They would stay to the end of the performance, help with the tidying up, assist the musicians in gathering up their belongings, and remain for a drink, a chat and an exploratory flirtation. Often a musician would disappear with one of them and return next morning or even afternoon.

I soon discovered the Finjan was not unique – most music clubs at the time had some form of Welcoming Committee; it came with the territory. For the girls, hanging out with musicians fostered the illusion of being part of an enticing, glamorous world, of being the Lady in the Gypsy Bard's song, aside from the special status afforded them by being part of the coveted 'in crowd'. And even if they could not travel with the musicians as seasoned groupies did, they could enter their world vicariously, in short bursts. They thrived on the details of that world; the stories, gossip, rumours, anecdotes, insights, anything that made them feel included. And they delighted in the intense courtships, in the aura of romance, in their own daring.

The musicians became adept at providing what the girls wanted, even if it meant an exaggeration or two, or even an intriguing improvisation. After the high of a performance it was difficult for them to face the low of an ordinary night, which often meant going to a lonely second-rate hotel room. They needed somewhere for the adrenalin to go. And they found that place in the excitement of a promising liaison, however short lived. Not surprisingly, they basked in the attention, the flattery, the sensual expectation, and even just the company. It was the perfect antidote to the lonesome times spent on the road without comfort or solace, alienated from friends and family. The Welcoming Committee girls offered a brief respite, a moment of grounding, in an ungrounded, solitary, insecure life. And the musicians seized that moment.

At first I thought of the Welcoming Committee as part of coffeehouse culture, part of the fabric of Finjan life. Later, I came to see it as being the mild, more genuine precursor to the groupie phenomenon – that obsession with musicians, with bands, with the 'sex, drugs and rock n' roll' ethos. The Welcoming Committee, however, flourished in the heyday of the music clubs, before the 'band' era, the 'big-event' music scene and the groupie phenomenon; the time when if you put a guitar between the thighs of an ordinary young man, he metamorphosed into a pop idol, worshiped and adored, and, whereas in his former incarnation he had difficulty getting a girlfriend, now he had difficulty keeping the girls away.

Unlike most groupies, the Welcoming Committee girls could actually be with real, live musicians, whereas the groupie girls could only scream, wail and throw their bras at an indifferent stage. For them, even the remotest connection with their idol, like a scribbled autograph, was a triumph. Except for those who made a career out of being a groupie, and the chosen few like models, female singers and other female celebrities, there was no possibility of physical contact. The pop idols were the Western 'untouchables', enforced not by culture or tradition, but by minders and bouncers. However, instead of being undesirables, they were, ironically, too desirable.

Our Welcoming Committee girls suffered no such taboos. The Finjan musicians were infinitely touchable. Although, like magnets, the connections were swift and unabashed, they were real. They often survived the brief encounters and were extended through phone calls and letters, even visits, until the next Finjan engagement. Some became genuine, fulfilling relationships that continued throughout the Finjan years and beyond.

One of these was the relationship between Brownie McGhee and Roz, which became a mutual blessing. Roz lingered on the fringes of the Welcoming Committee. Being somewhat overweight, she was excluded from its inner circle and tolerated only because she was our cashier. Brownie, however, had a strong liking for more ample women. Roz, who struggled with low self-esteem, suddenly found herself a sought-after paramour, and Brownie had a woman to bring warmth, loving and stability to his precarious existence.

The Welcoming Committee, although seemingly a random arrangement, was actually a self-regulating body with unspoken rules and an understood hierarchy. The fact that Amora was slightly older, more beautiful and instinctively knew her way around the male psyche, gave her star status. The other girls automatically made way for Amora, patiently enduring her auditions. As Leading Lady, first choice was her undisputed prerogative. The Finjan became her theatre, her stage and her playground. Amora had found her calling.

She was always present at a new performer's opening night to assess his desirability and to work her magic. I marvelled at her subtle moves, her choreography, her flawless script. I watched, fascinated as she opened each encounter with a delicate form of verbal foreplay, rife with innuendo but limited to intense eye contact, enigmatic smiles and, except for the 'accidental' brush of hair on an arm or shoulder, devoid of anything overtly physical. As the musician's interest became apparent, he was rewarded with the fleetest of touches that somehow managed to be both intimate and suggestive. The fleeting touch soon became less fleeting and, although not overtly sexual, had an enigmatic sexual implication.

One of her favourite manoeuvres was pretending to inspect the musician's wristwatch, which had suddenly acquired a special fascination. Then, turning his hand palm up, she would separate his fingers and draw her forefinger slowly over his palm, from fingertips to wrist, lingering just a few seconds too long to dismiss the move as accidental or without intent. The musician eagerly submitted, somewhat confused about the message, but hoping for the best. However, once she knew he was within her grasp, the curtain abruptly descended. She made no further effort, content with the knowledge that it was she who would advance matters, determine the outcome and re-write the script if she so desired; after all, she was writer, director and leading lady. With that assurance she was content to be the 'warm-up act' and could leave it to the other girls to develop or complete what she had started. That is, until she met Casey Anderson.

By the time Casey came to the Finjan, Amora had conferred upon herself unrestricted access to my home. Shimon, eternally grateful for her rescue of his ego after that bruising performance, had, on several occasions, invited her to visit us and each time had given her an especially warm welcome, which she had upgraded to an open-ended invitation to visit whenever she liked. 'I was in the neighbourhood so I thought I'd drop in,' she'd say, although our neighbourhoods were at different ends of the city. And, of course, the 'best friend' status, with which she had endowed our relationship, gradually extended that privilege to the point where she'd arrive without warning. I was surprised she hadn't requested her own key.

As fate would have it, she 'happened to be in our neighbourhood' the very day Casey arrived. I wasn't surprised. I had seen her stare at Casey's publicity photo with an almost glazed-over look. And I didn't blame her. I had been just as mesmerized.

It was impossible to walk by that photograph. It was shot in black and white with touches of sepia, which made it starker and more arresting. Casey was centre stage, wearing that same rough, bulky-knit sweater, his arms dark against the cream of the pushed-up sleeves. He was holding the guitar against his breast with a tenderness that belied the force, the drive, of his song and the intensity of his whole being, which one could almost taste. He stood there, tall and lean and hard, the embodied myth of the compelling black lover, powerful, passionate, defiant yet gentle. Amora couldn't wait to make that myth come alive, and I wasn't that far behind.

***

Casey barely had time to settle his guitars when the doorbell rang. It was Amora. She walked straight into the living room like someone on a mission, her eyes burning like black fire. She looked spectacular, with long silver earrings and an unassuming black dress that she made beautiful simply by wearing it. Casey was kneeling on the floor, his back to the door, arranging some papers in his guitar case. He stood up slowly and turned to face her. Amora froze. It was as though she had encountered some immobilizing force. The moment stood still, like a tableaux, a cameo etched in space.

'Oh my!' Amora said, her eyes absorbing him like suction cups, then narrowing with that riveting look that could stun a lion. But Casey was not stunned. The 'oh my', he no doubt registered, triggered no response. He simply extended his hand politely to greet her, but his eyes registered curiosity.

'Amora, Casey; Casey, Amora,' I said quietly, aware that I was shattering some special moment. They shook hands, Amora retaining his hand in a split-second message.

It didn't take long for Amora to regain her composure. Waving aside her usual watch–hand routine, which she instinctively knew was too amateurish for a pro like Casey, she said: 'You must be full of knots after all that driving. I know just what you need,' and walking over to face him, she slid her hands under his sweater, and within minutes of meeting him she was treating him to a special Amora massage. 'Are you as smooth all over?' she said, in a Marlene Deitrich kind of voice. I had seen it all before but never as the opening act. It was as though she couldn't wait to stake her claim and was cementing it with promises to come.

Casey had been caught off balance. For a few moments he submitted to the unexpected, but only for a few moments.

'Hey girl, I just got here, I haven't even properly met my hosts. Thank you, but I'll attend to me later,' he said, pulling away abruptly and adjusting his sweater as though to rid it of an unwelcome intrusion. There was an air of dignity about Casey that Amora had violated, and he wasn't pleased. Besides, Casey Anderson was not about to follow someone else's agenda, especially someone as beautiful and accomplished as Amora. He did not give her an inch and I was profoundly gratified and relieved.

For most of that first week Amora was consumed by a relentless determination. She 'happened to be in our neighbourhood' an awful lot during the day. And she came to the Finjan every night. She sat close to the stage so Casey could feel her presence. She waited for him after each set, praising his performance. She made erudite comments about folk music, about blues – it seems she was taking a crash course on traditional music. She tempted him with assorted invitations, which he would put on hold rather than accept or reject. She brought him small gifts, things she noticed he needed – special guitar strings which he had mentioned were hard to come by; a cigarette lighter, since he was always searching for matches; an Emory board, since he sometimes used his nails as a guitar pick. Casey accepted the gifts graciously but they didn't buy even a suggestion of intimacy. Although he seemed to enjoy Amora's company and allowed thank-you hugs, physical contact was strictly rationed, limited to a kiss on the cheek or a ruffle of hair.

The initial rebuff and subsequent indifference to her attempts at intimacy only made her more eager, more determined. Although Casey made no overt moves of encouragement, he allowed her to keep up the pursuit. I knew he was intrigued and although I hated it, I couldn't blame him. Amora glowed with that special fire, the heat of which was both inviting and dangerous, but even the danger was inviting.

By the end of the first week, with no significant gains, Amora must have decided it was time for bolder moves. On the Monday of his first day off, her visit was earlier than usual. I could sense her intent by the way she rang the doorbell, hard and long. She declined my offer of coffee and seemed edgy as she attempted some small talk, her eyes restless, her impatience palatable.

'Casey is still asleep,' I said, as I could sense her sniffing for his presence.

Her resolve was evident as without any preliminaries she knocked on the bedroom door, and walked straight in. It was very quiet after that and I tormented myself by imagining what was happening. After half an hour of indulging in wild, painful scenarios, I was granted a reprieve. They both emerged from the room looking entirely normal. There were no tell-tale signs, no indication of what had occurred and I had to satisfy myself with the possibility of an unremarkable encounter.

Despite Amora's frequent visits, Casey and I spent some precious times on our own, and I lived for those times. We went for rides in Maggie; we sat under the weeping willows on the summit of Mount Royal, ate the sandwiches I had lovingly prepared and talked by the pool. He told me about his time fighting in Korea; about his parents – both academics. I told him about my travels, about my frustration at being grounded, about my nomad aspirations, about the Finjan oasis. He sang me snatches of songs he was working on. On some nights, after his performance, when I managed by some ploy to outwit Amora and Shimon was busy with other matters, we went out to eat together. I had to be content with limited blessings.

I was not only agonizingly attracted to Casey's physical being, I also admired his mental being, his intellect, and was intrigued by the scope of his knowledge and by his probing mind. A lot of our conversations centred on folk music. It was mainly him talking and me listening and asking questions. He was especially interested in the evolution and history of folk music – history having been his speciality at university – and he had an extensive library of records and books on the subject.

He also knew a great deal about the influence of the early musicians, about the changing folk music scene, and about the current trend where musicians were writing their own material, which he too was engaged in doing. He not only sang folk songs, he researched different aspects of folk music, of blues, jazz, country and gospel. His repertoire included poignant ballads, black-black blues, driving work songs, calypso, even popular songs. And he was a master at each, infusing the songs with a style that was uniquely his. He had recorded nine albums and could draw from an extensive range of material, some of it gathered on his travels, much of it his own. It's not that I wouldn't have fallen in love with him if none of this was on offer, but it added a special quality to that love.

However, there was no doubt that the major draw – the primary element that turned infatuation into something more profound, something I could not escape from – was his performance on stage. I didn't miss a single one. They were the highlight of my day, of my life. I especially loved his musical arrangements. He had several guitars and played in a variety of styles. My favourite was his hard-hitting twelve-string guitar. Sometimes he used the neck of a glass bottle as a capo and the sound it made as he drew it over the strings was more than music, it was a cry into my heart. His voice was a panorama of my emotions. It could be gritty, sweet, tender or fierce. Both as a man and a musician, he was a fusion of the raw and the refined – for me a fatal combination. And when he stepped on to the stage, so striking, so perfect, the yearning I felt was overwhelming. It was a yearning for all the things I could never have.

All of Casey's skills came together in the way he performed on stage and the way he connected with the audience. Sometimes he was funny, sometimes informative, sometimes just plain thrilling. Sometimes, entranced by his music, he held the audience in a spell, so that at the end of the song there was a moment of silence before the applause, the audience needing time to absorb the magic. I loved every minute of every performance. He took me to a special place somewhere in the stars, where the man and the music combined into one powerful object of love. After the performance it was difficult to re-enter the real world. Casey was both my fantasy and my reality.

As part of the reality, he inspired me to do some of my own research, to compile my thoughts about the music and the musicians, even to expand the diary I kept into a Finjan memoir. Not long after he was gone, it was because of his influence, his inspiration that I wrote an essay on the popularity of folk music and especially on the appeal of the musicians who played it. It may even be because of him that I am writing this book.

In the essay, I wrote:

Folksingers are perhaps the last of the virile men. They deal with the soil from which men grow - hard work, physical and mental endurance and the kind of passionate love that makes men steal and kill. They sing of the earth, of violence, of chain gangs, of injustice, of big men and wide spaces. Their heroes are giants like John Henry, who raced with the steel drill to prove that no machine could beat a man, and who won the race even though the effort killed him. Their voice is their ammunition, the guitar, their weapon.

Yet the man who plays the guitar must also be gentle for the guitar has feminine qualities. Its delicately curved body is held close and loving. A man must be kind and tender to his guitar for it is his constant companion, going with him wherever he goes, sharing his moments of loneliness, of communication and of accomplishment. In effect, the guitar becomes these moments, for through and with the guitar, the musician becomes alive and most himself. He can sing his song to the world, or retreat into his guitar and keep the world away. The guitar is his connection with life; it is his lover.

It is the tenderness he exhibits on stage, combined with the love, the strength, the struggle for justice he sings about, which transmutes into virility. For in his song he travels the world where real men live. Although we have almost forgotten what virility is in a world where 'punch' means the nine-to-five timeclock, we are quick to recognize, to remember and to be stirred by any suggestion of it.

On stage, the folksinger presents a unique picture. His performance is personal, very much his own and therefore extremely revealing. He chooses his own material and makes that choice with care, for he must identify with the songs he sings. He is his own director. He alone decides how he will introduce and present his songs. And through his performance, which is unique and personal, he exposes his soul.

The sensitive, aware audience, is given the opportunity of seeing into that soul, identifying with it, feeling profoundly moved, not only by the song but by the person singing it. For he has no defences. It is as though he is making love, so unshielded, so naked is he. Not only does he sing his song, he becomes his song. And in becoming his song he becomes powerful, he becomes virile.

Perhaps in writing that essay, I came to a deeper understanding about my overwhelming connection to Casey, about what he represented to me and to other women; the feelings he stirred, the promises, the hopes, the visions. For I was by no means alone.

13

Amora's Game

THE MORE AMORA PURSUED contact with Casey, the more he avoided that contact; but he never put an end to it. He was enjoying the game, the flirtatious banter, the obvious ploys, or perhaps he was just honing his resistance skills. I felt sure Casey had no lack of high-powered, beautiful women in his life. Amora may have been big time for the less experienced musicians, but for Casey she was a pussycat. I don't know if she was in love with Casey or just obsessed with the idea, enticed by the challenge. I don't even know if there is a difference. But I did know that I was head over heels in love, in love like I had never been before.

Perhaps if conditions had been normal, I wouldn't have had the time to fall in love. But, as it happened, during the two weeks Casey was at the Finjan, circumstances combined to afford me that luxury. Firstly, we were in the midst of a university break, and I wasn't being plagued by late assignments. Secondly, my mother was off for two weeks to see relatives who lived in the country, and she had taken Ronit with her.

'Some clean country air will be good for her instead of all that smoking going on in your kitchen,' she'd said.

Most of the musicians smoked and my mother needed something concrete on which to focus her objections. Unlike Pistol Pete, she had never really given her blessing to the Finjan. But she was so helpful in caring for Ronit that I forgave her the odd jab or two.

Thirdly, by now my Finjan responsibilities were minimal, overtaken by staff. I had become almost redundant in the kitchen. My duties now veered towards caring for the musicians, duties I more than adequately fulfilled.

And, most important, Shimon was totally pre-occupied and spent little time at home. He was on the verge of opening a second Finjan in downtown Montreal, which he eventually did, and was consumed by this project. Between running the old Finjan, setting up the new one and fitting in the odd lucrative performance, he hardly had time to tie his shoelaces, let alone concern himself with my adventures. I was suddenly free of motherhood, wifehood and studenthood, and I devoted that freedom to falling in love with Casey.

But it was like running a race with your hands tied behind your back. The obstacles were overpowering. I was not only married, I was also the boss's wife. And there was Amora, who had a clear run; she was beautiful, she was bold and her skills were multiple. And then there was Casey himself; perhaps he was committed elsewhere, even married. I didn't dare ask. I was acutely aware that it was all hopeless. But knowing it was hopeless didn't help. When it came to affairs of the heart, reason didn't stand a chance, especially mine.

I think Casey knew how in love with him I was. Love must have been written all over my face, it crept into the way I looked at him, the way I talked to him. But he never let on. He was friendly, even affectionate, but there wasn't even a hint of anything more. However, he made sure Amora never entered the bedroom again. And I was grateful for small mercies.

Amora, too, must have known. And she wasn't as merciful as Casey. I don't know if she did it purposely, but she submitted me to her outrageous flirtations without an iota of pity. On one of the many days she appeared without warning, Casey and I were sitting in the living room, Casey absorbed in composing lyrics to a song, his back to me. It was one of those peaceful times, those rare times I was alone with him. I was loving it, running my imagination over the back of his neck, over the contours of his back, tripping on the feel of his skin on my fingertips, lost in fantasies.

Suddenly Amora appeared like a bolt of lightning; she was even wearing a silver dress, low cut and clinging. Peace vanished. When Amora was in a room, the air crackled with electricity; serenity gave way to turbulence. Without so much as a nod in my direction, and before Casey could acknowledge her presence, she went right up to him and ran her hands under his shirt and her mouth over his neck. I could only watch and bleed.

'You know, Casey, you're more than I thought you'd be,' she said, in that sexy Marlene Dietrich voice.

Casey spun around to face her, disengaging her hands. 'And you need a good spanking,' he replied.

'Are you going to be the one to give it to me?' she taunted. 'You know I'm going to sleep with you,' she added, with a small shoulder wiggle that made the tiny stars on her necklace quiver.

'Oh, so you think you know all about me. We'll see how much you really know,' he said, in a tone that was almost a dare.

I wished Casey had been seriously annoyed with Amora, that he would have put her in her place once and for all. But he merely returned to his song with almost a smile.

'Nice necklace,' he said.

If Casey was remiss about putting Amora in her place, he certainly wasn't remiss about putting me in mine. I had a tendency to step out of line once in a while, but I suppressed that tendency with concrete boots when it came to my dealings with Casey. However, on one occasion when Amora had been especially provocative and I was especially pleased to see the back of her, I seriously slipped.

'Why don't you sleep with Amora and put her out of her misery?' I said sardonically – although, of course, that was the last thing I wanted.

Casey just looked at me with withering disapproval and said, 'Do you know why they don't send donkeys to college?'

'No, why don't they send donkeys to college?' I said, my cheekiness deflated by the dagger in his eyes.

'Because nobody likes a smart ass.'

'Ouch.'

I never tried that line of reasoning again and Casey was never sharp with me again.

Finally, towards the end of Casey's second week, Amora scored a major victory.

'You're not going to leave here without visiting my home,' she said to him one morning. 'I want you to meet my dogs. I'll make a special lunch, I'm a really good cook. And I'll show you my etchings,' she added in that sexy provocative tone, batting her eyelashes suggestively.

'I bet they're all on the ceiling,' Casey quipped.

'Exactly.'

To my intense disappointment, Casey acquiesced.

'Okay, lunch, but no etchings. I think better on my feet,' he added.

'Tomorrow?'

'Tomorrow's good.'

'I'll leave my car here and we'll go in Maggie,' Amora said, 'unless you think I'm so hot I'll burn up the seat.'

'I can cope with hot,' Casey said.

'I'll be the judge of that,' Amora said, with that small shoulder wiggle.

I couldn't sleep that night, tormenting myself with a series of scenarios that I couldn't leave alone. I chewed on them like a dog with a bone, and even when there was nothing left, I still kept on chewing.

Next day, Amora rang the doorbell in a succession of short impatient blasts, signalling Casey to come out. I tagged behind to watch them leave.

'Hello beautiful,' she said, taking his arm and snuggling into him, gazing into his eyes with an adoration that was verging on the obscene. She looked dazzling in a silver and crimson gypsy dress with a lacey bit peeping out between her breasts, and long silver earrings; and she knew it. Her hair sparkled with tiny silver stars and her eyes were glowing with anticipation.

I hated the way Casey looked at her. And when she turned to face him, pressing up close and he took her in his arms, their embrace thrust into my heart. Until then, except for the thank-you hugs and cheek kisses, Casey had aborted Amora's attempts at serious physical contact. But this was an embrace from heaven – long and slow and promising. It curdled my blood.

Amora hardly knew I was there. I had already been demoted to a bit player in her drama and this scene was all hers, unfolding exactly as she had written it. For the first time Casey seemed to have relinquished control. It was she who pulled away, albeit only a few inches.

'What are we waiting for, let's get going,' Amora said, in a low suggestive murmur reeking of sex, while running her hands over his face, her fingers closing his eyelids and tracing his lips.

'It's your gig. You make the calls,' Casey said, gently removing her hands and stepping back.

He managed a quick kiss on my cheek and a breezy 'back soon' before Amora took his arm and walked him towards Maggie as though they were parading down the wedding isle, while I remained on the doorstep feeling like left luggage. Casey opened the car door for her with a slight bow and I watched her slide into the leather seat – my seat, my place – adjusting her skirt with the kind of familiarity that spells confidence. I could hardly stay alive.

I didn't cry when they left, I wept. I wept because of what I imagined, because of what I didn't know, because of what I couldn't have, because of where I couldn't be. And I employed the hours Casey was away to inflict the kind of masochistic torture upon myself that would have brought tears to the eyes of a self-flagellating monk.

I wrote and re-wrote the dialogue to every utterance of Amora's seduction of Casey, or was it Casey's seduction of Amora? I didn't know which was worse. He had looked at her as though he had never seen her before. And he was really into that embrace. I imagined the way he would touch her with those beautiful long fingers. And the way her lips would be all over that smooth brown skin I so longed to stroke. I even imagined her underwear. I remembered a long time ago, in the first flush of our 'intimate' friendship, she had complained about the thinness of her love life. 'I have all this pretty, sexy underwear and nobody to appreciate it,' she had said. Casey always noticed pretty things, and sexy was the ultimate bonus. That underwear ate into me like acid. I had to visualize every thread of it; the texture, the colour, the smell – I knew she kept rose petals in the drawers of her dresser.

Amora always smelled so good. When she walked into a room it was as though a bouquet of roses walked with her. Oh how I agonized over that underwear and that smell of roses. And it was all happening now, right now, at this very moment, where I could see it, feel the pain of it. I was in deep despair.

Casey returned several hours later. Amora was not with him. He must have seen her off without permitting her to come in. He was not visibly changed despite my close inspection. I knew to ask only those questions that I didn't care about the answers. 'Nice house. Nice dogs. Nice lunch. Lousy paintings,' was about all he said. And, perhaps, it was just that. But by this time I had suffered a lifetime of anguish and I wasn't going to give up even a tiny morsel. I was in love and my suffering proved it.

I'm sure Casey was aware of my agony, but he wasn't going to acknowledge it or pay it any heed. All he said was: 'It's difficult being an adult.'

'Don't patronize me,' I said, because I had to say something.

'Just stating a fact.'

But that night he gave me an extra close hug. 'Good night, sweet thing. You are a very special sweet thing,' he said, and there was something more than affection in his voice and a touch of keenness in his arms. Suddenly it was as though I had been blind but could now see. I had been deaf but could now hear. It was so easy for him to change my mood from despair to elation. I fell asleep fanned by angel wings.

***

In the last of Casey's days off, Shimon was away performing in Ottawa, until the following evening and Ronit was with my parents. Casey and I were alone. That morning over coffee, he said, 'I'm going to cook for you tonight.' I knew he loved cooking but rarely got the opportunity in the kitchenless hotel rooms he usually frequented. 'Dinner just for the two of us, and I'll do all the shopping, all you have to do today is sit there and look pretty.' I could have moved mountains.

Early that afternoon Casey sat on the sofa absorbed in working on his song. I sat in the armchair opposite him, pretending to read, but instead sneaking wistful, love-torn glances, studded with contemplations of our coming night together. I was exquisitely happy. Suddenly the phone rang. I went to the hallway to answer it. It was Amora. The room turned black. 'It's Amora, for you,' I called, without waiting for her to say anything. Casey came out to the hallway and I returned to the living room, my exquisite happiness dragging on the floor.

Amora was the worst possible news. Better to have been told that Canada was at war. I knew that somehow Amora wasn't going to allow me that time with Casey. I felt a rush of tears. Casey was gone for several minutes and I spent those minutes in state-of-the-art self-torture, all my senses turned to jelly. It made no difference that the hallway was out of earshot, I could hear Amora making an enticing offer. And I could hear Casey, hesitant at first but finally accepting it. I felt it, I knew it, I heard it. When Casey returned, we were both silent. I couldn't speak. He casually resumed working on his song as though only a minor blip had interrupted him. I waited for his excuse to cancel our evening.

My eyes were lowered and I was blinking hard, trying to keep the tears from spilling over. My agony was so fierce it must have infected the air we were breathing, for he suddenly detached himself from his song and said, 'Are you okay?'

'I'm fine,' I mumbled, hardly able to breathe. But he knew, and I knew, that he knew. He was good at knowing.

He looked at me hard for a moment. I must have looked the picture of misery – red puffy eyes, clenched mouth, gritted teeth, but I was too far gone to care. I had been fatally wounded by a single phone call shot.

'Come over here,' he said. Just that. '*Come over here.*' I crossed the room, head lowered to hide my tears.

He stood up, put his hand under my chin and raised my eyes to meet his. My face was wet, my eyes squeezed shut trying to hold the tears and my nose was runny. I longed to flee but was paralyzed with humiliation. I could feel him looking at me. No words. He just looked. I stood there riddled with anguish.

Finally, in a voice sweet with tenderness, he said, 'Are we still tight? Are we on for tonight?' It was as though a trap had been sprung, a reprieve granted seconds before the execution. The relief was instant and overwhelming. I could feel the blood return to my veins. It was as if I had just sipped from the cup of life. I opened my eyes to meet his and smiled through the tears. Gathering my hair from the nape of my neck in a ponytail, he brushed it all over my face.

'Silly girl,' he said, and folded my hands in his. 'Come here.' And that was the beginning.

14

Josh White and John Lee Hooker

J OSH WHITE, THE BLACK American blues singer, human
rights activist and close friend of the Roosevelts, was not only
one of our favourite musicians but one of our heroes. He was
the main musical influence on Shimon way back when we were
in South Africa. Both Shimon and I had listened to anything by
Josh White we could get our hands on, then listened again and
yet again. We could never get enough of him.

Like the traditional blues musicians – such as Lead Belly,
Sonny and Brownie, John Lee Hooker, Muddy Waters, Big
Biil Broonzy and so on – Josh White sang from the guts. These
musicians didn't sing what they had heard about, but what they
had lived, the suffering they had endured and the suffering they
had seen others endure, the betrayals, the anger, the passion; they

sang about the places they had been, the railroads, the prisons, the dust bowls. Sometimes their music was all they had. Some of the latter-day blues musicians, like Casey Anderson, had the ability to convey black sensibilities, to sing about those same emotions, those same places as though they had been there, lived them. But the original bluesmen remained unique; their music had a raw, authentic quality that could only come from actually living the life.

These original African American blues musicians were a major musical influence not only on the likes of American superstars such as Bob Dylan, Jim Morrison and Elvis Presley, but on British stars like Keith Richards, Mick Jagger and George Harrison. George Harrison is known to have said: 'No Lead Belly, no Beatles.' The Rolling Stones took their name from the track, *Rollin' Stone*, on a Muddy Waters' album. As a matter of fact, traditional black blues musicians were popular in Britain before they were 'discovered' in America, and British popularity was instrumental in gaining them recognition and acclaim in the US. I remember Brownie McGhee marvelling at the stunning reception he and Sonny had received in England. 'If I let them, they would have polished my boots,' he said.

The BBC was a significant factor in creating that reception, that popularity. When Josh White visited Britain in 1951, blues wasn't even a glint in the eyes of the music world. But some music guru in the BBC must have already caught the blues bug and initiated a one-off Josh White broadcast. Surprisingly, it was so popular that it resulted in a Josh White BBC series of programmes called *The Glory Road*, aired soon after. Black American blues hit the British scene with such impact that shortly after *The Glory Road*, it inspired the programme *Blues in the Mississippi*, which featured recordings by Muddy Waters and John Lee Hooker. The American south may have given birth to the blues, but it was British musicians who nourished it to maturity and sent it out into the world.

The relationship between Keith Richards and Mick Jagger grew into a formidable partnership fuelled by their mutual love of these blues icons. They became obsessed with turning everyone on to their music. Muddy Waters was Keith Richards's musical mentor, his idol. And in 1964 he actually met Muddy Waters when the Stones went to the Chess recording studio in Chicago to record *Key to The Highway*. To Keith's amazement, he found Muddy Waters wearing workmen's overalls, balanced on a ladder, painting the roof of the studio. It was as though he had found the Pope in a greasy-spoon diner, washing dishes. He was appalled.

The Stones became instrumental in the resurrection of these blues legends and, through promoting their music, they were instrumental in bringing the injustices and the horrors of American racism to the attention of the world. It was the music and the songs of these musicians that depicted the brutality of racism and which made that brutality tangible. And it was that music, those songs, which became mantras in the fight against racism.

Every time I listened to Josh White singing *Strange Fruit*, the haunting song about a black lynching, my soul wept. His guts were in that song. Lynching was part of his heritage, part of the fabric of his existence, part of the lessons he had endured in becoming a man. His voice was so clear, so poignant, so drenched in pain, and the pathos more powerful for being understated. Judging from the emotion in his voice, I can understand why he became a leading figure in the civil rights movement and a compatriot of Martin Luther King, singing on King's historic 'I Have A Dream' march on Washington in 1963.

Strange Fruit says more about the inhumanity of racism than thousands of political speeches. It brought the black cause directly into the musical mainstream. And, incidentally, it was written by a white Jewish man called Abel Meerapol. Meerapol, a schoolteacher from New York, was deeply affected by a photograph he had seen of a lynching and wrote a poem about it. Aside from being a poet, he was also a composer and wrote music to accompany his poem. He played the song to a New York club owner friend who then gave it to Billie Holiday, and the rest is history.

What is less known about Abel Meerapol is that he adopted the sons of Ethel and Julius Rosenberg when they were executed in 1953 for being communist spies – the first husband and wife to die in the electric chair. Meerapol was introduced to the orphaned children at a friend's house. Michael was aged ten and Robert six. The boys were not only deeply traumatized by the death of their parents, but somewhat abandoned by the community as, at the time, even the slightest connection with communism could lead to severe reprisals. However, several weeks after meeting them, they were living with Abel and his wife Anne.

'Strange Fruit' was first recorded by Billie Holiday in 1939, when the repressive McCarthy era was in full swing. It was an act of sheer bravery for Meerapol to write the song and for Billie Holiday to sing it. Since then, it has become an anthem of the civil rights movement in America, but at the time it was so subversive that Meerapol was called to testify before the committee investigating un-American activity.

The lyrics describe how, hanging from poplar trees in the USA's 'gallant' south, strange fruit are swaying in the breeze. For instead of trickling nectar or honey, they ooze blood. Instead of the sweet smell of magnolia flowers, they exude the rancid smell of 'burning flesh'. For these strange fruit are black bodies, left to rot in the sun, their eyes bulging, their mouths contorted in a gruesome death. The lamenting wail of the song's chorus – 'oh… oh…oh…' – is a sound of unbearable sadness, reminding me of the keening Irish women waiting by the shore for their drowned fishermen to be washed up in J. M. Synge's play, *Riders To The Sea*.

'Strange Fruit' was not the only song to reflect Josh White's legacy. When he sang about the humiliation of poverty, you knew he had been there, had slept in fields, had worn tattered clothes, had no shoes until the age of sixteen. And, like so many other black musicians, even though he was performing and earning money at a very early age, it was other people who profited from his talent. He knew exploitation from the inside out.

In his song 'One Meatball', he sings about the shame of being poor. The story he tells, the picture he paints, is a vivid one depicting emotions with which he was very familiar. When the hungry 'little man' nervously enters a restaurant with only fifteen cents in his pocket, he is dismayed to discover that fifteen cents buys him only one meatball. Trying to hide his embarrassment, he anxiously orders the one meatball. Even the other diners are startled when the waiter, in a loud voice, derisively informs them that this man has ordered only one meatball. When the arrogant waiter brings the little man his one meatball, which doesn't even merit gravy, he timidly requests some bread. We can feel his humiliation when the waiter shouts so everyone can hear that one meatball gets no bread. 'One Meat Ball' was one of the first songs Shimon performed.

I also discovered that Josh White was not only famous as a human rights activist, actor and celebrity, but as a ladies' man – he was the first black American sex symbol and a legend in that capacity. And he wore the sex-symbol label with pride. Casey, who knew Josh well, told me that Josh was completely confident of his power over women: 'It was something he took for granted, like the colour of his eyes.' Casey said Josh was handsome, charming, dripping with charisma and had a special skill with the female sex, an ability to make women feel adored. He had performed with Josh on many occasions, perhaps had even learned some of his own skills from the master and had witnessed Josh's abilities first hand.

He told me that during a performance, Josh would focus on some female in the audience that he fancied and perform in such a way that she was convinced he was singing to her. Appearing in a black velvet shirt, open to his chest, and black silk trousers, he exuded seduction. He embellished his technique with dazzling smiles, heartfelt gazes and his own, highly effective, body language until he was sure she got the message. After the performance she would be waiting for him.

'If Josh wanted a woman enough, he knew he could have her. The decision was his,' Casey said, and then added, 'except for this one time.' Apparently one night, a beautiful redheaded lady in the audience intrigued him. He tried his usually infallible manoeuvres, but with no success. The lady refused to comply. There were no responsive smiles, no exuberant clapping. As a matter of fact, the harder he tried, the more indifferent she became. And she was not waiting for him after the show. Josh was baffled, but just momentarily.

Casey had watched it all happening from the wings and after the performance said to Josh, 'What happened with that gorgeous redhead you were making eyes at?'

'Oh her,' Josh replied dismissively. 'She's a lesbian.'

Nothing else made sense to him. For him there could be no other explanation. However, in his own way – and it was certainly in his own way – he was a loyal and caring husband and father.

***

John Lee Hooker, considered by some to be the greatest blues singer of all time, was just beginning to gain that accolade when he came to perform at the Finjan. This was only a few years before he became a superstar and known as 'The King of Boogie', and had already released thirteen of the almost ninety albums he recorded. As was the case with all our musicians (with the exception of Sonny and Brownie), he stayed with us. Coincidentally, Josh White happened to be performing in Montreal at the same time. John and Josh were good friends who had performed and hung out together, and had lived through the same southern black Jim Crow horrors. It was extremely rare that they were in the same city at the same time and both were eager to meet.

Unfortunately, the day after John arrived in Montreal, Josh was due to leave. There was an overlap of only one morning, and it had to be very early as Josh was flying out before noon. As it was a unique opportunity for them to get together, they were determined to make it happen. However, if there was to be a meeting, it had to take place by 7 a.m. to give Josh time to catch his plane. John asked Shimon if it was okay to have Josh visit so early in the morning.

Was it? Was Jesus crucified? Although he rarely got to sleep before 2 a.m. and was useless much before noon, Shimon assured him that 7 a.m. was the absolute perfect time at which to arrange a meeting. Shimon would have crossed deserts barefoot in the heat of the day to meet the great man. How could the loss of a few measly hours of sleep compare with that? Suddenly, there was the possibility of Josh White, *THE* Josh White, coming into our very own living room.

How incredible was that! It was beyond belief. Even the idea was unbelievable. But would Josh White – *THE* Josh White – actually agree to come? We didn't dare breathe.

Next day, at 7 a.m. sharp, a limo pulled up to our door and Josh White stepped out, handsome and smiling. There was such an aura of splendidness about him and we were so honoured by the visit that I could hardly keep from bowing, and Shimon was on the verge of genuflecting. Somehow I managed to get us all into the kitchen before Shimon turned to stone.

Josh and John were delighted to see each other – it had been a long time – and their delight, laughter and good humour filled the room and my heart. Josh was so easy, so informal, so instantly loveable that it took only minutes to feel comfortable with him; that is, after my initial hostess blunder which I committed despite the fact I was trying so hard to do everything right. But, to be fair to myself, this was a blunder that my limited experience with old-time musicians made impossible to predict.

I had bought this special croissant dough that needed to be baked so that the croissants would emerge looking and tasting freshly made, all flaky and buttery. They were in the oven, piping hot and would be ready at exactly seven thirty. I normally drank instant coffee, but for this occasion I bought the best Italian coffee and dug out my rarely used percolator, which made a first-class brew. I had counted on the smell of percolating coffee and fresh croissants to enhance the specialness of the occasion. And, in case there was any awkwardness to begin with, the delicious aroma would act as a welcoming embrace.

But I needn't have worried. Josh was so pleased to meet us, so grateful we had made the occasion possible, so prolific with his thanks, it felt like he was honouring us, rather than we him. We sat around the kitchen table. John and Josh had lots to talk about – other musicians, gigs, concerts, studios, friends, family – and a lot of laughing to catch up with. Shimon and I listened in awe to the stories, the reminiscing, the plans for recordings, the gossip, feeling immensely privileged. It was as though we were involved in the making of history.

'Would you like some coffee, Josh?' I asked timidly, hesitant to interrupt one minute of the flow, yet reluctant to allow the coffee to get too strong and the croissants too well done.

'No thanks. No coffee,' he replied.

Although disappointed by the off-hand dismissal of my freshly brewed Italian coffee, my disappointment was dwarfed by the glory of the occasion.

'How about some tea?'

'No thanks.'

'Orange juice?' I asked tentatively. Surely he wanted something to drink?

'No orange juice.'

'Wouldn't you like anything to drink?' I asked, perplexed.

'I certainly would,' he answered, and I noticed a glint in his eye and a wink to John.

Suddenly I understood. It really shouldn't have taken me so long, but I was still a little slow on the uptake in such matters, although I was learning.

'You would like something a little stronger,' I said.

'You got it,' he laughed.

Luckily, Brownie had left a bottle of whiskey, his favourite drink, 'for next time'.

I got the glasses and Shimon got the whiskey. And, shortly after 7 a.m., we were in the kitchen drinking straight whiskey – no mixers, God forbid. 'You don't mess with good whiskey,' Josh said. A thimble full for me, a big bottom full for Shimon, and doubles plus refills for Josh and John. The croissants grew hard in the oven and the coffee blurped, ignored, in the percolator. But, never mind; we were in the kitchen with Josh White and John Lee Hooker, making history.

Just before Josh left, something very special happened. Perhaps it was the whiskey that gave Shimon courage, for it was not something he would normally have done. Back in South Africa, when Shimon had been trying to duplicate the chords Josh White played, he came across an elusive chord he found impossible to reproduce. He was entranced by the sound of the chord but, despite endless attempts, could not play it. He concluded that the human hand did not have the capacity to stretch that far and that Josh White must have used some device to capture the sound. He had remained intrigued by that chord throughout his guitar-playing career, and was even more intrigued when he learned that Josh White had seriously burned his left hand and had been unable to play the guitar properly for a long time afterwards.

Now, suddenly, by some miraculous happening, Josh White was right there, sitting beside him at the very same table. He took the plunge. With the humility of the initiate cross-examining the master, Shimon told Josh about his fascination with the chord and asked if he would demonstrate how he played it. Josh White did not bat an eyelash; he knew exactly which chord Shimon was referring to. Drawing Shimon's guitar to him like an old friend and spreading the fingers of his large black hand over its body, he struck the impossible chord. Just like that. The sound swelled, echoing, vibrating, reverberating, resonating; filling the room like the sound of the Great Amen. Shimon looked as though he had just seen God. And knew his guitar would be holy ever after.

***

If my initial *faux pas* in offering Josh White coffee instead of alcohol could be excused on the grounds that I was unfamiliar with the breakfast preferences of traditional blues musicians, I'm not sure under what pretext my second *faux pas*, far more serious, could be forgiven.

The story begins in my wonderful kitchen, with its windows almost to the floor overlooking an unkempt field where, by day, rabbits hopped through the weeds and wild flowers sparkled like jewels in the grass. My kitchen, surrounded by the open sky, where, by night, the moon and the stars came in through the windows to offer their blessings and enhance the music and the memories.

In summer, the field extended the kitchen into a macrocosm of possibilities. In winter, blanketed in snow, with long purple shadows, cold stars and streaks of northern lights, the kitchen left the field and became a secret refuge, withdrawing into an interior landscape, cosy, warm and intimate. The kitchen had a special energy, a particular ambiance conducive to discoveries, revelations, creations, a certain wellbeing where things flowed and stuff happened. It was in that kitchen that I spent hours with the musicians, drinking tea and listening to their songs and their dreams. It was the place where I came to know them, the embrace of candlelight making our connection magical, the place where I looked into their eyes and saw into their souls and forgot my obsession with travel. It was the place where we exchanged the wonders of being young and alive and together. I cherished that kitchen. It was my sacred place, my temple, my tiny oasis.

One morning I walked into my kitchen to find it defaced. Big black letters were scrawled across the large white wall opposite the window, proclaiming: 'This is the one and only kitchen in the whole wide world,' and signed 'Ron Eliran', the name of the Israeli singer then performing at the Finjan. I was so infuriated by those outrageous letters that I hardly registered the sentiment, so in tune with my own. How dare he mutilate my kitchen, defile my beautiful white wall? I tried to annihilate those letters. But scrawled with an indelible marker, they refused to be eradicated. When I confronted Ron, thinking he would be apologetic, he was unrepentant.

'Why did you do that? I can't wash it off. You've ruined my kitchen!' I moaned.

'I did it because it had to be done,' he said calmly and without an iota of remorse. 'You must never wash it off. Everyone who sings here must write something for the wall. It will be a wall of fame, a "thank you" to this wonderful kitchen.'

And so the 'Wall of Fame' was born. For me, it became a celebration of my kitchen, of the Finjan, of the musicians, of my substitute for travel, of my tiny oasis, of all of us together. After I left Montreal, I never saw that wall again, but wherever I went I took that kitchen, those musicians and the Wall of Fame with me.

The Wall of Fame was in full swing by the time John Lee Hooker came to play at the Finjan. And, when he was about to leave, I asked him as a matter of course to write something and sign the wall. I was taken aback by his adamant refusal.

'But everyone writes something on the wall,' I protested. Still he was unyielding. 'Please, John,' I begged, unable to fathom this stubborn rebuff in someone so amenable. No musician had ever declined to sign the wall. It would be like refusing to leave one's footprint in the Hollywood Walk of Fame. 'I really want you to sign the wall. I want to remember you being here,' I pleaded.

But uncharacteristically he continued to refuse and, characteristically, I continued to twist his arm.

'Why, John? Why won't you sign the wall?'

Finally, he offered a lame, 'I don't know what to write.'

'That's no problem,' I said with a sense of deliverance. At the time he had a hit song in circulation called 'Boom Boom'. 'Just write "Boom Boom", nothing else…just "Boom Boom",' I said, with relief.

He acquiesced, his resistance eroded by my insistence.

'Good man,' I said, handing him the felt-tip pen.

He clutched the pen like a child holding a too-fat crayon, and in slow awkward letters painfully scratched a wounded M, a flattish O, another O and a misshapen N facing backwards. Suddenly it hit me. He couldn't write. He was illiterate. And I had forced humiliation upon him. I watched, mortified as he pressed a second tortured M…O…O…N into the wall.

'Boom boom,' he said, smiling triumphantly as he handed me the pen, his ordeal over.

'Thanks, John, I really appreciate that,' I said, severely chastened. Now I'll always think of you when I look at the wall, I neglected to add, with stinging shame.

I saw John Lee Hooker many times after he played at the Finjan, and there was that time in New York when Bob Dylan and all of us bounced on his bed in the Chelsea Hotel. But no matter what we did, however good times we had, I never could get over wincing with shame each time I recalled the wall incident. Then, many years later, when I was already living in England, something, somewhere must have decided I had been punished enough.

I had been in Ireland attending the W B Yeats Summer School. One of the big plusses for me was frequenting the many pubs in town, whose main attraction was excellent live music. After the last lecture or seminar of the day, several of us would make our way to one pub or another to listen to music and indulge in Irish coffee. One night we went to my favourite pub and, to my surprise and delight, John Lee Hooker Junior was playing there. At the end of the evening, I went to speak to him and told him the story of the wall, and how that incident with his father was one of my major haunts.

'I know all about it,' he said. 'Dad told me – he found it funny. "She didn't know I couldn't write," he'd said, "and I didn't bother telling her. But I felt real sorry for her, she looked like the roof fell in." So don't take it so seriously,' he added. 'He didn't.'

And finally my haunt was over.

Part Two

In Search of a New Oasis

15

Jesse Winchester

I MET JESSE WINCHESTER in 1967, shortly after he came to live in Montreal and not long after the Finjan closed. The closing of both Finjans was as much a surprise to Shimon and me as it was to everyone else. Suddenly we found ourselves with an empty bank account. Opening the downtown Finjan the previous year had been the main culprit. It had been far too ambitious a project, especially for financially un-savvy people like us.

Converting the run-down premises above a delicatessen into a welcoming music club had been an expensive venture, far more expensive than anticipated, despite our experience with the original Finjan. Aside from the building work, which included erecting a proper stage and installing quality sound and lighting equipment, there were all the extras: furnishings, decorations and, most expensive of all, sound-proofing. Although the rent was high as we were on the main downtown street, we didn't have downtown visibility and exposure, being tucked away somewhere on the top floor. We were only allowed a small street sign that was up so high you needed training in neck mobility to see it.

Ferrying the musicians from the uptown Finjan to the downtown Finjan, which had seemed such a good idea, turned out to be exhausting and costly. Musicians' fees had also risen dramatically. As the old favourites became more and more popular, their fees became higher and higher. We didn't have the seating capacity to justify paying the increases. People seemed unwilling to pay downtown prices to hear musicians with no track record. Also, more low-key coffeehouses had opened up, which didn't charge an entrance fee and which were more laid back, more 'anything goes' and easier to access. And, most important, the new Finjan was unable to recreate the atmosphere of the old Finjan – the intimacy, the sense of being part of an adventure. The downtown Finjan was just too downtown. Despite Shimon's best efforts, limited as he was by multiple council and landlord restrictions, the ambiance and uniqueness of the original Finjan could not be duplicated. It had been a one-off.

Financially, things hurtled downhill at an unstoppable pace, racing to wipe out. We were suddenly in debt over our heads. After a brief but futile life-and-death struggle to make loans, cut expenses and raise the admission fee and drink prices, we admitted defeat. We simply could not pay our debts. Shimon closed both Finjans and declared bankruptcy. It was that bad and that sad.

Closing the door of the Finjan for the last time was like shutting down a piece of my heart. It was the oasis that sustained me when my travel dreams had withered. It was a love that was gone forever, a small death.

But surprisingly, our worlds did not fall apart. Although the shock was temporarily immobilizing, it took just weeks for

Shimon to transfer his affections to his second love – the art world – and to find a sign-writing/poster designing/graphic arts workplace which then developed into a silk-screening studio. Most importantly, he began to perform more extensively. Previously, managing both Finjans had quashed his performing ambitions. In the early sixties Shimon had released an album, *Songs of South Africa*, on the Folkways label, on which he played guitar and sang in both English and his mother tongue, Afrikaans, backed up by Peter Weldon playing banjo. (Peter Weldon later performed with the acclaimed McGarrigle sisters and, coincidently, recently contacted me after all those years, making the old Finjan days come alive again.) However Shimon was unable to capitalize on the potential exposure that recording a CD creates as he was too busy with both Finjans to perform or even to develop his musical abilities. Now he could do both once more and was able to accept engagements not only locally but also in Ottawa and Toronto.

As for me, even before the Finjan had closed, I had become increasingly involved in my university studies, having begun post-graduate work. In particular, I was intrigued by the dance plays of W. B. Yeats, dance being my initial love. And I was amazed to discover that although Yeats was celebrated as the greatest twentieth-century poet writing in English, he was considered a lousy dramatist. I thought he was an excellent dramatist and that his dance plays were especially brilliant, way ahead of their time in their use of multimedia and unique in the way they combined dance, music and masks with words that were often more poetry than prose. I longed to see his dance plays produced and single-handedly set about putting the record straight.

Although Yeats did not use dance as decoration but as an integral part of the play's essence – often the main action was expressed in dance – he provided very little choreographic information. I decided to remedy the situation by working on a series of choreographic notes for his 'Plays For Dancers', fantasizing about choreographing a live production. Not long afterwards I actually did just that, choreographing two of the dance plays for a production at the Centaur, Montreal's major English-speaking theatre. Although I doubt whether this influenced academic opinion, it did provide me with a creative challenge and a way of honouring Yeats as a dramatist. During this period, I also increasingly devoted myself to being a mother, something I had let slip. All these activities were major distractions from the pain of bereavement.

Some years later, I was able to produce and choreograph two of the dance plays in London for the stage, as well as for a BBC Yeats television special and a University of London recording. Coincidentally, Cedric Smith was visiting me in London at the time and I coerced him not only into writing the music for the plays and working with the musicians but into performing one of the main roles. His expertise as an actor and musician were crucial to the success of the productions. I couldn't have done it without him or without another Canadian artist friend, John Meighen, who made the formidable masks, as well as with Dorit, Cedric's lady, who was the principal dancer. A major delight arising from this venture was meeting Dame Ninette de Valois, founder of the Royal Ballet Company and Yeats's main dancer, who not only came to one of the performances, but who attended several of our rehearsals; and I was also delighted to meet Valerie Eliot, the widow of T. S. Eliot, who also came to a performance.

I must relate an amusing aside concerning my meeting with Dame Ninette de Valois. When I was first trying to choreograph the dance plays, back in my Montreal university days, I wrote to her explaining that I was attempting to choreograph several of Yeats's dance plays for both a Master's thesis and a theatre production. Since she was the main dancer in those plays when they were originally performed, I asked if she could give me some idea of the dance style she used, as there was little to indicate this in the printed version of the plays. I waited anxiously for her reply. When it finally came it said: 'I do not answer queries on Yeats.' Period.

Several years later, when I was living in London, Steven Cross, the director of the BBC Yeats television production, asked me to suggest someone he could interview for the programme, I suggested Ninette de Valois. I warned him that she didn't answer queries on Yeats but thought she might make an exception for the BBC. I made him promise that if she consented to be interviewed, he would take me along as his researcher. We were in the midst of rehearsing the plays and meeting the original dancer would be a massive triumph and a great help to me. As I suspected, she agreed to be interviewed and Steven Cross kept his promise.

The interviews took place in her home and I went along with a recording device hidden in my pocket. Ninette de Valois was delightful, warm, open and with a wonderful sense of humour. While chatting away, she would suddenly stop and say, 'I'm going to tell you something personal, but promise not to tell anyone else, it's just for our ears,' and go on to reveal some little treasure.

I was in heaven. I asked her a couple of obscure questions about the plays, especially about their dance element, and I seemed to know so much about them that she said, 'My goodness, you BBC researchers do your work thoroughly.' I only admitted during our final interview that I was actually choreographing the plays and not a BBC researcher. Like Diego Rivera, all those years ago in Mexico, she actually applauded my subterfuge. She was delighted that the plays would be performed once again and asked if she could come to a rehearsal. Is the world round? Of course she could! I also confessed that I had written to her several years previously, asking for information about the dance plays and she had responded with the terse, 'I do not answer queries on Yeats.' She laughed and told me that many years before she had been invited to give a lecture on the Royal Ballet Company in the US. She was amazed and delighted by the large audience attendance, far bigger than she could have wished for. That is, until question time. It turned out the audience was not the least bit interested in the Royal Ballet Company but had come to question her about her relationship with Yeats. She was really put out and decided, then and there, never again to answer any query on Yeats. I neglected to tell her that I had taped the interviews in which she had described their relationship. (However, I have never finished transcribing the tapes, although by now they would be part of history.)

***

Most important in stilling the pangs of loss after the closing of the Finjan was my continued involvement in the music world, which remained a major part of my life. I attended festivals, concerts, spent hours in coffeehouses listening to aspiring musicians, went to New York to connect with my musician friends, to Toronto to spend time with musicians there, and to Stratford, Ontario to visit Cedric, often taking Ronit with me. Also, when they played other venues in town, I made sure to connect with those musicians I had become close to. I invited them home to dinners, to parties and to jam sessions, or just to sit in my wonderful kitchen, where the memories were embossed in gold, and to indulge in catch-up sessions. The good times rolled on, albeit with less gusto and excitement. However, despite all the compensations, I noticed myself going the extra mile to avoid the area where the Finjan had been. The memories were too poignant and I needed time to integrate them into my being rather than have them consume me

Aside from spending time with the musicians I knew, I met many new ones, some of who became close friends. One of these was Jesse Winchester. It was the time of the Vietnam War and of fierce opposition to that war; the time of burning draft cards, of major US draft evasion, radical protest, the time of flower power. Jesse was among the thousands of young Americans opposed to the war and, when he received his military call-up, he decided to leave the country of his birth, his home, his family and friends, rather than be drafted into the army.

To its credit, Canada, officially declaring itself 'non-belligerent', stood up to its overpowering southern neighbour. It offered a home to US citizens opposed to the war – a means of evading conscription. Many Americans came to Canada in order to voice their disapproval of the fighting, but mainly to avoid serving in the military. They were considered draft dodgers and could not return to the US without landing in jail. Even when Jimmy Carter declared a pardon for all draft evaders in 1977, many of these Americans, grateful for the shelter and support Canada had given them, did not return home and, instead, became Canadian citizens. Jesse Winchester was among them.

Jesse was in his early twenties when I first met him. Although he had not been in Montreal long, he had connected with some of the local musicians and had found his way to one of our jam sessions. I remember that initial meeting with affection. Tentatively extending his hand to shake mine, he introduced himself with a slight bow, saying he was a musician from the US and had recently come to Canada. He seemed shy and uncertain but determined to gain my approval.

'I haven't been personally invited to your party, ma'am, and I apologize if you think me too forward, but I would be grateful if you would allow me to stay.'

I was a bit taken aback, both by his soft, lilting southern accent and by his formality. I had never been called ma'am before and was not accustomed to that sort of politeness. Most of the musicians I knew were 'hey babe' sort of guys and 'too forward' was not in their vocabulary.

'You are very welcome to my home,' I said, giving his hand a little squeeze as extra reassurance.

My heart went out to Jesse from the very first moment my gaze met his. I don't know if it's because he looked like he hadn't eaten a proper meal in a long time or because his eyes looked troubled. Probably both. Although he was less than six feet tall, his thinness made him appear taller, elongated and fragile. And it was as though his short, full beard and abundance of dark frisky hair were attempting to hide those troubled eyes. Of course, I was also taken by his southern gentleman manners. I not only found them respectful, but touching, even tender. He seemed like the kind of guy who would lay down his coat should we encounter a puddle. I didn't know anyone else like that.

I saw Jesse often after that initial meeting but, even though we became close friends and he lost much of that initial diffidence, he never lost his gracious gentleman persona. It was embedded in his genetics, part of his DNA. Not surprising as he had been born in Louisiana, then raised in Mississippi and in Memphis, Tennessee. He was a true Southerner.

I spent many evenings with Jesse, listening to songs he had composed and ones he was working on. There was a unique quality to his lyrics, a compelling philosophical overtone that intrigued me. Unlike many of the blues musicians whose songs emanated from the physical being – from hard work, breaking stones, picking cotton; from hunger, exhaustion, from riding freight trains and walking lonely highways – many of Jesse's songs emanated from the mental being, from contemplation of the human condition, from the 'to-be-or-not-to-be' questions of life, the incongruities of life, of love.

This was not surprising, as in his university studies he had focused on philosophy, a subject he had studied both in Germany and the US. He was especially keen on the German philosophers who grappled with those same issues. He spoke fluent German and once translated an article for me on dance from German into perfect English. His songs reflected that philosophical preoccupation, using simple imagery to convey deeper meanings, such as the need to bury a seed in dirt to make it grow, or how if you find yourself walking on thin ice, you might as well dance.

Although most of his songs were a tribute to and reflection of his life in southern US, echoing a sense of loss for that life, there was also a philosophical resonance to much of what he wrote; a haunting undercurrent of the fundamental questions of existence, of human frailty, human inconsistency, conflict, fickleness, and especially of the multiple aspects of love. In many ways, he was a philosopher-songwriter.

Jesse's music incorporated a variety of influences: blues, country, gospel and folk. His melodies were often rhythmic and catchy. I remember once attending an exercise class, which played Jesse's music to motivate us. We did stretches, skips, hops and jumps to the tune of his 'Yankee Lady'. Often, the deeper questions of human existence were embedded in easy-to-sing melodies, the juxtaposition of lyrics and melody making his songs even more powerful.

Jesse was very lonely during his first year in Montreal. He missed his home, his family and his friends, especially his female friends, and he was uncomfortable with the ethos of northern living, the attitudes, the social character, the behaviour patterns, the lack of niceties – all so different from what he was accustomed to. Although he made contact with several local musicians, he seemed timid when it came to acquiring gigs and had little musical outlet, rarely performing the songs he was working on. He was also a bit of a recluse and didn't make friends easily, especially female friends. One day, he said to me in a voice burning with a combination of frustration and pathos: 'Niema, I need a lady friend. Can't you introduce me to someone?' Ladies were not attracted to him. He was awkward, shy, remote.

Then suddenly all that changed. It began when he met Robby Robinson of the acclaimed music group The Band, who was by then a celebrity performer and friend and colleague of Bob Dylan. Jesse had gone to Ottawa to make a demo of his songs, and in a church basement used as a recording studio, the momentous meeting took place. Robbie had heard about Jesse and asked to hear his songs. He was the first person to realize he had encountered a huge talent.

In years to come, Bob Dylan would say, 'You can't talk about the best song writers and not include Jesse.' But it was Robbie who initially made that assessment. He took Jesse under his wing and, a few months after the meeting, produced his debut album, 'Jesse Winchester'. He also got Albert Grossman – the top agent in the music world who represented both Robbie and Bob Dylan – to sign up Jesse. It was a rags-to-riches story; a busking-on-street-corners to a stunning-acclaim phenomenon. The music world became Jesse's oyster.

Album followed album. Venues vied to engage him. His songs were on the radio; the newspapers wrote glowing reports of his performances; The Band opened for him in concerts. Although his status as a conscientious objector meant he was unable to tour the US, celebrity performers like Joan Baez, Emmylou Harris and Tom Rush performed his songs; and, of course, he performed coast to coast in Canada. In the flash of an eye, he had gone from unknown and unwanted to worshiped and adored. He had become a star.

And that's when his problems began. Instead of being ignored by women as an undesirable, he suddenly found himself overwhelmingly desirable. Stage doors were crowded with females not only wanting his autograph, but wanting him. However, instead of this pleasing him, it troubled him, confused him.

One day he said to me, 'I don't understand why I am dismissed one day and desired the next. I'm me. I'm the same me. It's not genuine. It's not the truth.'

'Why don't you forget the "why", forget brooding about it and just enjoy it?' I said.

'I can't,' he answered. 'It's not me they want. They rejected the *me*. It has nothing to do with me. It's all about them, all about something else.'

He felt caught up in some perverse human failing and had to understand why it was happening, to understand who he was then and who he was now. The questions overwhelmed and distressed him. He became increasingly disturbed as girls pursued him; women sent enticing invitations; sexually explicit notes appeared in his dressing room, once in the pocket of his jacket. He was obsessed with understanding the implications of the transformation, to know how to react to it, how to live with it. He became withdrawn, unreachable.

The straw that broke the camel's back came when, after one performance, a young, seemingly normal couple, with no outward signs of weirdness, confronted him. In a tone as though requesting a light for his cigarette, the male of the duo asked Jesse if he would agree to spend a night with his girlfriend. To make matters worse, he assured Jesse that he needn't worry because it was alright with him on the condition that it was just the one night. He explained that his girlfriend was obsessed with Jesse and he had promised to make that request and allow her to live her fantasy as a birthday present. That was the final blow. Jesse thought he was going mad.

'What does that say about them?' he said, 'and more important, even worse, what does it say about me?'

He was so distraught that he locked himself in a room, refused to come out, refused to perform and even refused to eat. He needed complete solitude to meditate, to work out a *modus vivendi*, a way of coping.

When Jesse emerged from this metaphysical hibernation some weeks later, although noticeably thinner, he seemed to have acquired a surge of vitality, of confidence. He walked taller. His eyes were brighter. He was easier, more relaxed. And his performances had a new energy. Something, somewhere, somehow, had given him new strength, new determination, new confidence. The transformation was miraculous although it was accompanied by an almost imperceptible steely resolve – 'steely' being foreign to his nature. I questioned him several times, but he refused to discuss the details of the transformation.

Many years later when I was living in England, Jesse informed me he was giving a concert in London. Of course he wanted me to attend. And of course I wanted to attend. After a superb performance, he came home with me so we could spend time together. By now he was a fully-fledged celebrity, especially in the US, which had welcomed the return of draft dodgers, and he had performed in countries all over the world, recorded sixteen albums and had a variety of celebrity icons singing his songs. We were delighted to see each other. It seemed like old times when we had opened our hearts to each other. There was so much to tell and to hear.

I had always wondered what had happened to him during that period of isolation when he had struggled with the extremes of female response to him. The female rejection he had endured before his musical success and the desire, the longing he evoked in women after his successes, had almost destroyed his will to live. I knew he had resolved the issue because he was now married. I was eager to know what wisdom he had gained which had given him the ability to take life by the horns and flourish?

I thought that after all this time he would be able to tell me. But all he did was quote a line from one of his songs:

'Whatever doesn't destroy you must surely make you stronger.'

16

The Healing of Leonard Cohen

W HEN I FIRST BEGAN university, in the early Finjan days, I
was thrilled to discover that Irving Layton, one of Canada's
leading poets, was giving several courses in English literature. I was
in awe of Irving Layton. I had every one of his books and his poems
were my favourite bedtime reading. He had seemed a remote,
intriguing figure, like Jack Kerouac or Alan Ginsberg; someone to
be admired from a distance, an idol, a hero, not a commoner like
myself. After all, he had twice been nominated for the Nobel Prize
for Literature. As a well-known Canadian poet had said of him:
'There was Irving Layton and then there was the rest of us.' It was
incredible I could actually encounter him in the flesh.

I hadn't intended to study English literature, but couldn't
forego the privilege of close-up contact with one of my icons. I

registered for every course he gave. As it turned out, he was not only a wonderful poet but also a fabulous teacher, exciting and stimulating, and eventually he became the inspiration behind my pursuit of W. B. Yeats and my friendship with Leonard Cohen, two major events in my life.

One day, in my first month at university, I thought I saw the man himself walking toward me on a street close to where I lived. Could it actually be him, I wondered, right in my back yard? But with his stocky physique, mane of black hair, prominent features and determined walk – as though he was on the attack, challenging the universe – he was unmistakable.

Should I approach him, introduce myself; tell him how much I admired him both as a poet and a teacher? I was too timid. I knew he wouldn't recognize me; he taught hundreds of students and I was sure he had no lack of acolytes. Besides it was such an unoriginal approach. I had to find something more original. But my mind, unable to process the glory of the moment, went numb. As he was coming closer my overwhelming desire to meet him trumped the unoriginality of my approach. As he was seconds from passing me, I was overcome by a no-guts-no-gain panic, and stepped into his path.

'Professor Layton,' I said apologetically, having almost bumped into him, 'I am one of your students and I want to tell you how much I enjoy your classes.'

'How wonderful', he said in his big booming voice, 'and how delightful for you to tell me. I have just been giving a poetry introduction to a class of teenagers and their desire to hear the bell ring ending the lesson was palpable.' He smiled. I smiled. What do I say next? My discomfort must also have been palpable. Fortunately, he suffered no such shortcomings.

'Do you live in this area?' he asked.

'Two minutes away.' Then suddenly, right out from left field, I said, 'Would you like to come by for a cup of coffee?'

'That would be very nice indeed,' he said. 'Thank you.' It was as easy as that.

And that was the beginning. He taught those teenagers every Wednesday afternoon, in a school close to where I lived, and every Wednesday afternoon he would come to my place for coffee. I loved it. At first, feeling so privileged made me awkward, but that didn't last long. He was so easy and open, so comfortable to talk to, so interesting to listen to and, besides, he seemed interested in hearing about my life. He was fascinated by the Wall of Fame and by the musicians, and he wanted to know all about the Finjan. He made it easy for my distant hero-worshiping to become a warm, relaxed friendship.

And it was through Irving that I met Leonard Cohen. Irving had an eagle's eye for spotting talent in younger poets and generously devoted his time and energy, even his money, to encouraging it. Leonard was eager to be spotted, especially by the sought-after Irving Layton. Irving, older, wiser and battle-honed, became Leonard's guru. Leonard, young, fresh, exceptional, became Irving's prize discovery. They were drawn together like the joining of night with day – Leonard of the night, Irving of the day. Leonard's 'brooding gypsy boy' complemented Irving's essential optimism; Leonard's pale aristocratic inheritance, Irving's robust peasant roots. Leonard revered Irving's talent as a poet: Irving considered Leonard to have 'the purest lyrical gift in the country'.

Leonard fascinated Irving. Leonard's tortured sensibility, his mystical yearnings, his affinity with pain, his patient Christ-like suffering, were diametrically opposed to Irving's pragmatic, vigorous solidity and his refusal to turn the other cheek. Leonard brought Irving in touch with an ethos Irving could not otherwise contact. And, in turn, Leonard drew strength from Irving's vast resources of stability and wellbeing. Leonard once said, 'I taught him how to dress, he taught me how to live forever.' Leonard's first album was dedicated to Irving, and one of Irving's poetry books was dedicated to Leonard.

Leonard began his career writing poetry, but he later expanded his literary activities to include novels and then turned to writing songs and eventually to performing them. Although from the beginning he achieved popularity in the US, especially as a songwriter and performer, he wasn't successful in Canada, except for amongst a small group of devotees. Every grant, every award he applied for was denied and everything he published, every performance he gave, received a negative review. Discouraged by repeated rejection, he left Montreal and moved to New York.

Years later, when, as a successful superstar with several gold albums to his credit, he returned to Montreal to give his first big concert, and was steeling himself against the anticipated negative response. Aviva (Irving's partner and my friend) and I found him in the dressing room, composing a terse reply to the bad review he knew would appear in the *Montreal Star*.

'Why do you bother?' Aviva asked. 'The London *Times* says you're great, the *New York Times* says you're fantastic; you get international rave reviews. Why do you care what the pathetic little *Montreal Star* writes?'

'Because,' he answered sadly, 'my mother reads the *Montreal Star* and she's convinced I'm a failure.'

From the very first meeting, Leonard fascinated me, and that fascination never lost its edge. I was intrigued by his bittersweet attitude to life, by his beautiful melancholy, his untamed imagination. Like Dylan, his imagination had a life of its own, an original way of seeing things and of yoking disparate ideas. But his was a darker vision, intense, haunted, as though he had visits with doom. Predictably, Leonard was intrigued by Dylan, by his songs, his startling imagination and his meteoric rise to fame. He was just beginning to write songs himself and was overwhelmed that I knew Dylan. He wanted to hear every detail about him, especially what it was like to be famous or even to know someone famous. Ironically, he was to find out all too soon. And, to compound the irony, in 1975 Dylan was to dedicate his album *Desire* to Leonard Cohen. Although it was through Irving that Leonard and I became acquainted, it was through music and poetry that we became friends. And that friendship led to some of the most memorable happenings in my life.

Leonard moved in and out of my life at intervals that became further apart the more famous he became. However, no matter where his fame led, he always returned to Montreal to celebrate Christmas with Irving and Aviva, Ronit and I also becoming part of the celebrations. Leonard believed in maintaining traditions, saying they were his anchor in the chaos of existence. Every Christmas we would usher in the Yuletide together.

Leonard would lead us in blessings for peace and love. He would ask each of us to bless the coming year by making a dedication, a pledge, asserting what we would give to it. Then he would lead us in various ceremonies and rituals, depending on what esoteric philosophy he was immersed in at the time.

One year he promised us connection with Universal Love. By the light of a single candle he taught us the Tibetan mantra *Om mani padme hum*: 'God in unmanifest form is like a jewel in the centre of a lotus, manifest in my heart.' Gazing into the flickering flame, we chanted that invocation over and over, until in a semi-hypnotic state, I could feel my energy merging with the cosmic forces in an overwhelming energy of Universal Love. It felt as though I was shining with love. Even Irving, a staunch sceptic, was captivated. It was Leonard who introduced me to Tibet, an introduction that was to become an obsession and which became one of the most significant adventures of my life, one of my most important oases.

When Ronit graduated from elementary school, Irving gave her a copy of Leonard's *Poems* with the inscription, 'Now that you have graduated, let Leonard do the rest.' He asked Leonard to autograph the book and Leonard added, 'Yeah, let me do the rest.' He was drawn to Ronit's undefiled girlhood and made me promise to 'keep her in white' until she was old enough to marry him. But in a photograph I have of them from that time, they already look like they were more than married. Such was the oneness between them, the similarity of expression, of unseen internal forces shaping the external image. Caught by the camera in a moment of intense connection, they were two aspects of one reality, Ronit looking outwards in innocent wonder, entering life, and Leonard with his arm around her shoulder, protecting her from what he had already lived.

Leonard once told me that I was a 'familiar'. I asked him what a familiar was and he said, 'That element that makes the magic happen.' Of course, I was delighted. But actually, it was Leonard who was the familiar. Leonard emanated a contagious magic. He was a master at evoking mystical atmospheres, creating strange moods where all things were possible. Like a magician, he wove a spell impelling both sceptic and believer to surrender to it, like with the Tibetan chanting. His poetry and his music had this same compelling power. I was especially receptive to these charged atmospheres and even more receptive to his seductive charisma.

One of the most memorable, most mystical, most 'on the edge of trance' experiences I've ever had, happened with Leonard in one of his most magical evocations. I don't know who was the familiar that night, Leonard or me, or both of us, but the magic certainly happened.

One cold Montreal evening, several years after the Finjan had closed, my friend Jim phoned, telling me he had procured some magic mushrooms that were very difficult to come by and asking if I wanted to try them. Although I was a coward when it came to drugs, the mushrooms intrigued me. They were highly valued as 'the love drug' and grown in Mexico where the native Indians used them for religious, spiritual and ceremonial rites. Friends of mine had gone to Mexico and swung in hammocks for months, waiting for the mushroom to mature. Leonard had introduced several mutual acquaintances to the mushrooms and they had reported huge ecstasies, delights of phenomenal proportions, life-changing insights. I decided to take the plunge.

I crossed the threshold of Jim's living room as though stepping on stage for my big performance. Jim, detecting my stage nerves, assured me he wouldn't indulge so that I could rely on his sobriety. I swallowed the mushrooms with total confidence. After about half an hour Jim's spartan living room became an enchanted palace. Everything seemed to be alive and in motion. A painting of flowers was suddenly composed of tiny points of light and although the points were moving, the flowers were still. I could see music become dancing sounds and could hear colours singing. It was an orgy of the senses. And I was in the heart of a magic lantern. I phoned the Laytons because I wanted to tell everyone.

'Everything is beaming diamond light,' I told Aviva. 'I'm in a wonderland.'

'Beaming diamond light,' Avivia repeated, impressed.

'Tell her to bring it here.' I recognized Leonard's voice in the background.

Jim and I arrived at the Laytons' in a cocoon of silver snowflakes, which melted into a log fire that was blazing warmth in colours of gold. The living room, usually lovely, was now exquisite with its Indian table top composed of tiny pieces of mother-of-pearl, radiating light like a chest of jewels. Irving and Leonard were sitting on the pale gold sofa and I knelt between them, gazing into their faces, exhilarated by crystal visions.

'What do you see?' Leonard asked.

Words came tumbling out of my mouth, hardly able to keep up with a kaleidoscope of changing mages.

'I see a spiral of words dancing from your mouth onto the table, then winding in the jewels and filling with light, and now they are sparkling into Irving's mouth and dancing back into yours; they are leaping higher and growing more and more luminous. It's wonderful.'

Leonard and Irving took turns asking, 'What do you see?' and then began to add their visions to mine, in a shimmering cascade of words until their words began to rotate in the kaleidoscope of images, brilliance upon brilliance, their laughter whirling in the air like sparklers, spinning, spiralling up and up, riding the contact high.

Suddenly Leonard raised his hand. The kaleidoscope stilled and his voice echoed from a cavern deep within him.

'Friends', he said, his laughter turned into solemnity, 'I must reveal to you a problem I have that I have been unable to share until tonight.'

'The problems of Leonard Cohen, a legend in his own time, do not exist,' Irving said. 'A man who can have everything he wants – success, money, fame, women – is no longer entitled to have problems.'

'Yes, it's true, I can have all the women I want,' Leonard said gravely. 'It's like magic. I enter a crowded elevator and point. When I reach my floor, the woman I pointed at, follows me.'

'And that's a problem?' Irving intoned. 'It sounds more like a blessing.'

'Yes, that's a problem,' Leonard said sadly,' 'because now that I can have any woman lay my finger on, I can't make love to any of them.' He paused dramatically. 'I have been unable to have an erection for almost a year.'

'But you, the guru of love...' Irving began to say.

'I'm a fraud,' Leonard said, his eyes darkening.

Suddenly I felt a wild exhilaration. I stood up and, drawing in all the magic of the room, of the people, of myself, I declared, 'On this night we have the power to magic your erection back.'

Leonard had laid his finger on me. His response was immediate. As though proclaiming a prophecy, he said, 'Tonight shall be remembered as the night Leonard Cohen's erection returned to earth. Henceforth virgins dressed in white shall light candles to commemorate the miracle, proclaiming, "Leonard Cohen's erection is alive. Magic is afoot."'

Leonard, the orgy master, cracked his whip and the sparks burst into flame. 'We shall have an erection competition!' He was inspired. 'The men will stand side by side, penises exposed and Niema will dance before them.' He spoke like a medium manifesting a vision.

The atmosphere was so charged, so buzzing with energy, so hypnotic, and Leonard was so powerful that there was no choice but to obey him. Irving and Jim did as they were told – refusing him would have been like the tide refusing the moon. While Aviva left the room to attend to baby David, Leonard lit several candles and then joined Jim and Irving. Music was playing and Leonard proceeded to conjure up the dance. 'First you will move sensuously, encouraging, coaxing erection. Woman as seducer. Then your dance will become a ritual of growth, of procreation; the goddess dancing a fertility rite to encourage a fruitful yield. The men will partake in a ceremony of manhood, a contest of virility.' Leonard wore the robes of prophet.

The music glittered through the candlelight and firelight, in an elaborate choreography of sound. Leonard raised his arm, signalling me to dance. I moved like a belly dancer in a harem, my body rubbed with oil, my navel flashing. Then I became the temptress, the enchantress, dancing a timeless seduction. My body was dancing but my head was hearing names: Cleopatra, Mata Hari, Jezebel. My blouse had come off at Leonard's instruction, but he had allowed my skirt, and the swish of silk against my legs was like a thousand caresses. My breasts, belly and thighs were rocking, swaying, tempting all maleness. My hips were pulsating deep into a journey of seduction. Leonard was shouting cries of encouragement. I was responding, searching for the golden stud, for Adam, Caesar, Alexander. Then, at Leonard's command, I moved into rituals of fertility, kneeling, blessing the earth, arms lifting in spirals from earth through rain and sun; palms reaching into the sky in an invocation of growth. I could feel the male energy bright with excitement but the penises hung like cobras who had forgotten how to be charmed.

Then slowly, very slowly, I danced to the sofa and folded into the gold, beckoning Irving and Leonard to either side of me. I felt newly born, my body fresh as morning sunshine but with the power of a healer. Beside me Leonard's penis lay like a broken bird. Carefully, I took it in my hand. As it nestled in my fingers I saw its mouth open and begin to sing.

'The bird is singing,' I smiled up at Leonard. Then I heard another call, faint, distant. I covered Irving's penis with my other hand. Yes, a mating call. 'Two love birds, two song birds,' I crooned.

'And you are creating the music,' Leonard said. I sat between them, cradling their music in my palms, feeling them fuse into a single instrument – and I, its maestro. I, who could hardly bang out Chopsticks on the piano, began playing like a master, fingering the pipes, simultaneously, alternately, my hands embracing, strumming, stroking, plucking flecks of golden light, my fingertips seething with tattoos of sound as music shuttled through my fingers. There was nothing else in the room, no people, no furniture, no anything; just Leonard, Irving, and me and the music. And I tossed my head and played for them and played for the universe, feeling the music in my nostrils, hearing it on my tongue, tasting it through my eyes. I was an inspired virtuoso playing a divine organ.

Both Irving and Leonard had closed their eyes, released into perfect attunement as the notes swelled, creating magical harmonies, mysterious chords, fierce rhythms.

'It's the sacred music of the spheres,' I said in wonder, as my hands tamed the wild sounds into cradle songs before the sounds beat wild again. And I, pulled by the pipes into the pools of music flowing between us, knowing every thought they knew, feeling every thought they felt. 'One hand on the crucifix, one hand on the song.'

I am the cauldron in which the energies are mixed and mingled, creating a profound oneness. I hear music, I hear poetry, I hear love. And yes, suddenly I am that familiar, I have special powers and for a moment I am making the magic happen. They create through me. And I, the altar, the temple, the wishing well of their poem, of their song, of their love. Touching where they cannot touch, feeling for them, through them, into them, their music exploding in my hands. Union. Communion. And Leonard is born in the palm of my hand – the birth of the Young King – and grows through Irving, through Tara, through Sheba, through me. Erect.

'Standing ovation,' Leonard shouts, rising, flinging his arms to the heavens. We applaud, celebrating Leonard's rebirth, as candles ignite all about us, and as candles ignite all over the world, in thanksgiving and commemoration. And the heavens sing Halleluiah.

***

Another time, some years later, Leonard was giving a concert in Toronto. I had known him several years by then and coincidently

I was visiting the Laytons, who had moved to the city. Of course we went to hear Leonard perform. What happened that evening turned out to be one of the major regrets of my life.

The concert was superb. The audience so responsive, so in tune with Leonard, that they burst into wild applause after the first bars of a song. There was a palpable sense of love emanating from the audience, an embrace of gratitude, of thanks, a feeling of being blessed just to be present. And I was at the head of the queue.

Leonard's songs, sung in his smoky, opium voice, evoked in me a combination of profound sadness and profound joy. He opened his heart in his songs and his heart opened into mine. For me, his songs were a journey into life – the pitfalls and the ecstasies. They brought me into the depths of soul life, into longings, into mystery, into a gamut of emotions. I was humbled, excited, frightened yet reassured. No other musician ever had that effect on me. Dylan's songs went to my head, making me think, while Leonard's songs went to my heart, making me feel.

After the concert, I went to the washroom to regain my balance, to allow my being to settle and return to safety. Then I went to the green room to join the others for drinks, nibbles and chat. Leonard was quietly radiant. He was almost back to being Leonard of the day, although he never really was of the day; there was always a shadow of the night hovering over him.

I didn't dare go near him. Whenever I heard him perform he was no longer friend Leonard, 'bread and butter' Leonard; he was transformed into Leonard the magician, Leonard the lover. His songs took me to the edge of discovery, of yearning, of trance. He was Leonard of the candles and wine. I was in tune with his heartbeat. The journey was not to the highs and lows of mountains, the thunder of skies, the rolling of waves, but to the peaks and troughs of emotion, of feeling, of longing.

I only exchanged a nod with Leonard and found a seat well away from him, but where I could watch him unobserved. I saw him joking with reporters, signing autographs, patiently answering endless questions; he was always polite, diffident, but I had the feeling he was not quite present. There was a barely visible mist shrouding him, keeping him separate. Then, when most people had gone, he came up to me:

'Where are you staying tonight?' he asked out of the blue.

'With Irving and Aviva,' I replied.

'My hotel is around the corner, only two minutes away, why don't you stay with me?'

Before I could stop myself, I shook my head in refusal, declaring in a kind of schoolmistress way, 'Leonard, no hanky-panky.' I don't know where that line came from or even why it came, but it amused Leonard and he laughed.

'Okay, Niema, no hanky-panky,' he said, raising his arms, palms up in a gesture of surrender.

And so I went home with Irving and Aviva. After that occasion, whenever we met, Leonard would greet me with, 'Okay, Niema, no hanky-panky,' and raise his arms in that same gesture of surrender.

As the years went by, I played that scene over and over, and increasingly regretted not accepting Leonard's invitation. Why had I refused it? I was aware I had missed a very special night. Like Dylan, Leonard had a head full of magic and I had been invited to share it. That night would have been with me forever. Besides, it would have enhanced the connection between us and, if nothing else, it would have been a night of fun. Leonard was good at fun. Why had I refused? I mused on that question, thought about it, analysed it, chewed it, gnawed at it. I desperately wanted to understand.

Was I afraid of falling in love with Leonard in some profound way that would ultimately require distance rather than connection? Was I trying to circumvent the agony of being in love, especially of being in love with Leonard? For I was aware being in love with Leonard was a fatal condition. I would have to share that love with a parade of women, even men. Leonard was 'everyone's man'. Everyone was in love with Leonard. He once told me both men and women would phone him, saying they wanted his voice to be the last voice they heard before killing themselves. He said this not as a boast, but as a bewilderment.

I hadn't fallen in love with any of the musicians since Casey Anderson, and that had been an experience etched with fire, one that I came to realize I had to escape if I didn't want to be consumed alive. There was no way we could be together and accepting that reality had been like slowly bleeding to death. Since Casey, I had come to know several musicians intimately, but I had been prepared to let them go. I had even been prepared to let Casey go when I finally admitted we had reached a dead end. But I knew I wouldn't have been able to let Leonard go. When he looked at me in a certain way, his eyes penetrating my soul, the earth rocked and I had to flee, to shield myself from the avalanche. No one else had that effect on me. Perhaps my guardian angel was protecting me from the anguish of impossible love, or perhaps I had finally become an adult.

Not spending that night with Leonard remained the big regret of my life; it was a haunt that pursued me, a lament that wailed through the years and gave rise to strange mystical happenings even though I normally shunned mysticism. I began to dream about Leonard, tender, caring, lovely dreams, and I began to have the uncanny feeling that it was those dreams that were keeping Leonard safe, and that I had to keep on dreaming them for Leonard's protection.

Yet the regret was my secret. I never told anyone about it, including Leonard. As a matter of fact, I saw very little of Leonard for several years afterwards. Not long after that night in Toronto, I moved to England, in the early seventies. Then he attended the Zen centre at Mount Baldy for five years with his mentor, Rashi, and became an ordained Buddhist monk. When he came down from the mountain, he discovered his manager, Kelly Lynch, to whom he had entrusted power of attorney, had robbed him of all his savings – over five million dollars. He was forced to tour again to fund his existence and this meant being terminally busy, writing new songs, rehearsing, touring, consulting with agents, music producers and musicians, and engaging in all the details that touring and recording demanded.

For some reason, the desire to confess my secret to Leonard grew increasingly relevant. I decided to contact him when he next gave a concert in London. It was just about this time I discovered that Leonard was ill and would not be touring in the foreseeable future. My desire to tell Leonard became even more urgent.

As it happened, I was planning on travelling to Santa Barbara to visit Ronit and decided that I would first spend time in Los Angeles, where Leonard lived. Since Leonard was not touring, I knew he would be at home, in the same place he had been living for years. But I never got that chance. When I tried to contact him, I was told he was very ill and not seeing anyone.

Leonard died a few days before I got to Los Angeles.

Several months before Leonard died, he received a communication from a friend who was close to Marianne Ihlen, whom Leonard had immortalized in the song *So Long, Marianne*. He was informed that she was in hospital, unable to speak and close to death. He was deeply moved and wrote to her.

A close friend read the letter to her:

Well Marianne, it's come to this time when we are really so old and our bodies are falling apart and I think I will follow you very soon. Know that I am so close behind you that if you stretch out your hand, I think you can reach mine. And you know that I've always loved you for your beauty and wisdom, but I don't need to say anything more about that because you know all about that.

But now I just want to wish you a very good journey. Goodbye old friend. Endless love, see you down the road.

Apparently when her friend read the line, 'if you stretch out your hand, I think you can reach mine', Marianne had reached out her hand to take his. She died two days later.

Marianne died 8 July, 2016; Leonard only months later, on 7 November, 2016.

17

The Man Who Wouldn't Talk

ALTHOUGH OUR FINANCES HAD taken a turn for the worse when Ronit was about eleven, I scraped together enough money to spend several weeks in Ireland on my own. By then I had completed my master's thesis and had begun a doctorate. I decided to attend the Yeats Summer School in Sligo, Ireland, a yearly event, with research for a doctorate as my excuse. But actually I needed to find a new oasis, a new adventure. I needed to travel. I had been growing increasingly restless and was straining at the bit. Whereas Shimon thrived on predictability, I withered. Whereas he needed a permanent home, I needed a temporary oasis. Without rancour or bitterness, we had been steadily moving in different directions, although retaining an affectionate attachment.

The trip to Ireland heightened my longing for the road. I returned to Montreal even more restless but unprepared for what awaited me there. Without warning, Shimon had left me for someone else, the someone who had done the lighting for our Yeats plays and to whom I had introduced him. Although I understood his motivation – my constant desire to move on, grinding against his desire to establish roots – I was devastated. Of course I knew there was more to it than that. There were my romantic interludes to consider. Shimon never knew about my adventure with Casey or about any other amorous diversions. But I assumed he didn't know because he didn't want to know. Having no interest or appetite for such diversions himself, he assumed it was the same for me. Besides, being completely immersed in his music and art, fully absorbed in each day's doings, he had no desire to rock the boat and as long as I was considerate of him, careful not to rub his nose in my adventures, he had no need to.

Shimon and I had a close, tranquil relationship. We never argued, never had explosions of anger or vindictiveness, never tried to hurt each other. There was a beautiful harmony in our being together. But emotionally we led separate lives. He, content and engrossed in working out the day, preoccupied with every moment; me, always reaching out beyond the day, reaching out for more – the nomad girl eager for adventure, for new oases, new loves. I would never have left Shimon, he was an essential part of my existence, and I was naïve enough and inexperienced enough to think he would never leave me. But his new partner had obviously evoked in him a passion I had been unable to evoke, had not even tried to evoke, being more of a sister and friend, than a lover. And although I was traumatized by his leaving, there was a tiny generosity in me that was pleased for him.

Feeling trapped, bereft and with little money, I spent the next two years chained to circumstances I was powerless to alter, my travel dreams shattered by unrelenting reality, my heart aching for the loss of Shimon. It had been so sudden, so final. Although Shimon tried to make things easier for me, his energy, time and commitment were no longer devoted to me. It was like an extended bereavement, which made the need to travel, to find a new oasis, ever more pressing.

Then suddenly everything changed. Amazingly, incredibly, I received a three-year Canada Council award, plus travel grant, to complete my doctorate in the university of my choice and in the country of my choice. The angels must have heard my weeping. My ticket to ride was magically reissued. With a heart split in two, one half broken, the other beating excitedly with a newfound energy, a newfound freedom, I packed one bag for myself and one for Ronit. Then, leaving Shimon with whatever worldly possessions I had, Ronit and I took off for England. By now Ronit had inherited some of my travel bug, and although she was sad to leave her father and grandmother, Pistol Pete having died some years earlier, the adventure excited her. Besides, she had the assurance that if things didn't work out she could return to Montreal.

Although Ronit had only a dim but fond memory of Pistol Pete, I was still suffering from the trauma of his death. It was me who had found him one afternoon in his favourite chair, the television still on. I assumed he had fallen asleep. But when I tried to wake him, there was no response. He was unconscious. In a panic I phoned the hospital and an ambulance was sent for him. It turned out he had had a stroke. When I next saw him he was hooked up to a profusion of tubes, bottles and machines, helpless. My Pistol Pete, so powerful, so mighty; and suddenly so defenceless, so vulnerable. It was unbearable. For the next few days my mother and I took turns sitting by his bedside. But he never regained consciousness. One day I entered his room to find him lying in his bed, all the tubes and other paraphernalia gone. Almost hysterical, and in despair I rushed to the nurses' station shouting, "My father's life saving equipment has been removed. Why did that happen? He needs it to stay alive. Are you trying to kill him?' One of the nurses put her arm around me, 'Im so sorry dear, but your father is dead, he died peacefully last night in his sleep.' Dead. It was as though she had given me a knockout blow and although I was still standing, I was unconscious. And, recollecting that moment, I can still feel the impact of that blow. Even though with time it has healed significantly, but never completely.

Initially, I intended to finish my university degree in Ireland since I was working on an Irish writer. But, after spending time in Dublin, I realized this was not a good idea. It would be too difficult for a foreign woman without a husband but with a child to live in Ireland. In a country where divorce did not become legal until 1997, where men lived with their mothers until they married in their late thirties or even forties, and where sexual repression was rampant, I would be too high profile.

Even my earlier trips to Ireland without Ronit had given rise to a plague of curiosity and endless questioning regarding my marital status, making me feel as though my very bones were being picked. Although I loved Ireland and the Irish - the poetry, the talk, the music, the hilarity, the madness - I knew I couldn't live there. It was too introverted, too incestuous, to give me the anonymity I desired. I decided on London where no one was interested in me, except for Ruth, my only friend there, and Rosy whom I had met at the Yeats Summer School and recognized as a soul mate., and of course Victoria, a Summer School highlight.

When I had been involved in the Montreal production of the Yeats plays as the choreographer and assistant director, I had met Brian Stavetchney. He had been the main actor–dancer in the plays and had quickly become devoted to Yeats and to me.

The more we worked together, the more I realized how perfectly suited he was to creating the elusive qualities Yeats was after in his dramas, like evoking those emotions which 'haunt the edge of trance', 'those perceptions outside the scope of reason', the 'intimacies, ecstasies and anguish of soul life' and the 'images that remind us of vast passions'. Yeats wanted his theatre to call up the world of imagination and spirit, to be magical.

Brian had magic about him. He was spectacular to look at, with a shock of frizzy, sunflower hair that framed his head like a halo. His long, oval face, high cheekbones and startling blue eyes were so striking that even in repose he appeared to be on stage. His face was always alive, as though sensing nuances the rest of us were unable to perceive, vibrations we couldn't feel, like a finely attuned animal, alert, responsive, tuned into another dimension. His body was beautiful, long and lean and golden. It was eloquent, able to communicate when he was silent and he moved it like a dancer even when he was still. He didn't speak much but when he did, his voice was soft and resonant, rich and melodic on stage. I came to regard him as some aspect of Yeats himself, some incarnation Yeats would have desired.

After Shimon and I separated, the relationship between Brian and me gradually became more intimate. I was in dire need of comfort and Brian was all too willing to provide it. When I left for London with Ronit, Brian came with us. And, when we eventually reached London, it was Brian who insisted on forming the Yeats Theatre Company and performing the dance plays, the first professional production in London since Yeats's death in 1939. I was merely impelled by his energy.

My plan had been for the three of us to spend the first part of the summer in Greece on the island of Lesbos, in a small fishing village called Molivos, before finding a place to live in London. Irving and Aviva would be there for the entire summer and Leonard would be coming for part of it – an extra bonus for me, although by now he was firmly 'friend Leonard'. Then Brian and I would go on to Ireland to attend the Yeats Summer School, an exciting bonus for him. Both Brian and Ronit had never been out of Canada and were thrilled to be going to Greece. Brian, who had never met Irving or Leonard, but who was a devout fan of both, was over the moon at the prospect of meeting them. Ronit was excited about everything: the plane ride, Athens, the boat trip to Lesbos, London, everything.

The plane to Athens had a stopover in London and we spent a few days there before continuing on to Greece. We stayed with Ruth and persuaded her to come to Lesbos with us. Not that she needed much persuading. I had met Ruth through Aviva; they had been childhood friends, but hadn't seen each other for years. Ruth was delighted at the prospect of seeing her friend and thrilled to spend time in Greece. It was agreed that when Brian and I went to Ireland, she would remain in the house I had rented for the summer and look after Ronit. Ronit was happy to spend time with Ruth and our other friends. It was win-win all around.

In Athens, we decided to rent a car and drive through the Peloponnese, so we could see something of the mainland before going on to Lesbos. Brian was especially anxious to see Olympia and declaim in the ancient amphitheatre. None of us spoke any Greek and once we left Athens and started travelling through unspoilt villages, we found few people who spoke English. It became increasingly difficult to communicate, even on the basic level of finding food and a place to sleep, until Brian conceived a brilliant idea. He would mime and dance our needs.

His performances worked wonders. The Greeks were so responsive that he went from expressing simple needs to conducting entire conversations. His talent for conveying complex ideas non-verbally was a thing of wonder. He was eloquent and inventive, with a remarkable skill for externalizing subtle perceptions through movement. Our trip was wonderfully enhanced by his ability to make contact with people and to elicit warm responses. He got so good at his mime–dance creations, polishing them into mini entertainments, and was so inspired by the reactions they provoked, that by the time we returned to Athens to board the ship for Lesbos he had made a massive decision. He decided to give up talking. In one of his last verbal communications, he explained that he wanted to develop the discipline of expressing himself only in movement, to experience an internal meditation, a 'noble silence'.

Brian had a captive audience on the boat trip to Lesbos and communicated with them and entertained them around the clock, developing his silence into a fine art. He was spectacular. He mimed skits, he danced stories, he invented games for both children and adults. He had everyone at his fingertips, watching opened mouthed, immersed in his gripping dramas or laughing when he switched to comedy. He could be a clown, a tragic Pierrot, or a confused chicken. During the two-day voyage, the passengers deluged him with wine, cheese, sausages and invitations. He was accepted as a family member but with special celebrity status.

Everyone loved what he was doing, everyone but me. Ronit revelled in his performances, Ruth was both amused and impressed, but I grew increasingly disenchanted. My initial sympathy for his experiment turned into resentment when I realized he wasn't going to talk, even to me. He was high on a solo flight from which I was excluded. When he wasn't performing he was silent, absorbed in thoughts I couldn't share. Instead of appreciating his noble silence, I became jealous of it. It was like a devotion to a new love, and I wanted him back.

Ronit, on the other hand, relished deciphering his complex communications: 'Brian says he's not having lunch with us, he's eating with that Greek family, you know the one with the little girl who wears that big bow in her hair. He says we should bring our wine and join them after we've eaten. The father is teaching him to play the Bouzouki.'

I grew weary of the sympathetic looks and sad smiles directed at me by the other passengers, especially the women, silently saying, 'Your husband is such a fine, talented young man – what a pity he's a mute.' The deception began to bother me. When the boat docked, I didn't mind making all the arrangements – the taxi into town, the bus to the harbour, boat tickets to Lesbos, food for the trip – while he entertained. But I did mind his total preoccupation with his new love.

By the time we got to Molivos, I felt totally alienated by Brian's refusal to talk and hoped that meeting Irving, Aviva and Leonard would induce him to forego his vow of silence. But it didn't. Up until that point, he had performed almost exclusively for Greeks and communicating with these Westerners only through movement represented a new challenge, stretching his capacities, requiring all his concentration, making him even more remote from me. I felt hurt, rejected, as his silence left little for me. I had become irrelevant. There was less and less contact between us as I stopped trying to interpret his infrequent attempts at communication. Finally I was just as silent as he was.

When Lloyd, a visiting New Yorker, began to pay me attention, I found it a relief to detach myself from Brian. I began to disappear with Lloyd and it was Lloyd who accompanied me on the outings with Irving Leonard and Aviva. Brian hardly noticed. There was a growing audience to play to in Molivos: visiting Westerners who were intrigued by his experiment with silence. I began to spend more and more time with Lloyd.

Then suddenly a note appeared from Ronit. It read: 'First Daddy, then Brian, now Lloyd. What do you think I am?'

I sprang to attention. I had been so entrenched in my involvement with Brian and Lloyd that I hadn't bothered to see how it was affecting Ronit. Thankfully, she had refused to become invisible. My motherhood vows, made in the cardboard-carton days, were in urgent need of renewal. Ronit was my priority. I decided to stop seeing both Lloyd and Brian and devote all my attention to her.

That evening, fortified by the zeal of a new resolution, I told Brian I didn't want him to come to the Yeats Summer School with me. Slowly, very slowly, his eyes widened, the blue turning to black and his mouth opened in a great 'Oh,' in the terrible sadness of a bewildered Pierrot. He rose to his feet and began to dance, slowly, intensely, his body vivid with regret. Then he took my hand and looked at me, his face a knife edge of pain. And in that moment I relented, aware I was punishing him for being himself. If I no longer wanted to be with him that was understandable, but I had no right to spoil his dream. And I said, 'Okay Brian, we'll go to the Summer School together, but once we get there, I want us to go our separate ways, have our own rooms, our own schedules.' His eyes filled with tenderness and he embraced me so completely my resolve was almost done in.

Until it was time to leave for the Summer School, my focus was entirely on Ronit's wellbeing and when Brian and I left, first to London and then to Dublin, I knew she was happy, even pleased to remain in Molivos with Ruth and the others, but without me. At almost fourteen, it was her bid for independence.

***

When Brian and I got to London, I insisted that he collect our tickets to Dublin. If he didn't want to talk, that was his decision; I wasn't going to serve it. He was no longer being indulged by a soporific Lesbos. This was the real world and I was determined to make him accountable. The fiasco at Heathrow airport strengthened that resolve.

Although I had warned against it, he boarded the plane to London wearing almost see-through macramé shorts, made by a Greek admirer, a thin cotton shirt with an embroidered edge, open at the chest and held together by a woven sash, and leather thongs. As he danced his way into the customs hall, I made sure to enter a different queue. When the customs officer asked him the usual questions he remained silent, but could not produce identification indicating he was mute. However, when the officer asked him if he was able to speak, he nodded in the affirmative. Yes, he could speak. Baffled and annoyed, the officer escorted him behind a closed door. With some difficulty, I discovered he was being held in the detention centre. When I was finally allowed to see him, I found him looking bright and cheerful despite a body search and rough handling.

I explained that he had taken a vow of silence. 'It's part of his religion,' I improvised.

The officers had no idea what to do with that information, but since Brian had enough money and a return ticket to Canada, and not wanting to be accused of religious discrimination, they released him.

***

When we got to Ruth's house, where we were staying, there was still time to get to the ticket office, which was close by. My insistence that Brian do this was more entrenched than ever. If he wanted to maintain his noble silence, to develop his 'art of silence', he would have to function in the real world without talking. I had already booked the tickets to Ireland; all he had to do was pick them up. I drew a map and wrote explicit instructions to guide him every inch of the way. Before he left, I made him promise to phone me.

'I know you won't talk,' I said, 'but I'll ask you questions and you click your tongue once if the answer is "yes" and twice if it's a "no". That way, I'll know if everything went alright.'

Brian hesitated. Would this be violating his vow of silence? But for the sake of peace, he relented.

On edge, I waited for his call. One hour. Two hours. Three hours. Four hours. But no call from Brian. Something must have gone wrong. By now the ticket office was closed and I had no idea if he had the tickets or not. We were due to leave early next morning. I was distraught. Why hadn't I left him in Lesbos dancing for the Greeks?

Suddenly the phone rang.

'Did you get the tickets?' I shouted into the silence.

One despondent click: 'yes'.

What a relief. But why had it taken him so long to phone?

'Are you alright?'

Two clicks: 'no'.

'No? Are you hurt?'

One click. *Oh my God, he's hurt.*

'Where are you?' He couldn't answer that. Quick – rephrase the question: 'Are you in the hospital?' One click.

My God, he's in the hospital. Suddenly a woman's voice: 'I'm nurse Murphy. A very kind couple found your husband unconscious in Regent Street. They called an ambulance and brought him here. He had injured his head and required several stitches. He's fine now and we're arranging for a taxi to take him home. He'll be right as rain after a good night's sleep. But do have a doctor check the stitches in a week or so. Nothing to worry about.'

I was so overwhelmed I couldn't think what to say. I thanked her and hung up. Within an hour, Brian was back, looking pale and subdued but proudly producing the tickets.

When I finally unravelled the story, told to me in frustrating mime and dance, punctuated by clicks and nods, I learned that all went well until Brian was on his way home. On Regent Street, one of the busiest streets in London, he suddenly felt inspired. He would treat the English to entertainment as he had so often treated the Greeks, and he began to perform one of his most popular skits.

Only London was not Athens. The English were not only indifferent, but disapproving, even hostile. They had seen enough crazies to avoid encouraging more. They hurried past him, averting their eyes, as though by looking at him they would be condoning some obscene activity. No laughter, no cheers, no anything. Brian grew more and more determined to make them respond, to bring them joy. Finally, executing a desperate whirlwind twirl, he went smashing into a lamp post and fell unconscious on the pavement.

My poor Brian, he was learning the hard way. I put him to bed with kisses.

Brian was a sensation at the Summer School. At an event that was based entirely on verbal exchange, Brian's vow of silence was a complete anomaly, dividing the Summer School into two camps: those opposed to Brian and those for him. Brian's vow of silence became a fascinating topic of conversation, almost warranting its own seminar.

On the last day of the Summer School, Brian and I performed a scene from one of Yeats's dance plays based on Irish mythology, *At The Hawk's Well*, in which the young hero, the warrior Cuhulain, is driven away from the well of eternal life by the Hawk Woman. Brian was Cuhulain; I was the Hawk Woman. The most powerful moment came when Cuhulain, standing with his back to the well, hears the water bubble up but is unable to drink it because of a spell the Hawk woman has put on him. In desperation he raises his arm and warns:

Run where you will,
Grey bird,
You shall be perched upon my wrist,
Some were called queens and yet have been perched
there.

Brian's voice shattered the silence – rich, intense, passionate, defiant, agonized. The audience held its breath. The magical power of the play exploded with the miracle of Brian's voice. The play, the dance, the poetry, Brian, me, we were all miracles together. And Brian had spoken. His silence was over. After a short stay in Dublin, we returned to London together, once again united.

18

Victoria

I T WAS DURING THE first year I attended the Yeats Summer
School, while Shimon and I were still living together, some
time before the Brian event, that I met Victoria. I had become
friendly with some of the Summer School leading lights, mainly
the Irish poets like Seamus Heaney, John Kelly, and especially
with Jimmy Simmons. Before attending the School, I had been
corresponding with Brendan Kennelly, who was then Director
of the school and who had advised that I stay at the Imperial
Hotel, a grand Victorian building by the river with splashes of
faded elegance, where all the literary elite was based.

I had been immediately drawn to the Irish poets. I adored
their fun-loving generous spirit, their informality, their refusal
to take themselves or anyone else seriously; their modesty; and
their sense of melancholy laced with humour. In many ways,
they were like my musicians. They had the same ability to

flood the soul with longings and excite the senses with startling imagery; they exuded that same quality of living life on the edge. They personified that line from Jesse's song that you might as well dance if you're treading on thin ice.

They were themselves a kind of poetry, as though the poetry of the written word had somehow shaped itself to their own beings. They were extremely articulate, taking pleasure in words, and with ordinary conversations becoming shot through with poetry – words leaping out of sentences, evocative, musical, delighting my ear which was accustomed to Canadian flatness. They were more gregarious than the musicians, more lusty, relishing the contact of a good scrum.

The hotel had a comfortable lounge with an open fireplace, which was host to nightly adventures of unlimited potential. After the daytime official activities were over – the lectures, seminars, readings, questions and answers sessions – the poets, critics and literary giants of the Yeats universe would gather here to sweep aside the world of letters, and indulge in social riot. And I gathered with them.

'This room is the only reason I come to the summer school,' Jimmy once confided to me. The drinking was bottomless and inspired a fierce hilarity spiked by monologue, dialogue, anecdote and raucous choruses, sung and spoken, reeking with nostalgia, causing uncontrollable laughter until tears rolled and collapse was imminent. After business hours, the academic aura dissolved into a grand drunken Celtic celebration, which I suspected, was the main attraction for the Yeats professionals.

As for me, it was hard enough to digest the fact that prominent Yeats scholars, critics and world authorities like Richard Ellman, Frank Kermode, John Unterecter and Norman Jeffares, before whom I trembled, were actually present in the flesh; but to see these eminent giants pissed and unpredictable, inhibitions soaked up by Guinness, was a jolt to my notion of the order of things. Had I witnessed Yeats himself dancing a drunken Irish jig, or belting out 'Danny Boy', I wouldn't have felt more privileged. I was being allowed a coveted behind-the-scene glimpse into a world I could never have imagined – and I savoured every minute. I rarely got to bed before the sun came up, lest I miss a single witticism, a single stagger, a single belch.

Early in the first week of this Summer School, the one to which Brian came with me, I was standing in the crowded corridor during a break between lectures, talking to fellow students, when Jimmy Simmons, who had a connoisseur's eye for the ladies, led me away with urgency.

'Come with me for a minute, I want to show you someone.' He pointed out a girl standing in a small alcove, half-hidden by a plant. 'I've been watching her from day one,' he confided. 'She's so beautiful it makes my heart ache.' He paused, contracted his brows, drew in his mouth and squeezed his eyes half shut, as though he was finding words for a poem. 'I can feel her fragility, her tremble. It's as though her body doesn't conceal her soul.'

I understood what he meant. She had a haunting beauty, her face mobile and vulnerable, her eyes surprised, slightly frightened, her mouth controlling a barely perceptible quiver, her body alert, slender, waif-like. She gave the impression of a doe poised to flee.

'She certainly is beautiful,' I confirmed.

As though aware of some threat, she inched further into the plant.

'I'd love to know her, to see what sort of creature she is, what land she comes from. But I'm too timid. I'm afraid if I talk to her, she'll vanish,' Jimmy said.

'So you want me to do it for you?'

He looked at me shyly and nodded. 'You won't startle her.'

'I'll be happy to talk to her.'

'You don't mind?'

'Not at all. She looks like someone I'd want to know.'

I started towards her.

'Not now,' Jimmy said, 'wait until I'm gone.'

I watched for her after the lecture and made my approach as she was leaving the building. 'Hi, I'm Niema,' I said in my brightest Canadian manner, extending my hand. 'Did you enjoy the lecture?'

She looked at me with a hint of a smile, her lower lip trembling slightly. 'Yes, very much. Did you? But it would be far better if the lectures were held outdoors instead of in the hall, don't you think?'

Although I shivered inwardly at the thought of sitting in the Irish damp, I agreed. I walked along with her. She didn't seem to mind. She told me her name was Victoria, that she was English, and that she knew very little about Yeats.

'What brings you to the Summer school then?' I asked.

'I wanted to get away from London... somewhere in the county with fresh air... and coming here seemed like an interesting thing to do... learning about Yeats. I admire his poetry... I've been reading a lot of his poetry lately. When I heard about the summer school, it seemed the perfect thing. To do.' She spoke in hesitant short phrases, as though unsure where they were taking her.

'Where are you staying?' I asked, anxious to move on to more relevant matters.

'In a little bed and breakfast.'

'Do you like it?

'Not really... The room is fine... but the landlady is a bit of a snoop, she comes into my room without knocking. I think she wants to catch me out... she probably thinks I'm hiding someone.' A small nervous smile hovered as she spoke.

'That's awful. Besides, you're away from all the fun and the poetry.' Then, impulsively, I said, 'Why don't you move to the

Imperial Hotel? That's where all the action is – poetry readings, singsongs, parties. All the Irish poets stay there and they're great.

'Is that where you stay?'

'Yes, it's wonderful.'

'I suppose there's nothing to stop me from moving,' she said, picking up on my enthusiasm. 'It would be a good idea to leave that landlady, don't you think?'

'Definitely. How long will it take you to pack?' I wanted to clinch the deal while I was ahead.

'Not long. Half an hour.' Her ability to take the plunge was impressive.

'I'll pick you up in an hour.'

She seemed really pleased, smiling and almost at ease. 'Thank you very much.'

I liked her a lot. She explained how to get to her place and I was off to relay the good news to Jimmy.

When I returned, Victoria was packed and ready. I helped carry her few belongings to the hotel, sat her in the lobby and went to check her in. Then something happened I hadn't reckoned on.

'Sorry, the hotel is full. Booked solid. There's nothing available,' the receptionist said apologetically. My heart plunged. How awful. Victoria had left her room at my insistence; she had trusted me. I was leading her on to bigger and better things, like some self-proclaimed pied piper, and now there was nowhere for her to stay. I felt humiliated.

'We may have a room in a few days,' the receptionist said, attempting to soothe my visible disappointment.

A few days. What good was that? I felt ill. How could I possibly tell Victoria? Then, suddenly, I had an idea. I had a large room. Why not invite Victoria to stay with me until another room became available?

'Can she share my room until then?' I asked.

'I can't see why not,' the receptionist said, pleased that a solution was at hand. 'I'll move her into your room and when something becomes available I'll move her out.'

'Can you put an extra bed into the room?' I asked.

'I'm afraid not. All the extra beds are accounted for.'

My room had only one bed, a fairly large bed, but still only one. I disliked sleeping with anyone except lovers. But never mind about me… I deserved to suffer. I was responsible for this mess. But what about the innocent Victoria? We hardly knew each other. I could feel my heart contracting with acute embarrassment.

I was nervous about telling Victoria, placing her in this impossible situation. Why hadn't I checked with the hotel first? Why am I always jumping off cliffs and yelling 'it hurts'? I began beating myself up big time. But my fears proved groundless. Victoria was delighted, bubbly and excited, like a schoolgirl on a new adventure. She loved the idea so much that a few days later when a room became available, she asked, very tentatively, if she could continue staying with me, saying she found it very comforting.

I was touched. There was a child-like sweetness about her. How could I refuse? Besides, I didn't want to refuse. Her bright intelligence, coupled with an original perception concerning the lectures and seminars, and even the lecturers themselves, fascinated me. I loved her wistful observations and her daring (she would ask the most provocative questions at question time), as well as her unpredictability, her strange blend of shy and strident, and the mischievous glint in her eyes when she knew she was being impossible. We became inseparable. Friendships made at the Summer School were quick and intense, like those made when travelling.

She took to Jimmy immediately. She liked his Irish lilt and the way he put words together. He made her laugh and she made his heart ache. They both adored the outdoors and, growing restless during lectures, would slip away for a walk. Sometimes I would go with them, but usually I didn't. Nevertheless, I took pleasure in their being together.

Although Victoria and I spent much time with each other, I knew very little about her. She seemed reluctant to talk about her life in London and I didn't press her. Then one day a postcard appeared in my room, addressed to her. I read it. One line said: 'I've been asked to lunch with Noel Coward and Zsa Zsa Gabor, she's passing through London.' It was signed 'Alan'.

'Someone is putting you on, Victoria,' I said, handing her the card.

She read it. 'No. It's genuine,' she said quietly.

'Genuine? How genuine can it be, having lunch with Noel Coward and Zsa Zsa Gabor?'

She looked embarrassed, as though caught in a guilty secret. 'I'm married to Alan Bates,' she said, lowering her head. 'He's an actor, he knows these people.'

'You mean *Zorba the Greek* Alan Bates?'

'Yes.'

'He's one of my favourite actors. I adore him.'

I could see she was becoming uncomfortable, agitated. 'I'd rather you didn't tell anyone... I'd rather people knew me as myself and not as the wife of Alan Bates.'

I was stunned. Had she told me she was married to the Duke of York, I couldn't have been more surprised – although Alan Bates was a much bigger celebrity than the Duke of York. She didn't fit my idea of a famous film star's wife, not that I had ever met one. She seemed so modest, so unpretentious, at times even awkward; there wasn't a smidgen of glamour adorning her person, and she seemed so interested in things untrendy, things without shine and glitter.

'How come you're married to Alan Bates?'

'Pure chance.'

'It's better than winning at roulette,' I quipped, in an attempt to dispel the disquiet I could feel gripping her. But then, gradually, the story unfolded.

She had been born into a poor East End family, but determined to escape the poverty, she taught herself secretarial skills and got a job in a London office, with connections in New York. Going to New York was her dream and she eventually saved enough money for an extended visit.

While there, she stayed with a friend in a shared flat. One day, her friend decided to have a party and asked each of her flat mates to invite three men.

'I didn't know three men,' Victoria said. 'But that afternoon I had seen a play with Alan Bates and I was very taken by him.'

'You and no doubt every other woman who saw the play. He's amazingly good looking.'

'I decided to do something daring. I decided to phone the theatre and invite him to the party. I left a message. I didn't really think he would phone back. But he did. I guess he was curious. It was strange really – had it been any other night he couldn't have come, but that was his one night off and so he came.'

'And you ended up getting married?'

'I didn't want to get married... It was his idea... I never intended getting married... I'm very jealous of my freedom and my privacy... Besides we come from very different worlds... I didn't like his world, especially the acting world – didn't fit into it, didn't want to.'

She paused, remembering something. 'When Alan brought me home to meet his parents – his family live in Derbyshire, D. H. Lawrence country, very beautiful – his mother was sitting on the patio... most elegant, sipping a glass of sherry... When he told her we were getting married, she dropped the glass... it shattered into a hundred pieces. I guess I wasn't what she had in mind.'

Later she told me that she and Alan had twin sons under a year old.

'How did you manage to get away from London, when you had twin babies?' I asked, remembering the bind of motherhood.

'Alan is taking care of them,' she said casually. 'He has some time off. I don't think being an actor gives one special privileges. Do you? He has to get up nights to change nappies just like I do. I'm an artist too, in my own way – everybody is. We share the responsibility of the twins. Alan agrees. He's very helpful.'

When I eventually moved to London, several years later, I saw Victoria often, and met Alan and the twins. We lived fairly close to each other and became good fiends. Alan was one of the finest, most gentle, most generous men I had ever met. I often marvelled at the patient way he dealt with Victoria's unbridled unconventionality, her wild riding-rough-shod-manner, her distrust of his fellow actors and her disdain and loathing for what she considered their indulged ego-inflated lives, and especially her exasperating principals. For example, she wouldn't have help in the house although she barely did the housework or cooking, disliking both. Chairs were piled high with clothing, papers and books. The bathroom walls were streaked with a blend of talcum powder, face cream and lipstick – the latest of the twins' artistic endeavours – but she refused to allow money to make domestic life easier. Eventually Alan had to get a separate flat so he could enjoy a semblance of order necessary for him to concentrate on his acting. I remember Victoria going to the doctor's for the twins' booster shots, waiting her turn in the surgery, with a baby under each arm, exhausted.

'Why don't you get a private doctor to the house? It would be so much easier on you,' I suggested.

'I don't believe in private medicine,' she said, her tone precluding further discussion.

Victoria had a gentle influence on my life, and her way of asking 'Neem, please...' could easily bend my resolve. 'Neem' was her pet name for me; spoken like an affectionate embrace, it silenced any objection:

'Neem, please take one of Tinker Bell's kittens; she's so pretty, her name is Tiger Lilly, Ronit will adore her.'

'No, Victoria. Ronit will adore her but I'll do all the cleaning up. And what about when I'm travelling? No, Victoria.'

'I'll look after her when you're gone. Oh please Neem, take her.'

I took her.

Victoria got me to alter an important aspect of my life. She got me to change my hair style. No easy matter. My hair was my one major vanity. All my life, I longed for it to be straight and bemoaned its crumpled curliness. Then I discovered that if I ironed it when wet, it was as good as straight.

One evening, Victoria and I arranged to meet Alan at a Greek restaurant for dinner. Both she and Alan were vegetarians (although she didn't consider plucking the odd bit of meat from my plate as a violation) and Greek cuisine had a good choice of vegetarian dishes. I had washed my hair for the occasion, and was preparing for the ironing ritual, when I was distracted by a phone call that took so long, my hair had dried. I was just about to wet it for the ironing treatment when the doorbell rang. It was Victoria.

'Sorry I'm early,' she said. Victoria was either early or late, rarely on time.

'Just give me ten minutes to iron my hair; it's dried while I was on the phone and gone all miserable and curly. I have to wet it first.'

She turned to look at me and her face became radiant, as though beholding a vision. 'Neem, your hair is beautiful... Please, Neem, you mustn't straighten it.' She paused dramatically and looked at me as though she had never seen me before: 'You look like an Egyptian princess.'

Had anyone else said this, I would have rushed for the iron. Egyptian princess, indeed! But coming from Victoria, I dared to be flattered. Surely Victoria would know. She not only had contact with the most glamorous women in the world but with royalty. I looked in the mirror. My hair had divided into a multiple of strands, and each strand had sprung into a coil. My face was stranded amidst a profusion of coils. I shrugged, unconvinced. Still, if anyone could recognize an Egyptian princess, it was Victoria. I never straightened my hair again.

Victoria always intrigued me. I knew I loved her, but I never understood the fierce ambiguities of her nature, although I learned to accept them, even to cherish them. She had an insatiable thirst for experience, for knowledge, for art, for literature and a total lack of interest in the routines that bind existence, in involvement with the rituals of living. Abstract concepts were her passionate preoccupation. They were far more important to her than daily realities. One moment she was consumed by the mystic philosopher Gurdjieff, the next devoted to iridology. The preparation of meals could wait, the laundry could be ignored, but the reading of John Donne or W. B. Yeats could not be neglected. Her spirit thrived on ideas; they were her nutrition, and her engagement with them was total.

One of her most fascinating characteristics was an exciting inconsistency. It was impossible to anticipate her. Just when I was convinced she was fiercely independent, she'd become awkwardly self-conscious, so insecure she seemed to dissolve into a puddle of dependency. She was like a musical instrument, so tightly strung, so finely tuned, the merest whisper could provoke a dissonant twang.

Once, when we were in Paris together, she seemed lost and awkward. (Alan had encouraged us to go to Paris and before we left had whispered to me, 'Make sure she buys some decent clothes.') We had gone to visit the Louvre and I could tell she was feeling crushed by the paintings; they had evoked some terrible insecurity. I could hear that twang encroaching upon the silence, see it in tiny darts around her mouth. She had a pained, trembling look and I was about to suggest we leave when I noticed a handsome Frenchman looking at her with that special brand of French appreciation. 'He fancies you,' I said, and was immediately sorry I'd said anything. Would this make her even more self-conscious, more awkward?

'I fancy him too,' she said, and with a marvellous directness, went up to him, smiled that small winsome smile and said, 'I would like to invite you for coffee.'

Victoria was not like some other friends who grew vague and undefined if we were separated for long periods. Time did not create distance. She was always there, close, integral, and when we'd meet after a long absence, there was no need to restate, to renew. We'd just pick up where we had left off, our friendship intact. The intimacy had never faded.

I was devastated by Victoria's death in 1992, almost twenty years after we met. Two years earlier, when the twins were in their late teens, they went to Japan for a modelling/acting session. I'm not quite sure what happened there, but according to Victoria, who was vague about the details, they went to a party where someone spiked their drinks, and Tristan, one of the twins, collapsed and died. Victoria was consumed by grief, almost dying with him. Not long before Tristan's death Alan's brother, who she was close to had died, and shortly before that both her sister and her mother had died. Already riddled with sorrow from the previous deaths, she was unable to endure the death of her son. She stopped eating, stopped wanting to see anyone, rarely left the house. She became silent, depleted, withdrawn, devoid of all interest in living. On the rare occasion she came to see me, she would look into the windows of my basement flat and if she saw anyone else there she would flee. The only one of my friends she agreed to see was Cedric, when he happened to be visiting. And he was even able to make her laugh. But her laughter had no joy and brought no relief. Alan became increasingly concerned as her health deteriorated and she became so frail she had difficulty doing anything. He finally convinced her to see their doctor friend, something she had fiercely resisted. She was prescribed vitamins, minerals, and an assortment of herbs and special remedies to regain her health and wellbeing.

At one point she told Alan she wanted to go to one of her favourite places, Club Med in southern France, to recuperate. Alan was delighted. Sunshine, fresh air and good food were exactly what she needed. He was working and unable to accompany her, but planned on joining her the following week when the play he was in closed. Meanwhile he spoke to her every day. He told me he thought she was doing fine, regaining her strength. However, on the eve of his going to France to be with her, he received a shocking call. Victoria had been found dead in her room. She had gone to Club Med, not to recuperate but to die; to die quietly, by herself, out of everyone's way, without fuss. When I went to visit him, he showed me everything the doctor had given her hidden in the back of a cupboard, untouched. Alan expressed his grief by dedicating his next play to her. He invited Tom and me to the premier. I can't remember the name of the play or what it was about because after his impassioned dedication, his sorrow reaching into my heart, intensifying my sorrow, I heard nothing else. Following Tristam's death, Alan founded The Tristam Bates Theatre in Central London, in memory of his son.

The Yeats Summer School had not only brought me new literary awareness, it brought me something more profound: new friends. One of the dearest was Victoria.

19

The Prince

BRIAN AND I HAD spent a few days in Dublin after the Summer School ended, before returning to London. By then, Brian had broken his vow of silence and was easier to live with. On our first night in Dublin, Brian went to a mime performance while I went to a pub renowned for its blues musicians. It was here that I met Major, the star performer that night. Major was immediately familiar to me, coming from the tradition of black blues musicians. Listening to his music and watching him perform was like coming home. He had that dynamic edge – that same swagger, that sexy assurance pregnant with innuendo which I knew so well from the Finjan days. I had no hesitation in approaching him. We hit it off immediately. We knew the same musicians, had been to the same Village clubs in New York, understood the same idiom. Meeting Major was like the embrace of a brother in a foreign land.

Major told me he was moving to London and looking for a place to live. I too was moving to London and would be looking for a place to live. He needed enough space for his partner, Susan. I needed enough space for my daughter, Ronit, and boyfriend, Brian. Under the influence of Irish coffee, music and each other, we agreed to share a flat. And, against the odds, that's what we did.

It was Susan who found the flat. Brian and I had one room, Ronit another, and Major and Susan, the third, a room with a lot more space. The only additional room was a kitchen with just enough space for a table and chairs. The rooms led off a hallway, which we decorated with posters, photographs and, at my insistence, maps. And my room had a photograph of the Potala Palace in Tibet, the same one I had in Montreal and which I couldn't be parted from. The flat was cold and damp with no central heating, but we managed to make it cosy and colourful. Our beds, which doubled as sofas, were strewn with multi-coloured cushions and covered with inexpensive Indian spreads; we improvised bedside tales made from orange crates and covered in the same materials; and our bookcases were constructed from discarded planks of wood, separated by bricks appropriated from building sites. Later, when I began travelling, Moroccan wall hangings, rugs and lampshade added an exotic touch.

Despite the lack of space, we had a constant stream of visitors – my friends from Canada and the US, friends of their friends, Major's musician friends, mostly from New York (his home town) and Susan's friends from the north of England. Sometimes we had wall-to-wall guests sleeping in the hallway, even in the bathroom where we could just about squeeze in a mattress. The flat was a befitting sequel to the Finjan, filled with music and musicians. I loved it.

It was during this period that Brian and I organized The Yeats Theatre Company, with Michael Yeats, Yeats's son, by then a senator in the Irish government, as our sponsor. We performed two of Yeats's dance plays with Cedric, who happened to be visiting, and who was coerced into composing and directing the music and acting in one of the plays; with John Meighan, a friend from Canada, making the wonderful masks; and Dorit, Cedric's lady, flown in from Canada to dance the major roles. The plays were a great success and the BBC recorded parts of them for their *Omnibus* programme on Yeats, while the University of London filmed them for their archives. Not long after the excitement of the filming and the television production was over, Brian left London for Paris. He had been accepted as a student and awarded a scholarship by his mime idol, Étienne Decroux, known as 'the father of modern mime', who had taught the renowned Marcel Marceau. Brian couldn't believe his good luck. He left for France with my good wishes, saying he would return in a year when the mime course was over. In the end, it was ten years before I saw him again and by then he had his own mime school in the French town of Nîmes.

***

I loved living in England, mainly because it was so easy to get away. In Canada, I could travel for hours, even days, and still be in the same place; but in England, in just a few hours, I could be in countries with different languages, different architecture, different food, different coloured people. I could even find myself in different histories: medieval times with castles or Roman times with fortresses. It was exhilarating.

By this point, I had already spent several weeks in Morocco with Susan on two separate occasions, when Ronit was visiting Shimon – and it was the beginning of a long love affair with that country which I continue to treasure to this day. Not long afterwards, Ronit and I spent nine months mainly in Morocco but also hitchhiking to Tunisia and Algeria. Nomad girl was in her element.

Ronit had been fascinated by my Moroccan adventures and had made me promise to take her there one day. That day arrived sooner than expected. When she was fifteen, Shimon had to cancel her summer visit. It was the perfect opportunity for an extended trip. I decided on nine months and received permission to take her out of school as she was a year ahead of her grade. I also managed to convince Aviva and my actress friend Annie to come with us, although they would only be staying for the summer. Aviva would bring her eleven-year-old son, David, and we would travel in Annie's Volkswagen – a tight fit, but never mind. I was the only one who had been to Morocco before.

The trip began with an amazing happening that set the stage for months of amazing happenings. This particular one arose because, on one of my previous visits to Marrakesh, I had met a girl called Jos. It had been a serendipitous encounter that makes one believe in miracles.

Jos and I took to each other immediately. She was a French Moroccan with a French mother and Moroccan father. Fluent in Arabic and French, she moved easily between both cultures. Her English was excellent and she was able to answer my many questions concerning Moroccan politics, customs and culture. It was through her that I gained some insight into the complexities of Moroccan society.

Jos lived in Casablanca but, when I first met her, she was in Marrakesh to make contact with a band of Western musicians who had been playing there, with the aim of hiring them. She and her father were about to open a nightclub in the fashionable Casablanca beach strip. The strip was inundated with nightclubs, but the entertainment was mainly in Arabic. Western musicians would give their club a unique status. However, by the time Jos arrived in Marrakesh, the musicians had departed and she was bitterly disappointed.

When I told her I had contact with musicians both in the US and in England and could possibly help her, it was as though darkness had turned to light. On returning to London after that trip, I arranged for two musicians, friends of Major's, plus Major himself, to launch the club. They were such a great success that Jos contacted me, asking if I could book musicians on a regular basis. I loved the idea. Visiting Jos was an important reason for this current trip to Morocco. I wanted to finalize arrangements and discuss dates, contracts, money matters and so on.

One of the first things on our agenda was therefore a visit to Jos and not long after we arrived in Morocco, we headed for Casablanca. Jos's villa was a surprise; I hadn't expected anything so grand. It overlooked the sea and was set in spacious gardens enclosed by a high picket fence. The entrance was through a heavy wooden gate that a gatekeeper opened and closed both day and night.

We arrived just after noon, exhausted. An early start and the oppressive heat had left us close to collapse. I felt dizzy, dehydrated. Jos insisted we shower and rest to escape the afternoon heat. I was ushered into a room with a chaise longue strewn with cushions. One of the servants brought a pot of mint tea and partially closed the shutters, darkening the room. I drank the tea and stretched out on the cushions, feeling light headed and slightly feverish.

Jos came to check on me. 'You look like the sun has got to you,' she said. 'The best thing is to rest.' With that, she kissed my forehead and left. As I drifted into sleep, the air heady with the smell of jasmine, my thoughts jumbled and unfocused, I felt myself entering some other realm as I floated in and out of dream-fantasies.

I don't know how much later it was, or if I was asleep or awake, or a little of both, but gradually I became aware of a physical presence in the room and very slowly my eyes opened to meet it. In the arched doorway, silhouetted by a ray of sunlight, was a man who must have emerged from my fantasies. He was actually tall, dark and handsome. For a moment I couldn't tell if he was a vision, a manifestation arisen from the depths of my dreams or a real being. I blinked and blinked again, but he remained tenaciously leaning into the doorway. Something about the way his trousers fell over his black leather boots, and his wide-sleeved shirt narrowed at the cuffs, reminded me of a Cossack I had seen in a film. I became reckless.

'Are you a Cossack?' I asked.

He laughed. 'No. I am not a Cossack.'

'Then what are you? Where are you from?' I asked, feeling light headed and slightly intoxicated.

'I'm Moroccan. I'm from Rabat. I apologize for disturbing you. Your presence was unexpected. I came into the room to retrieve something I had left here. I was wondering how to get it without waking you.' He spoke perfect English with an intriguing Moroccan–French accent. 'Forgive me for disturbing you. I will leave now.'

I didn't want him to leave.

'Rabat,' I said, ignoring his apology. 'I was there once, I didn't like it much. Do you like living there?'

'Not much.'

'Then why do you live there?'

'My house is in Rabat.'

'Do you have to live where your house is?'

'Yes.'

'Why is that?'

'It's that kind of house.'

'You mean you're so attached to your house that you can't leave it?'

'No. I am not so attached to it. But, yes, I cannot leave it.'

This was intriguing stuff. If the scenario was surreal, the conversation was even more surreal.

'What kind of house is it?'

'Would you like to see it?'

'Yes. I adore houses.'

'Then I invite you to see my house.'

'When?'

'Now.'

'Now? But Rabat is far from here.'

'But my automobile is very near.'

This was getting too bizarre.

'I'll tell you what. I'm going to have a little sleep and if you are still real when I wake up, we'll talk about it.'

'I will still be real,' he laughed. 'Have a good rest and I apologize once again for disturbing you.'

He went to meet the sunshine.

I closed my eyes but sleep was no longer possible. I lay awake, trying to work out what had just happened. Had I been awake or was I still dreaming? A little later, Jos came into the room. 'Did you sleep well?' she asked.

'I'm not sure. I think I was asleep when a tall, dark, handsome Cossack came into the room and tried to carry me off in an automobile to a house he can't leave in Rabat. And what's worse. I almost went.'

Jos laughed. 'He's not a Cossack,' she said. 'That was Bashir Tazi. He came to get something he had left here. He's a prince,' she added casually.

'What do you mean, a prince?'

'He is a member of the royal family. He lives in the royal residence in Rabat, in his own palace – Tazi Palace. He's a good friend.'

'Seriously?'

'Yes, seriously.'

I was silent, trying to digest this dazzling bit of information. 'Tell me Jos, how come you're hanging out with a prince, a prince who has his own palace?'

'I met him some years ago in Paris. He had travelled in the East and had become very sick and he was in Paris for treatment. We became friends and we cared for each other like brother and sister. This villa belongs to him. He is a good man. He does not act like he is from the royal family.'

'Have you been to the palace?'

'Yes, many times.'

'What's it like?' I asked, fascinated.

'Bashir will take you there if you wish.'

'I could have been halfway there already,' I said.

Aviva had entered the room at the tail end of the conversation. 'You mean we can actually get to see the Moroccan palace?'

'Yes, actually you can.'

'But we're leaving here tomorrow.'

'Perhaps we can arrange some other time. I will ask Bashir. He'll be back later on.'

Ronit, David and Annie had already gone to bed, exhausted, when Bashir returned with several magnums of champagne. Aviva caught a glimpse of him opening one of the bottles, expertly withdrawing the cork, the bottle between his thighs. 'He even looks like a prince,' she whispered. 'He's gorgeous.'

The evening was as sparkling as the champagne. After one glass, I was ready for anything. We laughed a lot. Bashir was easy, informal, funny and full of surprises. He told us his favourite Canadian was Leonard Cohen. He loved his music and his poetry.

'Leonard Cohen and Bob Dylan are the two great poets of Western civilization. Not only poets but prophets,' he said.

When we told him we were close friends of Leonard's, and that I was a friend of Bob Dylan's, our soiree gained a new dimension. Everything he had was at our disposal.

'I invite you to my home in Rabat,' he said magnanimously. 'This is an occasion for celebration. We will celebrate there. We can leave at once, my automobile and driver are ready.'

I leapt at the idea, believing as the mountaineer Mallory did, 'that the greatest danger in life is not taking the adventure'. But Aviva was not from the Mallory school. Things were moving too fast, she needed time to adjust to adventure.

'Now? It's almost eleven o'clock. We can't go *now*,' she said, slightly alarmed.

'Why not?' Bashir said.

She thought for a moment. 'We have to get up very early tomorrow morning. We're meeting our Canadian friend, Cedric, in Marrakesh tomorrow.'

'He will wait,'

'It's his first time in Morocco. We promised to be at the airport. I want to be there.' Her voice was terse with resolve. 'Besides, we have to go to Essaouira; we've rented a place there and need to make final arrangements.'

Bashir was quick to realize that whether her objections were real or fabricated, tonight's celebration was off. He thought for a minute.

'We will postpone your visit then,' he said, unperturbed. Consulting a pocket diary, he said, 'Today is Thursday, you should have your affairs in order in two weeks. I will send my chauffeur to pick you up in Essaouira, two Thursdays from today.' He calculated the exact date. '*Wacha* – okay? Be in front of Hotel Des Isles at ten in the morning.'

'*Wacha*,' Aviva agreed. She could handle an invitation two weeks away and we could cherish it for fourteen whole days. The rest of the evening flowed like silk, smooth, sensuous, magical, with Bob Dylan and Leonard Cohen amplifying the magic.

In Essaouira, we spent the next two weeks in avid anticipation while making arrangements for our palace adventure. David would stay with Scott, a Canadian poet friend who lived outside the town, and Ronit would look in on him. As the day approached, Aviva and I grew increasingly excited, despite being assured that nothing would come of the invitation by those with superior knowledge of Moroccan protocol.

'Moroccans make grand promises,' Scott cautioned, 'but no one expects them to be kept. The grander the promise, the less likely its fulfilment. It's just the way here.' He shrugged his shoulders.

But exactly as Bashir had promised, and despite the negative predictions, a green, chauffeured limousine arrived in front of the appointed hotel, and although we had been warned that Moroccans had no regard for time, it arrive not only on the right day, but the right hour. Aviva and I approached it obliquely, unable to comprehend that the chauffeur, complete with cap and uniform, was waiting for us.

'Prince Bashir Tazi has sent for me to take you to the Royal Palace in Rabat,' the chauffeur announced formally, standing to attention, cap in hand. We waited, unsure of our next move. Would the limousine turn into a chariot, the chauffeur into a coachman and we into pumpkins?

The chauffeur opened the car door, helped us climb inside, and, with the hint of a bow, pressed the door shut. We leaned back, submitting to the velvety cushioned seats, luxurious with arm rests and foot stools. By some miracle we were on our way to a royal palace, invited by a Moroccan prince. Two plebeians whose closest contact with royalty had been peering into the face of the Queen on a penny coin.

It was a long ride to Rabat and we savoured every minute. We smiled benevolently at people sitting by the road, waiting for buses. We stopped often to appreciate how hot it was outside, so we could better enjoy the air-conditioned interior. We were like kids playing lords and ladies, taking turns to order the chauffeur to stop, inventing reasons, enjoying the response. However, our attempts to prolong the journey were finally exhausted. Despite our efforts we had arrived in Rabat. Minutes later, the palace approached like a fortress, protected by high turreted walls, its massive gates studded with bolts and iron fittings, forbiddingly shut. Armed guards stood to attention before the gates. At the approach of our car, rows of uniformed men suddenly appeared, and with incredible speed, flung the gates wide open. We didn't even slow down. They sprang to attention at either side of the portal, saluting as we slid through the entrance, the gates silently closing behind us.

It was as though some genie had uttered 'open sesame'. All at once we found ourselves in the pages of *One Thousand and One Nights*. We had been transported into a perfumed Moorish garden with fountains climbing through trees heavy with fruit and flowers, through which rose domes and minarets, like secrets half revealed. We watched with awe as Bashir approached the limo. He was entirely splendid. A prince from the Arabian Nights. His silk kaftan rippled over his body, its pearly whiteness accentuating his cinnamon skin. His eyes were dark and penetrating, outlined by black kohl. His jewellery sparkled in the sun: earrings with five-pointed stars, silver and amber bracelets and the silver chain he had worn the first time we met. A filigreed Hand of Fatima rested in the hollow of his neck where the ivory silk parted. The white babouche on his feet shone with the same sapphire stars he wore in his ears. His jewellery and eye make-up only enhanced his masculinity and the thought occurred to me that Western men, with their avoidance of adornment, seemed insipid in comparison.

Aviva and I, normally life of the party ladies, able to rise to any occasion, remained seated in the car, stunned and helpless. I suddenly felt awkward, misplaced. Our presence seemed alien, our Western energy at odds with the Eastern mystery.

Bashir helped us out of the car and kissed us on both cheeks, touching his right hand to his heart, in the Moroccan greeting. 'Welcome to my home,' he said, and taking Aviva by one arm and me by the other, led us towards the palace. We responded submissively, hardly able to thank him. After ten trance-like steps, I became aware we were walking along a tree-shaded avenue, paved with marble flagstones, the branches of the trees leaning into an archway. The sun lit the entwined leaves, weaving lacy patterns of dappled greens, revealing glimpses of the palace, its elegant curves silhouetted against the sky. The air was heavy with the smell of jasmine and lilac. I felt graceless in my purple jeans and tie-dyed blouse. I should have been in lavender silks. We passed under a carved honeycombed archway and were suddenly in the palace courtyard. I stopped in my tracks, dropping Bashir's arm.

The courtyard opened to the sky. In the centre was a fountain, the water gurgling like a natural spring and flowing into a pool, limpid and still. Sunshine fell into the pool, creating diamonds. Creeping vines and plants bright with flowers were everywhere. The garden had entered the palace. They had become one. Surrounding the fountain, slender marble pillars reached upwards, curving into stone arches so delicately carved they looked like lace. Around the fountain, a ceramic pathway formed an arcade between the arched pillars and palace walls. The walls were decorated with elaborate arabesques of entwined flowers and ancient Arabic script, giving the impression of a rich tapestry. The ceiling was made of carved wood and chiselled stucco formed into patterns of crowns, stars and interlaced foliage. It was stunning. I was enchanted, immobilized by beauty.

I felt Bashir easing me out of my trance. 'We can return later', he said, taking my arm once more. 'Tea is prepared for you upstairs, you must be thirsty.' But I was transfixed, unable to leave the magic courtyard. Aviva's eyes too had turned glassy. We remained motionless.

Bashir attempted a more subtle approach. 'Come, I have a surprise for you.' And I wondered what surprise could possibly trump this courtyard.

He escorted us through the arcade in silent slow motion. I was enthralled by the poetry of the architecture, by the way heavy materials like plaster, stucco and stone had been transformed to produce an ephemeral quality. Several rooms opened onto the courtyard, their doorways ajar, revealing glimpses of opulence: Moorish carvings, sumptuous carpets, latticed windows, ivory, gold, jade, mother of pearl – each room was like the overflow of a pirate's treasure chest.

I tried to imagine Bashir as a child playing in the courtyard. The idea was inconceivable. The palatial dimensions precluded ordinary human activity. We followed Bashir up a wide marble staircase and entered a corridor tiled with gold and blue geometric patterns.

'These are my rooms,' Bashir said, leading us through a doorway curtained with beads. We removed our sandals. He led us to an alcove with silk-embroidered cushioned seats. 'Please sit. You must be tired after your long journey. I will arrange for the tea,' he said, disappearing through the beaded doorway. I sat down closing my eyes, over amped, unable to absorb further stimuli.

When I opened my eyes, several minutes later, I found myself in a dome of aromatic wood inlaid with tiny pieces of silver, mother of pearl and ivory. Aviva and I, who usually had so much to say to each other, were silent. A small table with an engraved silver tray had been set before us. On the tray was a teapot with the same engravings, slender glasses containing pine nuts and set in silver holders, and plates of small round cakes covered with slivers of almonds. Bashir appeared smiling, and sitting cross-legged on a cushion facing us, poured the tea in the Moroccan tradition, presenting us each with a glass. I gazed into the pale gold of the tea and, breathing in the scent of jasmine and mint, closed my eyes in a moment of perfect bliss.

'I have invited several friends,' Bashir said, his voice an intrusion from the real world. 'They will be arriving very soon.' Aviva looked up blankly. I stared at him as though he had said something obscene.

'Oh yes,' Aviva managed.

'When are they coming?' I said, forgetting he had already told us.

'Very soon,' he repeated.

Another, 'Oh yes,' from Aviva.

'I must go to receive them. Is there anything else you wish?

'No, thank you, Bashir. This is beautiful… really beautiful… It's amazingly beautiful here. We couldn't ask for more. Thank you, Bashir, thank you.' The rush of exuberance from Aviva broke the spell.

'You have no need to thank me. You are my guests. It gives me great pleasure to please you.'

'You are pleasing us, this is a super treat.' Aviva's voice was close to tears.

'That is reward enough.'

When Bashir left to welcome his guests, Aviva and I crept out of the alcove, anxious to explore the private chambers of a prince. We emerged into a large rectangular room with carved doorways leading to other rooms. Although similar in style to the rest of the palace, the room was less aloof, more friendly. Moroccan rugs, heaped with cushions, covered the floors. Against the walls were low benches strewn with pillows, facing several small tables which were tiled with Arabic letters that coiled in and out of each other. Enormous vases of flowers scented the air. At the far end of the room, a heavy brocaded material fell like a curtain from ceiling to floor. Byzantine lanterns hung from the ceiling. The room was lit by sunshine, the windows so low the gardens seemed within the room.

Further discoveries were interrupted by a confusion of voices. Bashir entered with a group of Moroccans, two of them female. They all wore traditional dress, the men in light summer *jellabas*, the women in long embroidered kaftans, their faces veiled by *yashmaks*. We were introduced in the traditional Moroccan manner.

'My friend Mohammed,' Bashir said. Mohammed clasped my hand in his, held it for a few seconds, then touched the fingertips of that hand, still warm with mine, to his heart, creating a connection between us. The ladies retired almost immediately to one of the adjoining rooms and reappeared in minutes, transformed from Ancient East to Modern West by lipstick, nylons and miniskirts.

We sat on the floor among the cushions. The servants brought bowls of melons, figs, grapes and oranges, all beautifully arranged. Trays with silver teapots, gold-rimmed glasses and plates of flaky pistachio pastries were set before us. The conversation was a lively mixture of French, Arabic and English. Then Bashir said something in Arabic that prompted several of the men to leave the room with him. The conversation ceased, replaced by a hushed expectation. All eyes were fixed on the brocaded curtain at the end of the room from which, we were told, our surprise would materialize.

Suddenly the curtain parted, revealing a stage filled with a miracle of electronic equipment. Synthesizers, Hiwatt amplifiers with echo chambers, speakers with glittering disks and vibrating cones, guitars with fuzz pedals, a drum kit – all the latest gear that I recognized from my music festival days. Bashir entered from a door backstage, carrying an electric guitar and wearing a T-shirt shimmering with sequins and skin-tight faded jeans. The other men filed in behind him, still wearing *jelabas* and tripping over the tangle of wires.

A tuning session followed with piercing electronic shrieks, instrumental moans, buzzes and beeps, as the sound man pressed buttons, flicked switches, turned knobs and checked levels. Somehow, the magic carpet had flown us to a big band venue in New York or London. Some mad Aladdin had rubbed the lamp the wrong way. Before I could grasp what was happening, I was jolted by a blasting shiver on the drums, a 'one-two-three' from Bashir, and an explosion of 'I Can't Get No Satisfaction.'

My instinctive reaction was to cover my ears, followed by an intense desire to laugh, but I fiercely subdued both. I didn't dare look at Aviva. The others were watching us with smiles of pleasure, no doubt anticipating enthusiastic reactions. I smiled weakly and tried to look pleased. The music was painful, but somehow we endured.

The absurd climax came when lead singer, Bashir Tazi, stepped centre stage and announced, 'And now a special song which I dedicate to my Canadian friends,' and burst into Leonard Cohen's 'Suzanne', his delicious Moroccan–French accent suddenly ludicrous. I sucked hard on my tea and oranges and wondered about Suzanne being 'half crazy'. I could see Aviva staring at Bashir, unable to suppress her dismay.

Then, just as suddenly, the mad genie retreated into the bottle, stunned by the deluge it had loosened upon us. The brocade curtain folded shut, the band vanished, along with the lipsticked ladies, and the electric nightmare was over. We were whisked back to the palace romance. Bashir returned alone in his white silk kaftan, changed back into a prince.

'Just a little amusement', he said, shrugging his shoulders, casually dismissing the misadventure. Bashir obviously had sensed our negative reaction because no further mention was made of it. He proceeded to attend to us in a manner befitting a prince instead of a rock star. He conducted us on a leisurely tour of the palace grounds, arranged for our refreshment with bowls of chilled rose water, which we dabbed on our temples and wrists, and jugs of iced melon juice, served in the garden. He picked purple flowers for my hair and a corsage of jasmine for Aviva, which he pinned on her blouse. After a superb couscous dinner in Bashir's quarters served by candlelight, with Prince Bashir the perfect host, it was as though the black bolt had never struck.

As soon as dinner was over, as though on cue, the chauffeur made an appearance. Bashir excused himself and returned minutes later, still wearing white silk but now fashioned into embroidered jacket and trousers. 'The night is just beginning,' he announced. 'We will celebrate it in Casablanca.' Although Casablanca was over fifty miles away and we were loath to leave the palace, we submitted to Bashir's wishes without protest. One doesn't contest the agenda of a prince. We departed in the green limousine, straining to catch a last glimpse of the palace as the gates closed behind us.

20

An Oasis without Shelter and without Fruit

S OON AFTER ALL OUR friends had left Morocco, Ronit and I,
in need of distraction from the sense of loss, decided to leave
Essaouira and head for the desert, hitchhiking to save money
and taking public transportation when hitchhiking became too
difficult. It was easy getting lifts to Marrakesh and from there we
headed south to Quarzazate, called 'the door to the desert'. We
spent a few days in Quarzazate, where we met Gerald, a Swiss
traveller who was also heading for the desert and with whom we
decided to join forces. It was always a good idea to have a male
in the mix, and Gerald was perfect: an experienced traveller,
easy going, fun and good looking.

From Quarzazate we took a bus to Zagora, which was about 160 kilometres away and as far south as we could go by a combination of public transportation and hitchhiking. We were on the edge of the desert where the paved road stopped and the special vehicles travelling to the desert villages were few and far between. We stood before a large road sign which read 'Tombuckto 52 jours' (52 days) with an arrow pointing into the desert and a picture of a smiling camel to cheer one on. I couldn't resist taking a photo of Ronit, wearing her jelaba, standing before the sign. I had always thought Timbuktu was another way of saying 'the end of the world', not an actual destination.

We had walked to this point from the Zagora bus stop, thinking we could hitch a ride into the desert, unaware it marked a dead end. While we were mournfully contemplating what to do next, two cars pulled up beside us. There was a driver and a passenger in each, all four being Frenchmen. They told us they worked for the Fiat Auto company and were testing Fiat cars in desert conditions. They were driving to a small village a little over thirty kilometres away, which wasn't even on the map, where a gala event was being prepared in their honour and would then be returning to Zagora. They asked if we would like to join them. We asked no further questions. This was one of the lucky things travellers make happen. Or so we thought.

After a slow, difficult ride, slipping and sliding, churning up sand, forced to create our own roadways, and with the drivers stopping frequently to check mechanical operations and make notes, as well as twice to push the cars out of a rut we had dug ourselves into (when they accepted Gerald's help but refused any female assistance), we arrived at the outskirts of the village. It was mid-afternoon; we had started out early morning. We had no idea what to expect, certainly not the lavish welcome prepared for the Fiat men and the enthusiastic greeting we received as their friends. Several men in full Moroccan dress, who appeared to know the Frenchmen, greeted them, and us, with embraces, kisses on both cheeks and ear-to-ear smiles.

We were led into a very large tent, the earthen floor covered with beautiful Moroccan carpets and cushions for seats, the ceiling hung with coloured lights and brass lanterns with inserts of coloured glass. A long, low table was laid out in style with Moroccan delicacies, some of which I had never seen before. There were only ten of us, but enough food for twice that number. We sat on the cushions and were served the finest Moroccan cuisine by young women in embroidered kaftans. When we were done eating, a troupe of musicians and two belly dancers paraded into the tent, playing music, singing and dancing. The Fiat men accepted the sumptuous welcome as normal. Apparently they tested cars several times a year at different desert locations and this sort of event was part of the arrangement. We had somehow stumbled into the best of Moroccan hospitality and relished every moment.

It was all so wonderful that when it was time to leave, all three of us decided to stay on. We had been told that a desert vehicle, which brought provisions to the village once a month, was due to arrive in a few days and would give us a lift back to Zagora. The idea of spending several days in the village, experiencing desert life, was a temptation not to be resisted. Gerald was especially enthusiastic as he would shortly be leaving Morocco and this would be his last opportunity for a desert adventure. So, replete with food, entertainment and good will, we profusely thanked both our French and Moroccan hosts and, leaving our knapsacks in the tent, went off to explore the village, get supplies and arrange accommodation before it got too dark.

The village was a short walk away, but to our surprise, there was nothing to explore. There wasn't a single shop, or, unlike every other village I had been to, any indication of visitor accommodation. There wasn't even a street. Narrow pathways wound between clusters of small, sand-coloured houses, their shutters closed against the heat, some crumbling back into the desert. Disappointed, we made our way back to the tent, thinking we would ask permission to sleep there and offer to buy some of the leftovers – we could live for a week on what remained on that table.

But to our dismay, when we returned, there was no tent. It was gone, vanished, along with everything in it. Thankfully our knapsacks remained, huddled in a clump, forlorn in the vast expanse of desert. Everything, including the Moroccan men, the musicians, the dancers, the serving girls and the leftover food, had apparently been carted off in a large desert vehicle, which I had noticed parked alongside the tent and which was no longer there. They had all been imports. Suddenly, we were alone in a bare landscape. Deserted. It was like the striking of an elaborate stage set; even the stage hands had gone and nothing was left except empty space.

It took several minutes to absorb our predicament. Then Gerald said, with a shrug of his shoulders, 'Pas de problem, we sleep in the desert.' And Ronit said, 'I finally get to use my new sleeping bag.' And I said, shifting into practical mode, 'The first thing we must do is get water.' Fortunately, during our village walk, we had noticed a water pump. So after returning to the village, where there was still no sign of life, and filling our water bottles, we wandered a little way into the desert and began setting up camp. Gerald created a refuge from the sun with a tarp he always carried, and then began collecting bits of wood for a fire – twigs broken from the few gnarled trees that had managed to survive. Ronit set about making tea (we always carried tea bags) and I began taking photos, including one of Ronit making the tea, to immortalize our predicament.

For five days we were left undisturbed in the desert sands, with nowhere to go and nothing to buy. Our only visitors were several young village boys, timid at first, but quickly becoming our best friends. When we mimed being hungry, they returned each day with a tin of sardines and a round of bread for which they refused payment. We rewarded them with ballpoint pens, Magic Markers, Post-it Notes and small packets of baby wipes, which they accepted with such expressions of joy that we felt like Santas dispensing treasures. One day they brought us a small clay pot filled with fig jam, and to our amazement it was wrapped in a bit of faded English newspaper advertising holidays in Cornwall. It seemed that someone, somewhere was watching over us. It was another example of what is known as 'telegraph Morroc', where information is dispersed without any obvious means of communication.

Gerald managed to open the sardine tins with his trusty Swiss Army knife. The first day we feasted on bread drizzled with sardine oil, saving the sardines themselves for a future meal. However, when we realized there would be a daily delivery, the entire tin was devoured in one go. We were puzzled by meeting only children in the village when we went for water, until we later learned that the men all worked in Zagora and returned home only on Fridays and religious holidays. The older boys and girls also stayed in Zagora, where they went to school during weekdays. The women, it seemed, stayed at home; not surprising as there was nowhere to go. We did see a large open-air oven, which we assumed was where the bread was baked, but we never saw anyone using it. We later discovered it was used only at night since the days were too hot for baking.

Once we met an elderly man who gave us a friendly nod, but who didn't want to engage in anything further. It was as though he considered whoever we were and whatever we were doing to be none of his business. Our Moroccan hosts probably had a similar attitude. It was a mark of desert etiquette not to interfere with the wishes of foreigners, no matter how strange both the wishes and the foreigners seemed. (And as for the Frenchmen, they had probably never been to the village itself and had no idea it was that desolate.)

We adapted to desert life with surprising ease. Since the days were hot but the nights cold, we covered our sleeping bags with sand for warmth. We ate dry biscuits from Gerald's stash and almond-covered ones from ours, supplemented by the sardines and bread; sardines had never tasted so delicious. After the initial shock of feeling abandoned we began to enjoy that abandonment, taking pleasure in creating a life without frills or diversions except for those we made ourselves. We built elaborate castles with motes and bridges, played OXO in the sand, ball with the children and learned card games from each other. (I always carried a deck of cards.) Ronit was already fluent in French but I booked a daily lesson from Gerald. We walked barefooted in the sand, enjoying the feel of each step. I especially loved the evenings, lying on my back, listening to the stillness and watching the night sky come alive. I revelled in the bliss of going nowhere and doing nothing. It was a doctoring of the soul.

Although this was an oasis that had no shelter and bore no fruit, it was its own adventure, its own happiness. And it provided concrete proof that much of happiness depended on the internal oasis rather than the external one. When the time came to leave for Zagora, I wasn't ready to go, and vowed to return to the desert as soon as I could. This was my first desert kiss and I wanted more.

21

The Gnaoua Musicians

RATHER THAN SATING MY appetite, the long months spent in Morocco only served to stimulate it. I went to Morocco as often as I could and convinced as many of my friends as I could to join me. Against the odds, I managed to persuade Cedric and then Aviva, both highly suspicious of the Moroccan experience, to chance it and join me. Both became instant converts. I became a one woman travel agency, with a one country destination.

My biggest coup was convincing my friend, whom I'll call Tanya, an excellent musician, to go to Morocco. Her interest was piqued by my description of the music, played with instruments I had never seen before. I described watching artisans making the instruments, stretching skins and creating ceramic bases for drums, then beating out intricate rhythms for hours on end.

I told her about the Gnaoua musicians who lived in the desert, but who could be found playing in the streets of Marrakesh, and who were a spiritual brotherhood originally descended from Negro slaves brought from West Africa. I described their music, and how they performed with drums, long-necked lutes called *gimbri*, and metal castanets, which beat out a trance-like rhythm with a distinctive African flavour. I knew she'd be intrigued by their spiritual approach to life, their supposed occult powers, and especially by their healing abilities, partially achieved through music. She couldn't help but absorb my enthusiasm – enthusiasm, like the lack of it, being highly infectious – and become caught up in my love affair with Morocco.

One day, she made me an offer I couldn't refuse. If I would go to Morocco with her, she would pay for my ticket.

Would I? I could hardly wait. Within minutes of saying yes, I had booked our tickets. My plan was to fly to Marrakesh, spend some time there, mainly checking out the music scene, and then to travel into the desert where the Gnaoua people lived. My friend Chris a high-profile lawyer, needed a break after an especially difficult case and wanted to join us at some point. Having a male accompany us into the desert would ease the doubts of those who feared for our lives – two women travelling on their own being considered an invitation to disaster.

I booked accommodation in my favourite hotel, the CTM, on the Place Djemaa el Fna, the central square cum market place in the old section of Marrakesh. The Place Djemaa el Fna was for me a microcosm of Morocco, a symbol of its enigma: that mystery which struck some deep responsive chord, but which remained unknowable; that fascinating plunge from West to East. It bustled with an incongruous mixture of Arabs and foreigners – Moroccans from the cities in modern dress, carrying brief cases; Berbers from remote mountain villages, in long hooded *jelabas* and yellow *babouches*, carrying bundles of belongings and come to have letters written for them by the scribes, to buy spices and herbs for medicines, to listen to stories told by the storytellers;

Western tourists clutching cameras, intent on reproducing the local colour for home viewing; hippies wearing sandals and a tangle of Moroccan and Western clothing. Best of all, the square was always filled with music – Eastern rhythms with unfamiliar cadences, syncopations and rhythmic structures.

The CTM Hotel was on one of the streets that formed the square, and the roof terrace hung directly over it. From that vantage point, we could be within the buzz and throb of the square – the collage of vendors, jugglers, fortune tellers, acrobats, water sellers, musicians, snake charmers – and immersed in the Moroccan experience, yet removed from the hassle of the crowd.

We arrived at the Marrakesh airport in the middle of Ramadan, the holy Muslim holiday where people fast from dawn to sunset and feast from sunset to dawn. By the time we had cleared customs, night had fallen. The taxi drive into Marrakesh was exceptionally quiet. Few vehicles were on the road because of Ramadan. In the night stillness, we slipped silently through the gates of the city. And then, all at once, we were in the Place Djemaa el Efna.

The rush was overwhelming. The lethargy of Ramadan had erupted into an explosion of celebration. Marrakesh lay like a carpet spread out at our feet, woven with unruly threads into the flamboyance of the square. The energy was wild with dancing, music and everywhere eating, eating, eating. It was like encountering all the tastes and smells and sounds of Morocco squeezed into a bullring of jubilation.

As we made our way into the thick of the Place Djemaa el Efna, I could sense Tanya's foreboding. The strangeness of the men in their long, dark, hooded winter *jelabas*, the absence of females, the dimly-lit stalls, the crowds, all induced a feeling of vulnerability. But gradually, as the potential assassins became harmless grandfathers, uncles and sons, and in any case they were clearly too engrossed in the celebration and too hungry to pay us any attention, I sensed only her fascination.

Huge pots of *harira*, the special soup prepared for breaking the Ramadan fast, bubbled on camping stoves in pavement stalls. Men sat on benches surrounding the stalls, relishing the soup, their sharp features lit by candlelight and gas lanterns. Music wailed and thumped and blasted through the square. The smell of roasted candied almonds, barbecued kebabs, newly baked Moroccan bread and freshly picked oranges mingled with the music in great gusts of steam and sounds and smells. Flashes of fire glowed as torches were lit and cooking fires set alight.

Throughout the square, men were gathered in circles, each circle enclosing its own drama – fire eaters, dancers, drummers, snake charmers, story tellers – all accompanied by music, their stages either a small carpet or the pavement itself. The gas lanterns hanging in the stalls added a surreal dimension, conjuring up images from ancient tomes and scenes from the Arabian Nights. We pressed through the people, the donkey carts, the monkeys, the snakes and the fragrances in silence, overwhelmed by the intensity. As we approached the gate of the CTM Hotel, we could hear galloping along the edge of the square. White horses with fierce-looking, hooded riders carrying daggers and rifles, lined up at either side of the entrance. Then suddenly rifle shots rang in the air and the spectacular introduction to Morocco was over.

At the CTM, I was welcomed like a favourite sister with a tray of mint tea, almond cakes and excited greetings. Even Fatima, the cleaning lady, shrieked a delighted welcome and embraced us with unabashed joy. Mohamed, the manager, wouldn't allow the houseboy to touch our bags. He insisted on carrying them to our room himself. It was like coming home, only better.

Before going to sleep, although drained emotionally and physically, I had to retreat to the roof terrace to gather up the fragmented day. It had been a long day, charged with emotions, fraught with tension, with responsibility and with soothing the frayed edges of travel anxiety. I had promised much, created vast expectations. Would I be able to fulfil them? As I had done so often before, I gazed up at the Atlas Mountains, at the snow-covered peaks lit by the moon, and down at the square, its heightened activities lit by lanterns, torches and candles, and then at the luminous tower of the Koutoubia Mosque, the beacon of Marrakech, reaching into the stars. And suddenly I knew. I wasn't sure what I knew, or how, but I knew. All would be perfect.

Later, as I was falling asleep, in that lull between exhaustion and wellbeing, a rush of pleasure engulfed me, a great comfort, a great assurance; and I was overcome by something akin to bliss. Tanya, Morocco, Ramadan, Place Djemaa el Fna, Fatima, the Koutoubia – we were all perfect together. And I was back in Morocco.

Early next morning, even before croissants and coffee at my favourite café, I searched for Abdul and found him at one of his choice haunts. Abdul was my man in Marrakesh. I had met him several years previously and since then had sought him out again and again. He was an unofficial guide who had become a friend. Aside from deterring unwelcome attention just by his presence, and providing a protective escort in dodgy circumstances, he possessed a broad, almost scholarly knowledge of Morocco. He was also privy to a wealth of its fictions; mysterious encounters, covert trysts, dark scandals. Abdul was closely woven into the texture, the fabric, the very essence of Marrakesh life.

By the time Chris arrived, Abdul was an indispensable member of our team. He would relate tales of intrigue, corruption and decadence between mouthfuls of couscous and sips of mint tea, and disperse fascinating anecdotes about esteemed visitors like Churchill and Jimi Hendrix, along with his discourses on Marrakesh art, holy places and cultural events.

'You see that bench over there,' he once said, when we went to a small garden for tea, 'we must sit there,' and he led us to a bench hardly visible behind a tree.

'Why this bench?' I asked. 'It looks the same as every other bench.'

'Because this is the Jimi Hendrix bench. Me and Mustafa and crazy Mohammed used to sit here with Jimi, playing music and smoking ganja until the morning, because he liked to see the sun come up in Marrakesh. He said it was the same colour as his grandmother's favourite dress. Now we play music here every year on that day; for us, it is a Jimi Hendrix day.'

Abdul introduced us to master instrument makers who showed us instruments we had never seen before. Tanya bought a beautiful old gimbri, the lute-like Gnaoua instrument which combined melody and percussion. It had an intricately carved wooden body and an attachment containing several rings which added a jingling sound. He then took us home to meet his mother, sisters and brother – a rare privilege as Moroccan women were difficult to connect with, being almost invisible in public places; and the family invited us to share the Ramadan harira soup and prepared a meal in our honour.

Best of all, Abdul was a musician, intimately involved in the Marrakesh music scene. His closest friends were musicians. He was able to organize musical sessions, some with top Moroccan musicians, where we met the musicians and listened to their music close up. One great session took place in his home with us curled up on his bed. But the best session, the one that qualified as life enhancing, took place by chance.

One day, Chris, Abdul and I were walking down a Marrakesh alleyway, when we came across a group of Gnaoua musicians sitting on the ground, their backs against a wall, playing music. We stopped to listen. Suddenly, one of the musicians stood up and, taking my hand, led me to sit with the group. Giving me one of their special hats and a clicking instrument like a glorified castanet, he signalled me to play with them. I found myself accompanying the musicians, timidly at first and then more boldly, encouraged by their nods of approval. Although I had no idea what I was doing, I became absorbed in the music, caught up by the compelling rhythms, while Chris took a photo to capture the scene.

I was disappointed Tanya hadn't been with us. When I mentioned this to Abdul, he invited two of the musicians whom he knew, both drummers, to a drumming session so she could meet them. and listen to the drumming. I was delighted.

We gathered the next day in Abdul's room with the two drummers we had met, plus another drummer friend of theirs. The Gnaoua musicians had brought their own drums and Abdul gave one each to Tanya, Chris and me from his extensive collection. I had assumed the Gnaoua musicians would be playing by themselves, but apparently this was to be a special session where we all played together. It was getting dark and Abdul lit a single candle. In the semi darkness the room seemed to lose its moorings; it became any place. And even before the drumming started I felt the boundaries of the now fading.

At first, the Gnaoua musicians led and we followed. The rhythm was slow, one sound beating into the next, with the vibrations creating a new sound and a more complicated rhythmic pattern, which we then followed and repeated over and over and over, our drumming becoming entwined in theirs, the rhythmic phrase remaining the same but the volume changing, suddenly fierce, suddenly sweet. And then, emerging from the drum beats, the throb of a voice, repeating words I did not understand but which became part of the drumming; the sound of voice and drum beats becoming a chant. Over and over the chant went on, filling my head, until all was the chant. It moaned, it wailed, beating, pulsating, with words, with sound, until it became a kind of music. I closed my eyes and was drawn into a place where there was only drumming, only chanting, and I was inside the drumming, inside the chanting, every moment a perfect lifetime. And then, in some semi hypnotic state, I was chanting with Leonard, surrendering to Leonard's presence, chanting *Om Mani Padme Hum*, feeling that universal love he had promised. Was I asleep? Was I awake? Was I somewhere else? I didn't know.

Then suddenly it was over. There was no ending; it was just over. The only sound was the silence. I felt exhausted, but radiant. And I knew that in some strange way I had been purified, washed clean. It was several minutes before we rose to leave. And we parted with only embraces. There were no words.

The rest of our time in Marrakesh was both intense with activity and languid with refuge from activity – serene hours in the sunshine dreaming our separate dreams, lounging in gardens among the flowers, meditating over glasses of mint tea ceremoniously poured from silver teapots, visiting museums and workshops. But, for me, the crowning experience was the drumming with the Gnaoua musicians. That was the essence of Morocco.

Marrakesh was all that was expected, and more. It had all been perfect. I had fulfilled my promise. But I had more promises to keep. It was time to move on. The desert was calling. Other oases were calling…

22

Tibet – Oasis of My Dreams

M OROCCO WAS AN EASY adventure to explore because it was so accessible. However, there were places embedded in my travel dreams that I longed to experience but which were entirely inaccessible. The most compelling of these was Tibet.

Since those days back in Montreal, when we celebrated the New Year with Leonard Cohen and he introduced me to Tibetan chanting, I had developed a strange, inexplicable fascination for Tibet. I began reading everything I could about Tibet. I had managed to find a photograph of the magnificent Potala Palace, the home of successive Dalai Lamas, and hung it over my bed, like a benediction. I was drawn into that photograph, never tired of contemplating it (and that was the photograph I had taken with me when years later I went to live in London.) I longed to see the Potala Palace, I longed to go to Tibet. It was a longing so deep, it was almost an obsession.

But it was an impossible longing. Tibet was known as the 'Forbidden Kingdom'; no foreigner was allowed to cross its borders and it had little contact with the rest of the world. Until the twentieth century so little was known about Tibet that most maps left it blank. The mysteries of the remote mountain kingdom were kept jealously intact. Then, suddenly in 1984, the miracle happened. China, who controlled Tibet, opened its borders to foreigners. I made an instant decision to go and to go quickly – before the Chinese authorities changed their mind. By now I was in need of a new oasis. I had finished my university studies, Ronit was all set up to begin college, and, best of all, I had a partner, Tom, who was almost as excited as I was to experience Tibet. As it turned out Tom, and I were among the first individual foreign travellers to enter the Forbidden Kingdom.

However, getting there was no easy matter. We had to fly to Lhasa, the capital of Tibet, and there was only one way to fly to Lhasa, which was from Chengdu, a town in southwest China. But nothing could deter me. After almost insurmountable difficulties, arranging visas and tickets, we found ourselves in Chengdu, boarding a fragile-looking plane that didn't inspire confidence, and heading for Lhasa. The other passengers on our flight were all Chinese, official-looking men with brief cases and thermos flasks. The flight was one of the most terrifying and one of the most beautiful I had ever experienced.

Most of the flight was uneventful. We were flying above a blanket of grey clouds, unable to see anything below but sailing along so smoothly, I was sorry I had ever doubted the plane's virility. However, twenty minutes before landing, the clouds suddenly parted like a heavy curtain heralding a drama, to reveal a spectacular scene – the Himalayas. The sky was lit by sunshine, the blue laced with delicate white clouds. The mountains were magnificent: snow-capped summits creased with purple shadows, glinting with frozen lakes, etched by glaciers. Rugged peaks speared the clouds, piercing the fragile webbing with powerful thrusts. It was a stunning vision, awesome, grand. Amongst these formidable mountains lay Tibet – seemingly inaccessible.

I was totally entranced by the miracle that allowed me to float above the Himalayas, delighting in the nuances of colour and texture, when suddenly the small Chinese plane dived into the mountains, wrenching us from the splendid panorama in the heavens and plummeting us into a gorge. The mountain walls, hung with ice, loomed steeply, tight against the plane, obliterating the sun. The floor below was a dark desert, with sand rising into strangely sculpted dunes, creating a death valley. The valley curved and the plane leaned sharply and veered around the side of a mountain, like a racing car swerving around a bend on two wheels. Hunched against the possibility of wings scrapping against rock, I sucked in my breath, cold against my teeth, as we dipped through the precipices into a frigid moonscape. When we had been flying at high altitude, the mountains appeared superb, majestically aloof. Now, deep in their midst, they were desolate and frightening.

The landing was even more terrifying. It was as though the pilot was on a kamikaze mission. Abruptly, we plunged deeper into the mountains. A river with a shoreline of rock appeared beneath us. We were falling fast toward the water and there was nowhere to land. I sat glued rigid against the window as we dropped lower and lower, sweeping through crevasses with cold blue hearts, skimming over the river, engines screaming. We were so close, I could see ripples on the surface. It seemed certain we would hurl ourselves into the river, or smash into the mountains. My body clenched like a vice, braced for the inevitable, when suddenly, magically, a thin ribbon of runway appeared at the base of the mountains. With engines roaring, we glided to a stop. The pilot received a standing ovation.

***

We disembarked from the plane's reassuring comforts into a disturbing landscape. A few yards from the plane, the runway returned to the desert as though it had never existed. There was no trace of welcome. Nothing to greet us except for several busses squatting in the sand. I took a last look at the shining plane and followed the other passengers into the sand.

The Lhasa bus was old and worn with thinly padded purple seats. Purple is my favourite colour, so a good omen. The road to Lhasa was totally unpredictable, only partially paved, with road works in progress and inevitable long waits. The landscape was parched and inhospitable, with a few stark villages among the barren mountains. The only colour came from makeshift prayer flags, bits of torn rag impaled on twigs. There was nothing green. What a bitter place to live.

A sudden lurch, as the bus stopped abruptly, jolted me out of my speculations. Road works. We got out and lined the roadside, watching the workers wielding sledgehammers to smash the huge boulders blocking the road. Realizing it was going to be a long wait, I decided to go for a walk. After only minutes, the road, buses and passengers were swallowed by the landscape. I found myself alone in a valley of twisted rocks – tombstones in an alien cemetery. The silence was like eternity.

I crept carefully among the boulders, conscious of their hostility, feeling soft and vulnerable as they grazed my skin. I was the only living thing, trapped in a soundless universe unchanged since creation. I shuddered as though someone had walked over my grave. Hurriedly, as though pursued by demons, I retraced my steps, startled by the voices of passengers squatting by the roadside. I boarded the bus, tentative and silent.

As we approached Lhasa, the mountains seemed friendlier. I began to see signs of foliage at their base – meadows, trees, flowers. I drank in the moisture, nourished by the green life. Then, suddenly, in the distance, shining in the barren hills, golden domes: the Potala, with its miracle of smooth, rounded shapes, rising in the blue sky, glowing like a vision. After the harsh mountain peaks tearing at the heavens like broken claws, the domes were a welcoming embrace, a circle of comfort. Then, all at once, the full force of the Potala Palace. I held my breath. As though aware of the impact, the bus slowed down.

Brilliantly etched by sunshine, a powerful structure of white, red and gold dominated the mountains. The image was so intense that for a moment my eyes shut tight, as if encountering a dazzling light. But as I succumbed to the sense of wonder, an unexpected surge of joy swept through me. It was more than the excitement of seeing something I had imagined for so long. It was an exhilaration, an elation, beyond the scope of reason. I was aware that I had entered an unexplored spiritual realm. I felt like the wandering Jew first glimpsing the Wailing Wall, or the Muslim pilgrim finally entering Mecca.

Instinctively, I knew that the Tibetans had some special secret that enabled them to survive the unsparing Himalayas and create, from bare rock, this Potala Palace. And, most important, I knew there was some personal secret, some personal revelation hidden and waiting for me between the starkness of the mountains and the beauty of the Potala. I knew I would have to experience both extremes to unlock that secret, to fathom any of the mysteries of this mythic mountain kingdom. I had no idea how I would do this, but the possibility excited me. Travellers made lucky things happen. I held the image of the Potala carefully in my mind, closing my eyes to better preserve it, as the bus moved into the Forbidden City.

23

The Sky Burial

WE HAD BEEN IN Tibet for several weeks before I had the courage to attend a sky burial. By that time, the Banak Shol, the Tibetan guest house where we were staying, had become like home, yak butter tea had become palatable and I was adorned with Tibetan jewellery, but I was still unable to face a sky burial. Texas Dave, a fellow traveller who had become a friend, said, 'It's like being in Pamplona and not attending a bull fight.' As a matter of fact, I had been in Pamplona and hadn't attended a bullfight. But I was finally convinced that this was different – a unique ancient ritual at the heart of Tibetan culture and belief. Experiencing such an event was the essence of travelling, and to miss it would be like travelling with blinkers. I might as well be on a tourist bus, sheltered and shielded not only from Tibet but from myself. I knew it was something I had to do and I braced myself for the occasion.

But when the day arrived, I woke up before the alarm, filled with apprehension. Grey streaks in the dark sky created a dull, gloomy light, and it was chilly, which added to the bleakness of my mood. After gulping a hurried cup of Chinese tea, Tom and I set off, cold and silent. We had been given directions to the burial site, about an hour's walk away. We were to turn left at a rubbish dump, and at that point should see a fire on the hill. That was our goal.

We headed into the countryside. It was very early morning and the road was dotted with peasants going into Lhasa on foot or in small donkey carts, carrying grain, hay, vegetables and other goods to market. Traffic was sparse, with several trucks filled with workers, a few army vehicles carrying soldiers and the donkey carts. We were in a valley green with barley, surrounded by stark, barren mountains. Then the rubbish dump. We picked our way through rusty cans, metal bits, rotting clothing, and other unsavouriness.

Finally, we saw a fire burning on a hill and climbed to a small rocky plateau. This was the burial site: a stubby patch of ground on top of a rocky hill at the base of bare mountains that looked like wrinkled old elephants' hide. Below were the tin roofs of Chinese barrack-like buildings, glinting in the rising sun. Five Tibetan men and a boy of about ten were seated around the fire drinking tea, talking and joking. Their mood was easy, even jovial, in contrast to our sombre, funereal demeanour. They were wearing ordinary work clothes – worn jackets, peaked caps, rough cotton trousers. They smiled and motioned us to sit. Nearby was the 'altar', a large flat rock with bowl-like depressions. It was separated from where the Tibetans sat by a shallow gully, strewn with bits of discarded clothing, and hunks of hair.

Pascal, a lovely Frenchman I had really connected with, and who spoke Tibetan, arrived with three other Westerners and joined us. It was his second visit. We sat on the edge of the gully, facing the altar rock. Pascal gestured towards the mountains. I looked up. Neat rows of silent birds were perched on ledges – vultures. Their colours blended so perfectly with the mountains that at first they were hard to distinguish. Ravens swooped in and out of the gully and gathered nervously in black patches on the altar rock. A white square bundle, tied with a rope, sat among the ravens. A small dog struggled up the rock and chased them. The rising sun slowly turned the drab greys and dull browns of the mountains to patches of pale gold and dusty pinks. I became pleasantly warm.

About fifteen Westerners trickled in, newcomers to Tibet. No Chinese were present. There had been some unpleasant incidents with the Chinese. In the past some had jeered at the burial procedure, proclaiming it barbaric. Now Tibetans stoned them whenever they appeared. Westerners still seemed welcome, although this surprised me as they too had created incidents.

Despite the fact that Tibetans strictly forbid photographs, some Westerners were desperate to capture the sky burial on film. Several days ago, one such desperate Australian had hidden himself, his telescopic lenses and his elaborate camera equipment high in the hills, determined to take the prized photos. His frenzied preparations frightened the birds away, an intensely evil omen. He was discovered and bombarded with stones. Next day, the Westerners who attended were stoned. Yesterday, some had filtered back and were allowed to stay. Today, we were greeted with smiles. Tibetans are wonderfully tolerant and forgiving. Still, I felt certain that our days at the burial site were numbered.

A little after eight o'clock, the sun touched the altar rock. This was the signal for the burial to begin. One of the Tibetans donned a grubby white coat and a white surgical-type cap. He was the man in charge. He said something to us in Tibetan. Pascal translated: 'While they work, no pictures.' Then the man in charge, two of the Tibetan men and the boy, climbed on to the rock. The other two Tibetans, relatives of the deceased, remained by the fire. The man in white was thin and wiry and wild looking, with flashing black eyes and black hair sticking out from under the cap. He untied the bundle. A woman, naked except for an unbuttoned faded red blouse, tumbled out. She looked pregnant, youngish, with long black hair. (Later, we learned her body had been carried a long distance on someone's back, since there are only a few places in Tibet where sky burials are performed.).

The man in charge dragged her body over the rock and laid it face down in the centre. He began, without ceremony, by pulling off the woman's blouse and flinging it into the gully. Then he yanked a large knife from his belt and, with surgical precision, cut a slit down her spine. Starting from her shoulder blade, he stripped the flesh away down the left side of her back, using swastika-patterned cuts. (For Tibetans, the swastika is the symbol of eternity.)

This done, he neatly hacked off her left arm with his knife. The severed arm was tossed to the young boy who, squatting on his haunches, pounded it to a pulp with something that looked like the back of an axe, using one of the depressions in the rock as a container. It was hard work for a boy and he grunted and groaned as he worked.

The man in charge continued to hack the left side of the body, panting loudly, like someone chopping wood. The two men, also squatting, were thrown flesh and bones, which they too pounded in the bowl-like depressions. The sounds of panting and puffing combined with the squishing sounds of flesh being pulverized and bones being smashed. *Tsampa*, a mixture of barley flour, tea and yak butter was added to the flesh and bones to form a paste. Everything happened quickly. The men worked with a practised skill, pausing only to sharpen their axes, or for a short cigarette breaks. So engrossed was I by their expertise, I almost forgot what they were doing.

Work began on the woman's right side, the flesh efficiently sliced from the ribs. The man's white coat became splattered with blood as he severed the limbs, detaching them from the rest of the body. By now the rock looked like a butcher's shop, bloody with tattered flesh and strewn limbs, and the woman like a butchered carcass. I turned away many times, unable to watch, then turned back, unable not to watch.

Several vultures flew off the mountains and began circling the altar rock, gliding over our heads. The man in charge continued working. He flipped over what remained of the body, a torso with no back or limbs. Then he chopped hard, with one resounding blow through the chest cavity, and reaching inside, pulled out the heart. Holding it up, he shouted something to the two Tibetans by the fire. They nodded and he chopped the heart to bits. Then he slit the stomach open and removed the organs. These were cut up and kept separate.

The work was easier now. While they worked, the men talked, laughed, and joked, but did not break their work rhythm. The Westerners were silent. Lastly, the head was separated from the neck with one neat blow. The severed head was held up high. I recalled John the Baptist, only this man was no Salome and the seven veils were bloodied rags. Next, the man in charge held the head by the hair and deftly scalped it. Then, tying the long black hair into a knot, he flung it into the gully. After that he picked up a large flat stone and, holding it overhead, muttered a short prayer and smashed the skull twice.

One of the seated Tibetans then brought tea on to the rock for the workers. The vultures circled closer. An old monk dressed in crimson and saffron robes appeared close to us. Facing the rock, he said a prayer, his hands held together, and prostrated before the rock. A Chinese man carrying a briefcase, dressed in navy blue trousers and a sparkling white shirt, appeared from nowhere. He climbed the rock and handed the man in charge a cigarette.

They discussed something. Apparently a small group of well-dressed Chinese had been given permission to attend the burial. At a signal from their leader, they hastened to the edge of the plateau and sat with us.

At this point, the man in charge faced the mountains and turned to the vultures, calling: 'Shoo...tzshoo...' At the signal, about a dozen vultures, the vanguard, left their mountain perch and swooped on to the rock. The rest remained, not breaking rank. He threw them bits of flesh as they gathered around him. They were huge, beautiful birds with white necks and legs and speckled tan and white bodies. Their wings fluttered and spread to reveal white undersides with dark brown tips. Some were so close we were able to see their bright blue eyes. The vultures waited with constraint as the work continued. The boy bundled the chopped organs into a cloth. Several vultures, unable to maintain discipline, tried to steal bits of flesh from the boy. The man in charge angrily chased them off the rock with kicks and abusive shouts, as though punishing them for bad behaviour. When he was finished, the boy carried the bundle off the rock, the two men leaving with him. Then the man in charge faced the mountain ledges, raised his arms to the vultures and addressed them in a shrill singsong voice: 'Tria...soya...tria...soya...'

Suddenly hundreds of vultures filled the sky and hovered in a quivering cloud above our heads, their wings beating a nervous fluttering sound, and descended on the rock, completely covering it. As the vultures vied for space, the ravens clung to the edges. The birds were served with the preparation of flesh, bones and tsampa. The tsampa had been added to make the mixture more palatable, for it is a bad omen if anything is left uneaten. The vultures ate greedily, fighting over scraps of flesh, slipping off the rock, pushing each other in their haste to consume. The ravens joined the feast cautiously; uninvited guests, they had to be content to scramble at the outer edges, snapping up any morsels the vultures accidentally dropped.

At this point, several Westerners attempted to photograph the vultures. The man in charge became incensed. He leapt off the rock and rushed at two German girls, brandishing his knife and shouting. He pointed the knife at the heart of one of the girls. Livid with rage, he grabbed both their cameras and ripped the film from them; tearing it to shreds, he flung it in the fire. He was like a rabid madman and shouted at us to leave. I began to go, disturbed and frightened. Those who brought cameras quickly hid them. Several people left immediately. The rest were suddenly signalled to stay by the other Tibetans.

The birds finished eating but did not leave the rock. They fluttered about in staccato hops, timid and nervous. I wondered why they lingered.

The answer came quickly. The bundle of organs was returned to the rock. They had been waiting for these choice morsels – dessert. Voraciously, they devoured every last bit. Finally the feast was over. The vultures took to the sky, bearing the deceased with them, upwards to the heavens. The rock was empty. An hour ago, there was a body on the rock; now there was nothing. The Chinese and then the Westerners began to leave. The man in charge sat with the other Tibetans around the fire in animated discussion, his black eyes flashing. Tea was served. There was no sign of mourning, no tears, no wailing, no prayers. Attending a sky burial for a Tibetan seemed to be the equivalent of going to the morgue for a Westerner. Family members were present only to ensure that everything was done as it should be.

The two men now climbed the rock to check that all had been eaten and to clean it for the next burial. They joked and laughed as they worked. I sat, too stunned to move. This had been the strangest, the most bizarre thing I had ever witnessed. Powerful images raged through my brain. What amazed me was that despite the horrific nature of what I had seen, I felt no revulsion. One reason must be the inevitable distancing of oneself from the intensity and nearness of the experience. But more important was a feeling that the sky burial fit in with the isolation and strangeness of the setting. Somehow, in that alien environment, it all made sense. When I looked around me I was surprised to see everyone had gone. I was the last one to leave.

24

Tashi

THE OTHERS WERE WAITING for me at the bottom of the hill. Our plan had been to visit Sera Monastery, close to the burial site. But Pascal suggested we accompany him to a teahouse where he was to meet Tashi, a Tibetan friend whom he'd met while travelling in India. Tashi would soon be returning to India, where he lived, his parents having left Tibet in 1959, when thousands of Tibetans fled the Chinese; and Pascal wanted to give him a going-away present.

I was the only one who wanted to go to the teahouse instead of the monastery. I was glad to postpone Sera. My head was seething with the sky burial, reluctant for more input.

'You'll be glad to meet Tashi,' Pascal said. 'He's a very special person, very magical.'

'I could do with a bit of magic, I'm all magicked out.'

'Then Tashi is the man.'

Pascal collected his bicycle, which was propped against a rock. 'We're going a shorter way on a path through the mountains. Would you like to ride with me on the bicycle?'

'If you don't mind doing all the work.'

'I don't mind. You can't be too heavy. In any case, we must walk much of the way, but it is very beautiful.'

I climbed on to the seat of the bicycle and we took off along a dirt path, wobbling and bumping as Pascal steered between stones and gravel ridges. To steady myself, I held his waist. His body felt firm, solid, reassuring, under his thin cotton T-shirt. As he struggled with the terrain, his shirt rode up and my fingers spread slowly, embracing the contour of his muscles, filling my senses with their life force, blotting out that other body on the rock.

The makeshift path soon became too difficult for cycling. We walked, Pascal pushing the bicycle, my head blisteringly with images that leapt at me from every rock. I felt fearful, troubled, resisting some unnamed threat.

'Are you thinking of the sky burial?' Pascal asked hesitantly, reluctant to intrude.

But I was grateful for the intrusion. 'Why do you suppose they allow us to watch it? Especially since we are so insensitive, coming with cameras, taking photos. It's such an intensely private ceremony, you'd think they wouldn't want to share it with a bunch of gaping foreigners.'

'For them it is not private,' Pascal said. 'It is their most common way of burying the dead. For a Tibetan, once a person is dead his body is not important, only his soul is important and the sky burial protects his soul. It makes sure that it is taken to heaven by the birds. Tibetans are not afraid of death because they believe that if they have gained merit in this life, they will be born to a higher form in the next life. My friend Tashi will explain it to you, it's part of the Buddhist philosophy.'

We continued walking, me still struggling with the sky burial and now with the Buddhist philosophy. Pascal interrupted my thoughts.

'In the West we allow our bodies to be eaten by the worms. But, of course, we do not see the worms doing it. For me, I would prefer to allow my body to be eaten by birds and to rise into the sky, it has more poetry.'

'I guess it does,' I said, unhappy with both options.

We walked in silence. But I was convinced there was something wrong, something voyeuristic about Westerners attending the sky burial. Our Western culture doesn't equip us to deal with it. For us, it can only be horrific, with nothing religious or secular to temper the horror, no context in which to place it. To see a body mutilated, chopped to bits and fed to vultures can only signify brutality, the ultimate disrespect for the ultimate personal disaster.

We hold that the body is sacred in death. We adorn it, paint it, beautify it so that our last vision of the deceased is a pleasing tranquil one, as though by prettifying death, it becomes less terrifying: 'He looks just like he's asleep, so peaceful.' That last vision shapes our memory for all time and we want it to be uplifting, whole, unhampered.

I thought about Pistol Pete, who had died suddenly of a stroke all those years ago. It was me who'd found him sitting in front of the television, supposedly asleep. I remembered switching off the television and gently attempting to wake him so he could get into bed. When he was pronounced dead at the hospital, I refused to believe it. Later, when the doctors wanted to perform an autopsy, I panicked. 'Don't touch my father,' I warned, fierce with anguish. 'Don't cut him up. Leave him in peace.'

And now I thought about our reverence for cemeteries, for graves and gravestones. Burying a loved one in a special place where they can be visited, communed with, paid respect to, is vital for us. We chisel their name so deeply with epithets that several lifetimes cannot obliterate it. Sometimes they are profound, like the one W. B. Yeats wrote for himself: 'Cast a cold eye on life, on death. Horseman pass by!' Or humorous, like W. C. Field's 'I'd rather be in Philadelphia.' Or even commanding like Marx's 'Workers of the world unite.' The dead want to be remembered and the living make pilgrimages to remember them. I thought about how important Pistol Pete's grave is to me. I cross the ocean to visit it, perform small rituals beside it, and tend it with the care and love I wish I had given to him before he died so unexpectedly.

Thoughts about my father's death were so painful, I broke the silence to dispel them. 'Pascal, don't you find it strange that Tibetans have kept foreigners out of their country for centuries, but now that we are allowed in nothing seems sacred, not even the sky burial?'

'The Tibetan people never kept the foreigners out; it was the Tibetan authorities, especially the lamas and monks. They wanted to keep their culture pure, not contaminated by foreigners.'

'Maybe the lamas and monks were right. Lhasa was probably the last forbidden city. Perhaps we should have left it that way, left one ancient civilization alone and left ourselves one mystery.'

After a long while Pascal said, 'Perhaps.'

The grip of searing images and disquieting thoughts gradually eased as I became aware of the sun, warm between my shoulder blades. It was a perfect day, a perfect place – an unfamiliar and intriguing landscape. We were in a valley of stones, the mountains stark on either side, cut with deep shadows and sudden patches of light. The sky was a bright hard blue. I was in a place that, as yet, held no memories for me, but as I contemplated the harsh landscape, the boulders trembling in balance, I could almost remember something and I felt the stirring of an uneasy excitement.

The path widened and Pascal helped me mount the bicycle. 'You must be exhausted,' I said, feeling the strain in his body as he forced his way through the hills. 'Even I'm tired and you're doing all the work.'

'I don't mind, I'm used to the altitude, you're not.'

With me clutching Pascal, we cycled into Lhasa and headed for the teahouse.

The Lhasa teahouse was somewhat disappointing. It was a bare room with a dirty, uneven stone floor and tables and chairs scattered at random. Several Tibetan Muslims, wearing small pillbox hats, sat poring over papers and slurping tea. The owner, distinguished by a soiled white apron tied over a round belly, greeted Pascal with a huge smile and a flood of enthusiastic Tibetan, then rushed out to bring tea, his gestures large, like an opera singer.

The tea was served Muslim style, in covered cups with lids like pointed roofs, and crystals of rock sugar in a saucer. It was neither the sugarless Chinese green, nor the milky and sweet Tibetan black. It was made from lotus seeds, drunk without milk and sweetened with rock sugar. Delicious. It redeemed the tea house.

Tashi arrived after our first cup and was welcomed by the owner with even more enthusiasm and still larger gestures. His area of the table was wiped clean and the tea brought even before he was seated. I was immediately drawn to Tashi. He was in his late twenties, tall and lean with straight black hair falling over his ears, high cheekbones, black eyes and an extraordinary beauty. He wore a white shirt, the sleeves pushed back, dark cotton trousers, sandals and one long, exquisite, silver and turquoise earring.

Pascal and Tashi embraced with affection, a great fondness between them; then Pascal reached into his bag and produced two medical books in English – Tashi was studying traditional

Tibetan and also Western medicine in India – and a book I had given Pascal, about the Canadian doctor, Norman Bethune, who had worked in China.

'For you, Tashi, a present for going away.'

Intense delight spread over Tashi's face, flooding it with magic. 'Thank you, my friend.' My eyes did not leave his face. It was like gazing into a deep, still pool – tranquil, calming, yet tinged with excitement.

Pascal introduced us, and as Tashi reached for my hand, it was as if a bridge sprang up, joining our eyes.

'Niema?' he said, surprised. 'That is a Tibetan name.'

I was even more surprised. 'Really? What does it mean?'

'The sun.'

'How strange. Whenever possible, I sign my name followed by a smiling sun.'

For a moment we were silent, our hands joined, our eyes linked, each remembering something. Then he said: 'I had a younger brother called Niema.'

Dimly, I registered the 'had'. 'Really?' Again. 'Is it a boy's name?'

'Sometimes. It can be either.'

'When I was young, I very much wanted to be a boy.' Then I added lightly: 'Maybe I was a Tibetan once, or maybe I am yet to become one.'

Tashi searched for something in my face, then said: 'Yes, it is possible.'

I waited for him to continue, but he smiled and said nothing, his interest returning to the books and the tea, while mine was riveted on him.

When Tashi had flipped through the books, unable to postpone the pleasure, and the ceremonial sugaring and stirring was over and we had settled into the sipping, he asked: 'Where have you been this morning?'

'We are coming from the sky burial,' Pascal said.

'Ah, the *jhator*, that's the best way to be buried. I will be buried that way. When I die I wish to go up to heaven with the birds.' He smiled serenely, as though anticipating some great joy.

'The idea of vultures gobbling up your body doesn't bother you?' I asked, mention of the sky burial evoking a fresh flood of the images that were now embedded in my consciousness.

He turned to me with a wonderful serenity. 'I wish my body to be eaten by vultures. You see, in Tibet there are no cemeteries because for a Tibetan, the body is of no use when the soul has departed. It is good to feed it to the birds. It is an act of altruism, of compassion, and compassion is the heart of the Buddhist belief. The word *jhator* in its exact translation means giving alms to the birds.'

I was clinging to every word, fascinated, not wanting to interrupt, but the pragmatist in me had its way: 'Someone told me that the sky burial exists because it is the easiest and cheapest way of disposing the dead.'

'It is true, we cannot waste soil for burial or wood for burning, but the consideration of economics is not the reason for the *jhator*; the main reason is altruism. You know, even high lamas, who by our custom have the right to be cremated and their ashes shaped into small figures and venerated in a chorten, a Tibetan shrine, in their own monastery, ask instead that their bodies be fed to the vultures as an act of charity and compassion.' He sipped his tea and I waited, eager for more of Tashi, of Buddhism, of Tibet. Instead he ordered more tea.

Fearful that the conversation would slip away, I asked, 'Why do vultures deserve acts of charity?'

'You see, because the Buddhist believes in reincarnation, he has a love for every living being, a universal compassion for all creatures. Birds must eat too. And for us, vultures are very special birds. They do no living creature any harm, they eat only what is already dead, they never kill. They are sacred birds.'

'Sacred birds?' The idea came like a surprise thump. 'That's so different from how we think of them. In the West, we have an instinctive fear, a dread of vultures. The circling of vultures is an image of doom.'

'They are birds which bring bad news,' Pascal added.

I nodded in agreement. 'Exactly. Vultures are involved with the ugly side of life, greed, mutilation, death. To eat a human body is unthinkable for us, it's a terrible violation, loathsome, vile. To call someone a vulture is the ultimate insult. I was actually shocked to see how beautiful vultures are. I've always thought of them as ugly, repulsive, as though their morbid calling would spill over into their appearance.'

'Not only beautiful,' Tashi said, 'but well behaved, well disciplined. They follow civilized rules of behaviour.'

Again I was impelled to interject, recalling the pushing and pulling. 'Their table manners leave much to be desired, they devoured that girl's body with a speed hard to believe.'

'Perhaps there has been no *jhator* for some days and they were very hungry. On some days several people are buried at one time, but on other days there is no one to be buried. The vultures have come to depend on humans for their food, just as humans have come to depend on animals and birds for theirs.'

Tashi was right. I remembered Texas Dave saying he had gone to the sky burial two days running but nothing had happened. 'No body showed,' he had laughed, 'hope you have better luck.' I hadn't found it funny at the time but now I made allowances for the vultures.

'I guess if I was ravenous, I'd grab too,' I conceded.

'As a rule, vultures are very orderly,' Tashi continued. 'I am sure that although they were very hungry, they waited patiently for their leaders before they ate.'

'Yes, that's right, they did. I wondered about that. Did the man conducting the burial call to their leaders? Did he know who they were?'

'Yes, he called to them. He must know the leaders because he works through them, and they must know his calls and work with him. The man and the birds must cooperate together. The vultures know this as well.'

'My opinion of vultures obviously needs a complete overhaul, especially now that I've not only met a vulture fan but the vultures themselves.'

Tashi smiled and I sipped my tea with the feeling that I was in for considerably more overhauling, yet knowing that this too is what travelling is about: the imprinting of disturbing images and emotions, and the formulation of questions that may require a lifetime to answer.

Determined to get some of the answers now, I said, 'Tashi, there are so many things I'd like to know about the sky burial, so much I don't understand, it's totally overwhelming.'

'I am glad to explain if Pascal does not object, because he has already asked these questions.'

Poor Pascal had been sitting there all that time, allowing me to ignore him. But Tashi was more considerate. 'Of course I do not object.' Pascal said, with a magnanimous wave of the hand. 'For me it is always interesting to hear more. It was I who promised that Tashi would explain.'

So, with Pascal's blessing, I devoted myself to Tashi and the *jhator*.

'Tell me, Tashi, why don't relatives of the dead person go to the sky burial? Is there no funeral service for the family and friends of the dead?'

'It is because the main burial rites are performed before the *jhator* takes place. You see, when a person dies, his body is blessed, then covered with a white cloth and put in a quiet place where he remains for at least three days while special burial rites are performed for him. We believe that even though he is physically dead, his mental consciousness – if you like, his soul or spirit – is still in his body and therefore he is not really dead, but only in the process of dying, in a meditative state, between ending this life and beginning another one.

'He can remain in this state from a week to a month if he has reached a high level of spiritual development. In India, I have known dead people to remain in this condition for over two weeks, even in the hot season. They are like ordinary dead bodies – they do not breathe, their hearts do not beat – but because they are not really dead, they have no bad smell.

'While the person stays in this dream-like trance, monks and lamas surround him with beautiful thoughts and chant recitations from a sacred book to assist him to receive death, for to be born well one must die well. They also say prayers for the release of his soul from his body. His family and his relatives and his friends make special contributions, like incense, *tsampa* and white silk scarves, called *khata* scarves, which are a symbol of purity, hoping to secure a better rebirth for him.'

'If he is not really dead when he dies, how do you know when he is really dead? My great horror is being buried alive. I have a recurring nightmare about being buried alive. I am submerged in a deep hole, helpless, as earth and rocks tumble over me, muffling the sound of my cries. I'm gasping, fighting to breathe, terrified, until overcome by the avalanche I am sealed forever in the earth, still alive.' I hadn't intended revealing this nightmare, I hardly ever do, yet I felt compelled to continue, 'I once read a story about a man who was thought dead because he was unable to move, but he was not dead, his mind was alive, he could hear and understand. He was about to be buried, but at the last moment he managed to shed a tear. It was terrifying. How can you be sure you're not cutting up someone still alive?'

As I disclosed my obsession about being buried alive, I was conscious of a shadow crossing Tashi's face, darkening his features, shrouding them in pain. But almost before I was aware of it, the shadow passed and he answered my question as though it had never been there.

'Because we are certain when a person is dead. You see, a fluid, usually a whitish fluid, comes from the dead person's nose and his head leans to one side. When this happens, it is the sign that the soul has left the body and the body is ready for the *jhator*. The burial cannot take place before this occurs.'

'And then is the person buried right away; is there some special procedure?'

'Once the signs have been received that the person is really dead, the family consults lamas and astrologers and they advise them of the most favourable time for the *jhator*. Then the body is wrapped in a sheet and the head of the family carries it to the entrance of the house and there he makes three circles. This circling and then further prayers to ensure a good rebirth for the departed soul, is the family's final farewell to their loved one, after which the body is handed over to special lamas. Then monks and family representatives take the body to the *jhator*; the family members themselves do not go. The farewell has been said to the soul, to the spirit; the body is of no interest.'

More tea was brought and I feared the owner's intrusion, but he slipped away with a sensitivity I could not have predicted. My attention was so focused on Tashi that he continued without pausing for tea: 'As you saw this morning, incense and cypress wood are burned at the *jhator* and prayers are chanted by the monks. They also sprinkle *tsampa* on the fire, and the *tsampa* causes a heavy smoke which the vultures know, even if they are far away. From then on, as you saw, everything is in the hands of the special lama who is in charge of the ceremony. He decides when to pray and when to call to the birds when the time is right. At the end of the *jhator*, the family representatives serve food, tea and chang – that's Tibetan beer.'

'And is that the end of it?' I asked. 'Is there no ceremony or celebration, or mourning afterwards like the Irish wake, or the seven days of mourning the Jewish people call shiva?'

'No, that is not the end of it. Buddhists believe that there is a forty-nine-day period called the bardo, between death and rebirth, when the soul has left the old body but has not yet found a new one. On every seventh day of these forty-nine days, monks and lamas say special prayers, recite mystic chants and perform ceremonial rituals to guide the dead person's soul through the bardo, until he has reached his new incarnation. The family mourns for one year, they avoid celebrations and wear no jewellery or other ornamentation, and their friends are quiet and respectful in their presence.'

'Is that what happens to all Tibetans when they die? Do all Tibetans get buried by the *jhator*?' I asked, my head jammed with fragments of religion, tradition, facts and images, yet eager for more, as though the amassing of enough detail would somehow complete the picture, make it comprehensible. Besides, meeting a Tibetan like Tashi, who was not only knowledgeable and sensitive, but who spoke excellent English, was a rare event, unlikely to be repeated.

'Oh no, although the *jhator* is the most common form of burial and most Tibetans are buried in this manner, it is not the only one. There is also ground burial, water burial and cremation. And when a high religious person dies, he is buried in a special way: his body is rubbed with special ointments and spices and then is embalmed in a stupa, a religious monument like a small temple. Have you been to the Potala Palace?'

'No, not yet, I'm saving it for a special time.'

'When you visit there, you will see the stupas where seven Dalai Lamas are buried. They are wonderful stupas, shaped like bells, about thirty feet high, with gold plating and decorated with precious gems.'

'I'm really looking forward to seeing the Potala, it means a great deal to me, but the other forms of burial you mentioned, are there only certain people who are cremated or buried in water?'

'Yes, great lamas and high officials are cremated, unless they have expressed a wish for *jhator*. People who die from smallpox or leprosy or any other contagious disease are buried in the earth, and generally it is small children, babies, who are buried in water.

'But there are exceptions. Sometimes, for some special reason, a person is not buried according to custom but by some other means, like the lamas who request the *jhator*. One exception of special interest is the baby brother of the Dalai Lama, who died when he was only two years old. The lamas and astrologers advised that he should be preserved rather than given the customary burial for young children, so that he would be reborn in the same house. They advised that a small mark be made on the baby's body so that when he is reborn, he could be recognized.

'When the Dalai Lamas's mother next gave birth, it was to a baby boy, her last child, and he had the same mark on his body. The proof was there: the baby who had died was now reborn in a new body, to begin a new life.'

The story must have been new to Pascal, for we both listened with the intensity of children mesmerized by the fantastic. Neither of us wished to doubt it, it was too perfect.

After a long silence, I said, 'Will your *jhator* take place in India or will you return to Tibet?'

'I will return to Tibet when I finish my study of medicine and healing. I am a Tibetan and I wish to live and work and die among my own people. You see, my parents brought me to India when they escaped from the Chinese, but most of my family remains in Tibet and I come often to visit. I grew up in India but I was raised there in a Tibetan village, as a Tibetan. My family is close to the Dalai Lama, they are very much involved with Tibet, and although they may never return here themselves, they wish me to return. There are many young Tibetans living in India who are considering the same possibility, although most Tibetans exiled in India will not return to Tibet until the return of the Dalai Lama himself.' Tashi paused and felt his tea cup. 'It's cold. I will order some more tea.'

'Please do,' I said, contritely. 'I've talked you as dry as a desert. I'm sorry.'

Actually, I was feeling a little deserty myself and somewhat dizzy, whirling in an eddy of fragmented impressions. The intense concentration, the shifts of interest from Tashi to what he was saying, had left me lightheaded and depleted. Pascal had already excused himself, saying he would return shortly. I suspected he too needed a break. It was time for me to go.

'Thank you, Tashi, but I won't stay for more tea. It's been a real pleasure talking with a Tibetan, especially one who explains things so well. I am very grateful. Tibet is strange for me, so filled with mystery, so difficult to understand. There are many questions I want to ask, so much I want to know. Thank you for being so patient and forgive me for getting carried away.'

'No, forgiveness is not necessary and please do not thank me. It has been a privilege for me as well. Pascal is acquainted with my cousin, Lobsang, and Lobsang's brother is a high lama in the Sera Monastery, I will arrange for you to visit him. The lama speaks a little English, Pascal speaks a little Tibetan, between them you can find some answers.'

I had made my parting speech, but I made no move to leave. I was pulled towards Tashi, compelled to stay. Pascal was right; his presence was magical and I clung to it. I wanted more of him and his Tibet. But somehow I managed to tear myself away from both. Having monopolized his attention, I graciously decided to allow Pascal some time alone with his friend when he returned.

'I'm going back to rest. Please tell Pascal I'll see him at the Banak Shol, the *jhator* has exhausted me,' I said, gathering myself for departure. Besides, it was true. But as I began to get up, something extraordinary happened, something I was totally unprepared for. As Tashi rose from the table, our eyes locked and I was overcome by a terrible poignancy, an acute sense of loss, of bereavement.

I heard myself saying, 'Have we known each other for long?'

His eyes held me motionless. 'Yes.'

An unbearable swell of love rushed at me, so intense, so naked, that I had no way of dealing with it. I felt panicky, unable to move, unable to breathe. I was impaled, bound by an unknown force, my face wet with tears.

'Go now, with love.' Tashi's voice spread over me like a balm, healing, giving me breath. The wild grief was over. His eyes released me, his kiss gentle on my forehead. 'Do not fear the strangeness of Tibet, allow yourself to be embraced.'

I left the teahouse in slow motion, as if on the verge of remembering something from the deep past.

25

The Mani Stone

I DIDN'T SEE TASHI again for over a month. In that month, Tibet gradually began to reveal itself to me; the monasteries, the celebrations, the countryside, the villages, the encounters with people and most of all the special moments at the Potala Palace. I was immersed in Tibet, living in another dimension, another world. But underlying the unfolding of Tibet was Tashi. I carried him with me.

I was patient about seeing Tashi again, enjoying the certainty of the coming pleasure. I knew I would see him and postponing the pleasure was in itself pleasurable, heightened by the assurance of still greater pleasure. It was like anticipating a journey. I longed for it to happen but never wanted to rush the moment. The waiting had its own delights, an excitement, a quickening heartbeat entwined in the calm of certitude. I enjoyed living with that certitude, with that promise, holding it in my mind where I could savour it at will. The waiting brought him closer.

Then, late one afternoon Pascal startled me. 'I have arranged a meeting with Tashi at the teahouse. Are you free to come?'

I was flustered, unprepared. 'Tashi? When?

'Now.'

'Right now?'

'Yes. He is already there. I was just with him.'

My tongue tangled, but my head managed to signal 'yes'. I rushed into my room, couldn't focus on what to do there and rushed out again.

We rode on Pascal's bicycle and he left me by the teahouse, saying he had things to do. I entered alone. The teahouse looked empty. But Tashi was there. He was more beautiful than I remembered, his ear pierced with turquoise, his body lean, his smile magic. Seeing him, I wanted nothing else. Some troubled yearning I hardly knew existed, was quietened, yet I was wonderfully excited. His glance drew me like gravity. Was I laughing? Crying? Did I speak? He rose to embrace me and I held him with such intensity that to separate from him would tear my flesh. It was not the wild elation of the first five minutes of being in love. It was the sustained power of a profound love, eternally there, yet begun at this moment. As I recognized it, I heard other voices. His embrace quietened me. Gently we drew apart. Two men were drinking tea.

As if it was pre-arranged, Tashi and I left the teahouse and followed the road to the Potala Palace. His serenity flowed through me. I was stilled, wanting only to walk with him, just like this, on and on, yet wanting to postpone the next step indefinitely. All the questions I had wanted to ask, all the things I had wanted to know, did not exist. I had no questions; I wanted no answers. The menagerie of desires was satisfied.

By the Potala we found a rock and sat down. It seemed curiously familiar. Had I sat here before? Had I come this way before? I thought I heard Tashi speak but knew he was silent. As I sat contented, I was compelled by Tashi, by the Potala, by Tibet, to some realm where we had existed together. United.

Tashi reached into his pocket, withdrew his hand and slowly opened it. In the centre of his palm was a stone the size of a pressed rose. Its icy blue colour caught the sun as he handed it to me. As soon as I took it in my hand I knew it was no ordinary stone. Tashi watched me with a total serenity that made no demands, but which only enhanced the experience, as my fingers moved over its worn surface. At first it felt cool like silk, but as I held it, folding my fingers and palms over it, it was as though my hands were drawn into it and filled with energy. It was warm, significant. I seemed to know it. Perhaps it recalled the stone a Chinese masseur once used to stroke my forehead, my temples, my cheekbones, suffusing me with calm energy.

I fingered the ridges embedded in the stone, deliberate, like script. Eventually, I said, 'Is this Tibetan writing?'

Tashi nodded.

'What does it mean?'

'This is a Mani stone,' he said. 'A very special stone that has the characters of a prayer carved into it. The stone contains the prayer to Chenrezig, the Bodhisattva who looks with compassion in a thousand directions; his compassionate spirit is reborn into each Dalai Lama. The prayer to Chenrezig is "Om Mani Padme Hum", the six holy sounds and the characters of Mani are carved into the stone.'

'It's beautiful,' I said. 'It's the mantra that was taught to me by a very dear friend.' And I thought how right it was to bring Leonard into this moment. 'I love holding it. It feels like it has an energy, a power of its own.'

'Yes. It does. It was given to me by a very great lama and contains his love and his blessings. Because of that I wish to give it to you. It is my gift to you.'

'But it was given to you,' I protested.

'And to you,' he countered. 'It will remind you of Tibet and of Tashi.' As though I could ever forget. He continued: 'And it has special healing powers; it will heal your fear of being buried while you are still alive.'

His voice was quiet with caring and I recalled how his face had darkened with pain at the telling of my nightmare. He wanted to protect me from my fear. I was deeply moved, deeply grateful.

'Thank you, Tashi, I am so overwhelmed. What can I say?'

'You must say nothing. There is no need.'

He was right. There was no need. He understood more about me than I understood about myself. I sensed that he possessed an attunement with the profound rhythms that shape and connect events. I held the stone in both hands, like a prayer, and lowered my head to it. Tashi reached out, his fingers spreading through my hair, his fingertips coming to rest in the hollow of my neck. I held them like a nest cradling new birds. The exquisite surprise, the exquisite familiarity, stirred something within me to ecstasy. It was an ecstasy I could never have imagined. The sensation was so vivid that when Tashi withdrew his hand, it remained. My head stayed bowed, unwilling to disturb it. We sat for a long while under a still heaven. It was perfect being there, not talking, not touching, a deep bond between us, a recognition of the unlimited alternatives for love and affection that exist in life, and the even more profound bond that made of this moment, a lifetime.

'There is a story I would like you to know an old Tibetan tale,' Tashi said, 'but sadly I do not have it with me here in Lhasa.'

'Tell it to me then.' All at once I had an urgent desire to hear it.

'I do not wish to spoil it with speech. You must read it slowly, carefully. When I return to Dharamshala, I will send it to you. I will make arrangements.'

'Please. Promise you will send it, that you won't forget.' My urgency surprised me.

'I cannot forget.'

We walked back under the silence of the sky, my mind spreading slowly like the moon on the sea, quietly embracing Tashi and Tibet. When we reached the Banak Shol, we turned to each other. I was supremely happy.

'Go with my love.'

Tashi's voice was absorbed by the mountains, the rivers, the skies. Did he say that now, yesterday, many years ago? I entered the Banak Shol, holding the Mani stone and trying to remember.

26

'The Brothers' – A Tibetan Tale

――――――

TASHI KEPT HIS PROMISE. About two weeks after I returned from Tibet, I received a letter from Pascal. Inside was another envelope, containing the story. Nothing else. No message, no explanation, not even Tashi's signature. I read it slowly, carefully, as Tashi had wished:

Once long ago, in the land of snows, where the hills turn to the east, there lived two brothers: the older one a man of twenty winters and the younger, a boy of ten summers. These brothers lived alone in a humble cottage, their parents having died of a terrible illness that befell their part of the country when the younger brother was born. And so it was left for the older brother to raise the younger and he tended him with great love. The younger brother received the love and returned it with great veneration, for his brother was the source of his sustenance, being not only his mother and father, but his teacher and protector.

From the time they could remember, each brother held a great wish in his heart, and every morning and every evening and many times in between, they prayed, reciting mantras and chants, moving the worn beads of their rosaries in their fingers, each asking the deities to grant him his wish. The older brother prayed to become a healer so he could save his countrymen from illness and disaster such had befallen his mother and father, for he never forgot their suffering. The younger brother prayed to become a storyteller, for he spent long hours listening to the travelling bards, the Lama Manis, telling tales filled with wonderment and magic, and singing epic verses about gods, fierce demons and flying steeds, tales with a special power, gained over the long years of telling. The tales of his land and his people and of the great holy men stirred his imagination with adventure and romance and made him proud. A great longing arose in his heart to learn these tales so he could tell them to his brother during the long dark nights, and perhaps, if he learned them well, to the people throughout the land. But he knew that to become a storyteller he must have great knowledge and great skill.

It came to pass that a famous lama arrived in the village near the place where the brothers lived. 'I will go to the wise lama and ask to speak with him,' the older brother said. 'I will tell him of our wishes, and perhaps in his wisdom, he will know how to help us.' So saying, he went into the village and asked permission to see the lama. Although there were many people waiting to receive the lama's blessing, his wish was granted.

After he paid homage to the lama by offering an auspicious greeting scarf, the whitest and longest khata scarf he could find, and prostrating at his feet, he spoke thus: 'I would like to become a healer so that I can help all living beings and heal the people of my land, and my younger brother wishes to become a storyteller and learn our great tales so that he can tell them to the people throughout the kingdom and bring them knowledge and joy. What shall we do?'

The lama saw that the older brother's heart was sincere and that his motives were of the purest, and so he said to him: 'You and your brother must journey to the centre of learning in the great and holy city. There you will learn the knowledge to complete your tasks from the wise and holy men who reside there. When you reach the sacred city, you must make a pilgrimage to the palace where the greatest lama resides and ask for his blessings for your endeavours.'

Having said this, the lama took from his bag a small stone of an almost ice-blue colour that had the characters of a prayer carved into it. The lama then blessed the stone and gave it to the brother, saying, 'Receive this Mani stone with my blessings. Your journey is a long and hazardous one and many have failed to complete it, but if you hold the Mani stone in your hand and think upon it, it will keep you from fear and give you strength.' The older brother received the stone with deep gratitude, for it was a sign of the lama's love and compassion and his wish to help them.

And so, after sewing the Mani stone into the sleeve of his chuba and stringing cubes of dried cheese into a loop for chewing, the older brother filled two travelling bags with provisions, took the younger brother by the hand, and together they set off to the holy city. The journey was indeed a difficult and hazardous one. They walked for *many days and many months through harsh and desolate lands ruled by strange spirits, through rocky wilderness and barren plains. They crossed swirling rivers and were discouraged by the looming fierceness of the mountains as they struggled up their slopes. Often they were frozen with cold and starved with hunger, for they had little to wear and their provisions soon ran out. They were forced to live on wild berries and sometimes a little hard cheese or roasted barley begged from the few travellers they chanced to meet. Often they thought they could go on no longer, so weary did they become and so many were their trials. But they held the Mani stone and thought upon it and chanted the holy sounds of its prayers and they received the strength to continue.*

Before they could reach the holy city, they had to pass through the valley of the solitudes, a silent valley where many demons dwelt among the bleak rocks and danced silently upon the stony wastes. The ghostly glow of the moon chilled their hearts with fear, for they knew that few ever left the valley of the solitudes. Upon entering the valley, each brother, in turn, took hold of the small ice-blue stone given to them by the lama and held it, thinking upon it, feeling its power and sending their prayer to the deity, and then they were no longer afraid. And with their fears thrown from them, they passed through the valley, unharmed.

Always the thought of the great palace moved them forward and the Mani stone eased their fears and gave them strength, for in it was the lama's love and the deities' protection. And so they climbed and walked and stumbled with prayers on their lips and courage in their souls.

When they first saw the golden spires of the great palace in the distance, their hearts stopped in awe and reverence and their pace quickened. Thus they reached the holy city, and when at last they beheld its gates, they fell to their knees in prayer and thankfulness, for their hearts had been filled with deep longing to reach this city, and were brimming with happiness to enter its gate. When they had prostrated three times and given thanks to the deities who had guided them on their journey, and brought them safely into the holy city, they asked a beggar how they could find the great palace. The beggar pointed upwards to the heavens, and there in the sky, shining more purely than in any of their dreams, rose the palace. They gasped in wonderment.

They reached the palace with ease, for the palace itself seemed to lead them to its walls, beckoning to them like a blessing. However, since night was falling, they thought it wise to wait until morning before seeking entrance. They made camp for the night in a place close to the palace, finding shelter beside a rock and laid down to rest with joy and contentment in their hearts.

But suddenly in the night their contentment was broken by a fierce storm such as they had never known. The sky became dark and angry, the winds howled and bent the trees to the earth, bolts of thunder crashed with a mighty roar and in the flashes of white light they could see the trees and the rocks trembling with fear and feel the earth shake beneath their feet.

'We must go to the palace and seek shelter,' said the older brother, 'for surely the storm shall destroy us.' They began running to the palace, the black sky fierce with white light, the earth rumbling and roaring until the mountains became loose and huge rocks crashed down from above.

But as they ran, hand in hand, the earth seemed to slide apart and the younger brother was wrenched from the older brother and swallowed by its force. He tried to shout for help but his mouth was frozen and could not form the words. Finally his mouth opened in a piercing scream that took moments to tear itself from his being. The older brother heard his scream but could not reach him. Earth and rocks hurled from the mountains, falling into the dark hole where the younger brother was struggling. The younger brother tried again and again to climb the walls of the hole but was quickly pushed back by the earth and the rocks piling over him until he was weary with the struggle. He grew full of despair, gasping and choking as the earth filled his nostrils, driving the breath from him, until only a feeble whisper came from his lips.

With a sudden energy, the older brother jumped into the deep crevice and, lifting the younger brother onto his shoulders, pushed him to safety. The rocks and earth tumbled into the hole with such speed and such force that the older brother could not fight them. Filled with terror, the younger brother stood helpless as the earth swallowed his brother who had saved him from that very fate. But before the hole was sealed and the darkness descended upon him, never to be relieved by dawn, the older brother shouted, 'Go to the palace and wait for me there, for the chaos will surely subside and one day I will come to you.' When the younger brother remained motionless, unable to move, he shouted again, 'Go now, go at once, go with my love.' Then there was a great flash of light and in the white light, the younger brother ran to the palace, obeying the wishes of his older brother. But even as he ran, he could feel that his heart was truly broken.

When the holy men who dwelt in the palace heard what had befallen the younger brother, and beheld his sorrow, they were consumed with pity and asked him to remain among them and live in the palace. Although the younger brother was aware of the great honour bestowed upon him, and although the holy men, in their compassion, did their best to please him, and although he was blessed by the highest lama in his private chambers and served tea from the jade teacup, his heart could not be eased. His sorrows grew and multiplied, the weight of unhappiness fell heavy on his shoulders; for his brother, who he deeply loved and who was all things to him, was now gone.

Sorrow sapped his strength and fear weakened his body. He never departed from the palace walls, for the fear of falling into the earth and being engulfed by it never left him, not by night and not by day. Visions of the earth and the rocks burying first himself, and then his brother, invaded his sleep and woke him with sudden anguish, and when he was awake he pined for his brother and grieved for his loss. The holy men grew worried and knew they had to help the younger brother, for surely he would die from the sadness and the grief. They consulted healer upon healer, but no healer had the knowledge of a cure. Then word came that a young healer with special powers had appeared in the land and that this healer was seeking permission to see the younger brother, because he had special knowledge that could relieve him of his suffering. Immediately a messenger was sent to bring the healer to the palace.

When he arrived the younger brother was brought before him. The healer laid his hand on the younger brother in the place between his shoulders and felt the grief knotted in his flesh. Then he gazed deep into the eyes of the younger brother and saw the place where the fear lay hidden. When the younger brother felt the healer's touch and looked into his eyes, he was sure he could recognize something. Suddenly he could feel a powerful stream of *love enter his being and his heart grew light with love; the terrible fear was driven out, banished from his heart and with it the sadness and the suffering. His being was filled with great bliss. Then the healer took from the sleeve of his chuba a stone with almost an ice-blue colour, which had the characters of a prayer inscribed upon it: 'Think upon this stone', he said, 'and love will be with you and your fear shall never return.' So saying, he placed the stone in the younger brother's hands and departed from the palace.*

The healer wandered far and wide, healing the people of his land, and the younger brother, the Mani stone always on his heart, became famous as a storyteller. People from near and far came to hear him tell tales and they received knowledge and joy. Although the two brothers lived in different parts of the kingdom, they remained united because their spirits were as one, for there was much love between them and there was much love for the land.

The older brother's name was Tashi, the younger brother was called Nyima.

27

Meeting The Dalai Lama

THE COMPULSION I HAD to visit Tibet did not diminish after I had been there. On the contrary, it increased. It was like discovering a new love. I was constantly preoccupied with thoughts of Tibet, thoughts of the amazing encounters I had experienced and especially with thoughts of Tashi. I was haunted by the Tibetan tale he had sent me. I read it over and over and then over again, until I almost knew it by heart. I longed to see him, to understand, to know and just to be with him. I knew I had to return and made plans to do so as soon as I could get the money together. But alas, that was not to be.

Not long after I returned to England, Tibet exploded into a state of chaos. The peaceful Tibetan pro-independence demonstration of October 1987 was brutally put down by the Chinese. When the Tibetans demonstrated, chanting independence slogans and calling for greater political and

religious freedom, the Chinese government airlifted hundreds
of armed police into Lhasa. Police fired into the crowds of
protesters, killing and wounding at random. There were killings,
beatings and mass arrests.

Tibetans retaliated by stoning Chinese, raiding their shops
and burning their belongings. The Dalai Lama pleaded for an
end to the violence but to no avail. Police moved in to occupy the
main temples, while heavily armed security forces patrolled the
streets. Monasteries were sealed off. A cordon of roadblocks was
thrown up around the city and a curfew enforced. All foreigners
were expelled. Tibetans with stones were no match for Chinese
with live ammunition. Once again, Tibet was inaccessible – and
I was left with my longing and my story.

Almost two years later, when I had saved enough money
for the trip and I knew that some foreigners had trickled back
into Tibet, another demonstration put an end to my plans. The
demonstration in March 1989 was even more brutal than the
previous one. Rioting spread throughout the Tibetan quarter
in Lhasa. Police with machine guns abided by a shoot-to-kill
policy. Automatic gunfire was sprayed into Tibetan homes.
After days of horrifying violence, the Chinese declared martial
law. Thousands of armed troops entered the Tibetan quarters.
By evening, the entire city was ringed with troops. Truckloads
of soldiers armed with Kalashnikovs patrolled the streets,
headlights blazing. Everyone had to carry identification at all
times, and all meetings, petitions and public gatherings were
banned. All foreigners were expelled once more. Lhasa became
a garrison town.

My plan to return to Tibet was now impossible. Even when
things had eventually settled down and foreigners were allowed
back into the country, I did not want to return. The Chinese
now outnumbered the Tibetans, and Lhasa was more like a
Chinese city than a Tibetan one. Individual travellers were no

longer permitted entry. Visitors had to be in groups headed by a Chinese guide, who arranged all visits, all movement. It was no longer possible to stay in a Tibetan guesthouse. Contact with Tibetans was strictly limited and controlled by the Chinese guide. Tibet, as I knew it, was no more. It would break my heart to see this new Chinese Tibet.

I have never returned to Tibet. I have never heard from Tashi. Neither has Pascal, although he tried contacting him on numerous occasions. The mystery of our connection, the mystery of Tashi, has remained to haunt me, but also to sustain me, to nourish me. I eventually concluded that perhaps there are some mysteries I do not need to understand, but just to accept as part of living, part of being. That's the best I can do with such a massive unknown.

But although I have been unable to return to Tibet, I was granted a massive compensation. I heard that the Dalai Lama was coming to England in April 1988 and giving a talk in Westminster Central Hall, which was open to the public. At least I would be able to catch a glimpse of him. I was fascinated by the Dalai Lama. Although exiled in India, he had been present everywhere in Tibet when I was there. His presence had been in some ways more real, more alive than if he had actually been there. Tibetans lived and breathed the Dalai Lama. The mere mention of his name evoked a great reverence, an adoration, a visible bliss. I could think of no other leader who was so unequivocally loved. But experiencing first-hand the response he elicited from Tibetans still did not prepare me for the impact he was to have on me.

Westminster Hall is a large formal venue with a stage set at some distance from the audience. But when the Dalai Lama stepped on to that stage, the distance, the separation, vanished. Formality was suddenly transformed into intimacy. The Dalai Lama's manner was so easy, so unassuming, so warm, that it felt as though everyone had disappeared and he was talking just to me. The British government, bowing to Chinese pressure, had forbidden him to discuss anything political, but what he did discuss was almost irrelevant. The Dalai Lama himself was his most powerful message. He projected an almost visible purity, compounded by simplicity and humility. He himself was compassion and love – the pillars of his Buddhist belief. He himself was the serenity and the peace he wished for all mankind. And I felt in the presence of a great spirit, a truly special being – the jewel in the heart of the lotus.

But if he projected a sense of divinity – and there was no doubt that he did – he was also profoundly human. When he talked, he laughed easily, infectiously, speaking with his hands, his body, his heart and often laughing at himself in bursts of humour. He smiled a great deal, wonderful wide smiles, and even when he wasn't smiling, I could sense a smile waiting to explode.

It seemed incredible to me that this man, who was forced to flee his country, who was forced to witness the terrible cruelties inflicted on his people while impotent to help them, could still radiate such gentleness, such humanity, such joy. Experiencing him was not only a great privilege but an especially significant one. For if I had been unable to go to Tibet, Tibet had come to me. Once again I was touching Tibet.

I was not to know then that an even greater privilege was awaiting me, once my book *Touching Tibet* (originally called, *Flight of the Wind Horse*) was published in 1990 and the Dalai Lama had written the foreword to it. Having the Dalai Lama write the forward was not my idea. I never dreamed that such a privilege was remotely possible. When the publishers proposed I write to the Dalai Lama and ask him, I refused. How does one write to the angels? Besides, it was 1989, the year the Dalai Lama` was awarded the Nobel Peace Prize, he would be too busy to read my letter, let alone write a forward, even if I knew how to contact him, which I didn't. However the publishers continued to pressure me and suggested I visit the Office of Tibet, which happened to be close to where I lived. Reluctantly, I finally agreed. I made an appointment with Madam Takla, the Dalai Lama's representative in England. What happened next was one of the great surprises of my life. Madam Takla was not only welcoming, she was interested in my book. Over tea we chatted about the book, about my impressions of Tibet, about the current situation there. In the end she suggested I send her the manuscript, she would read it, and if she approved would send it to the Dalai Lama. The Dalai Lama's letter containing the forward, arrived only days before publication. I don't know if he actually read the book or just glanced through it, but I do know that his brother, Tenzin Choegyal, did read the book, for he wrote a cover blurb. I couldn't have wished for more.

Coincidently, in October, 1990, the year the book was first published, I was visiting my family in Toronto several days before the Dalai Lama was due to give a series of talks in Toronto. The Tibetan community was hosting a reception and dinner for him at the prestigious Royal Ontario Museum to honour his visit. It was to be a very private affair. As a special tribute, I was not only invited to the dinner, but to meet the Dalai Lama personally. I had never dared hope for a private audience with the Dalai Lama. I was thrilled.

Because the guest list was restricted, it was understood that I was to come on my own. However, the day before the reception I received a call from *Now* magazine, a Toronto weekly detailing events in Toronto. Somehow they had got wind of my invitation and asked if they could send a photographer and a reporter to photograph me with the Dalai Lama. I was aghast, refusing point blank. I was still reeling from the compliment of my invitation:

what a cheek to show up with a photographer plus a reporter, like a publicity-hungry celebrity! The very idea was appalling.

However, with journalistic tenacity, the editor phoned the organizer of the event. Later that day, a Tibetan member of the organizing committee, whom I had previously met, phoned me. 'Niema,' she said, 'if you want a photograph with the Dalai Lama, you are welcome. It's no problem. Please bring your photographer. We will arrange a special place for the photograph, to be sure that only you and the Dalai Lama will be together.'

When I protested, embarrassed, saying I had nothing to do with the request, she said, 'Please Niema, you are most welcome, you have done so much for us.'

I was astounded. What an unbelievable privilege. Instead of considering the request inappropriate or an imposition, the committee was extending its blessings. I relayed the news to the *Now* editor, but insisted that only the photographer was to attend, no reporter, and that he was to leave immediately after taking the photo.

'Agreed,' she promised.

However, when I arrived at the reception, both the photographer and a reporter were already ensconced. So much for journalistic integrity. The Tibetans, ever gracious, ever generous, were serving them tea. It turned out that the photographer had become a Buddhist and a devoted fan of Tibet. He had even changed his name to a Tibetan one. His great dream in life was to meet the Dalai Lama. This intrusion was all his doing.

As I was led to the location chosen for the photographic session in an alcove set off by majestic pillars, and was shown the impressive lighting arrangements, I grew increasingly excited, warming to the idea, even forgiving the pushy press. A photograph with the Dalai Lama in this grand museum setting was not to be taken lightly. The photographer, even more excited, stood by breathless in anticipation, elaborate camera equipment at the ready.

Then the moment arrived. The Dalai Lama entered the hall, followed by his bodyguards; he was constantly under threat from the Chinese who would have loved to be rid of him. He was guided directly to me, his bodyguards holding back. He took both my hands in his, enfolding them very carefully, as though he was being given something precious, and repeated my name with such affection as if meeting me was a great privilege. He smiled one of those wonderful smiles I had seen him bestow on others, only this time the smile was for me. He told me how pleased he was to meet me, and how pleased he was I had been to Tibet and had written about his country. I felt myself beaming, but could only nod. I did manage to thank him for writing the foreword to my book despite the fact that he must have been very busy, having recently won the Noble Peace Prize.

But our communication that day had nothing to do with words. I hardly knew what I was saying. I could only feel the warmth of his hands holding mine, and could sense that some sort of new dimension, a new capacity, a new joy had entered my life. Then he placed a white *khata* scarf around my shoulders, the Tibetan blessing, and his eyes held me in an embrace. For a perfect moment, nothing else existed. I was his entire focus, he was my centre of gravity. I had never felt the giving of someone else so completely, so entirely, so unreservedly.

Then, suddenly, some commotion penetrated my state of bliss, and from the corner of my eye the photographer came into view. He was staring at the Dalai Lama in dumbfounded rapture, living his dream of a lifetime. The camera had dropped to his side, a total irrelevance. Not a single click had escaped its prostrated shutter. Perhaps some flash of the here and now struck him at that moment, or perhaps it was the reporter's frantic signals. For, with a sudden start, he returned to this life, and in a frenzy of activity snapped photo after photo. But it was too late. The bodyguards were closing in. The angles were all wrong, the Dalai Lama had released my hands and was moving away. The perfect photo opportunity was no more.

Afterwards, the photographer apologized profusely. He had been overcome. He had had a revelation, an epiphany, an out-of-life experience. But whatever it was he was having, it didn't stop both him and the reporter from staying to dinner. And I was too euphoric to care. I had received the Dalai Lama's personal blessing, a gift to treasure for a lifetime, and a *khata* scarf to make that blessing tangible. and which goes wherever I go. It is draped on my living room lamp and now as I write this book, I look at it and remember.

Although the photograph that appeared in the next issue of *Now* was a disappointment, it did not diminish the gift. I had experienced what could never be captured on film. The moment would never fade. It was held in my heart. It was etched on my soul. I can see it, feel it, forever.

28

The Bee Gees

B Y THIS TIME THERE had been significant changes in my
life. Ronit had moved to Santa Barbara and was living with
a partner; both my mother and brother were living in Toronto,
my mother in her own flat, my brother nearby, in a lovely house
with his wife, Gitte, a very special lady from Denmark, whom
he called 'My Danish Pastry'; Susan and Major had moved, after
their baby was born, and Tom and I were living with a succession
of friends who rented their room; and I was teaching in a boy's
school, which was more of a babysitting job than a teaching one
– the boys were more interested in climbing the curtains and
throwing spitballs than in learning anything. I was also writing
my second book.

But all was not well. My spirit was ailing. I was growing restless.
My oasis was getting stale and my nomad nature was chomping
at the bit. Except for visiting Ronit in the US and my family in

Canada, which I dismissed as sojourns, real travel had dwindled to a pin head. There were no more adventures. The last one had been several years before, when returning from Tibet, Tom and I had taken the trans-Siberian train from China to Russia and then on to Warsaw and Berlin, before returning to London.

We had spent time both in East and West Berlin. The wall had divided Berlin at that time and the Communist East had seemed hard pressed, not exactly poverty stricken, but poor. The atmosphere was grey, severe, with no obvious night-life or signs of exuberance. As the showpiece of East Germany, it featured museums, grand buildings, even department stores, but these were neglected and run down and the merchandise was drab and sparse. By contrast, West Berlin was flourishing. We stayed in West Berlin with musician friends, in the heart of glitz and glamour – bright lights, all-night cafes, prosperous, alive with the buzz and money of the Capitalist West. It was as though glittering West Berlin was an island in a sea of East German dowdiness. It was like a kind of New York Coney Island full of amusements, merry-go-rounds and roller-coaster rides, stranded in an arid, shabby, landscape. East and West Berlin had become two realities in one body.

Then, suddenly everything changed. My musician friend, Tanya had been growing increasingly popular. By the early nineties she had her own band and had released five albums. She decided it was time to go on tour and wanted Tom and I to go with her. We were both hired to do all the merchandising arrangements (the sale of merchandise often providing the revenue for the tour), which involved creating and erecting fold-up displays, working out prices in foreign currencies, ordering, banking, calculating, selling her albums and, eventually, her knapsacks and tee shirts.

For me this was a new kind of travel experience. There were no run-down buses crowded with people in exotic dress, carrying baskets of food, even live chickens and speaking foreign languages; no hostels where the locals stayed; no bargaining in street markets; no tasty treats in holes-in-the-wall stalls. Now everything was spit and polish. The tour busses were sleek luxurious affairs with sleeping bunks, a recreation area, washroom with shower, mini-kitchen that included a well-stocked refrigerator, cooker and dishes. Sometimes we slept on the bus but usually in posh hotels, populated mainly by rich tourists, the likes of which I had entered only to rip off toilet paper in former travel days. Everything was taken care of by a tour manager, everything was provided, we had only to submit and let it happen. Except for the luxury liner from South Africa to the Canaries I had never experienced first class anything, now it was first class all the way.

The touring lasted for several years, the first a European tour, beginning in 1994. Then a North American tour and finally a tour to Australia and New Zealand. It took me a while to adjust to this new kind of travelling – whirlwind touring. Although we travelled to countries all over the world, we hardly experienced their cities or their people. We lived in our own bubble world with the same people and the same agenda, in the same settings, but not only in different countries but in different continents. We became a tight family with its own concerns, its own rituals – pizza at midnight, punctuality at all times, rivalry jokes between the crew bus and the musician bus – a virtual family, isolated and protected from the bumps and grinds of the rest of the world. Our world of concert halls, fancy hotels and people who spoke our language, had no threats or dangers. When the door to the tour bus closed, all foreignness was shut out. We were children enfolded in the reassuring arms of mother bus and father tour manager.

Touring was actually simulated travel. It had the earmarks of real travel, like lots of movement, in planes, in busses, even in boats, but essentially one remained in the same place, doing he same thing and having the same experiences. However, sometimes there was the opportunity for genuine travel, if one could escape in the interval between tours. Tom and I had that possibility after the New Zealand tour. We went to Fiji where we booked our own bure, a Fiji style dwelling.

The drive to the bure was spectacular – dramatic sea views, hills, wildflowers, blue skies and sunshine. Our bure was one of several lining the sea at each end of a large tranquil bay – white sandy beaches, palm trees, flowers, even a small swimming pool. It was built in the old style – magnificent high ceilings laced with bamboo and crossed with dark brown wooden beams. The walls were bamboo and the floors polished hard wood – truly a work of art. It was situated on a narrow projection, two sides of which jutted into the sea, the windows looking into the water, like a sailing boat. This was an oasis to delight any nomad girl and my nose quivered with the excitement of a new adventure.

It wasn't long before we met Eroni, the Fijian man in charge of the bures who lived in a village close by. Eroni was a big man with massive hands and feet, intelligent, sensitive, with a smile that lit up the universe, and he spoke English. He became our companion, our guide, our guru, our map and our peep into the Fijian world. In order to prevent the villages being overrun by tourists, an invitation from a village head man, not easy to obtain, was necessary before anyone could visit a village. Eroni not only invited us to his village but encouraged us to partake in its social life. We danced with the villagers, attended special occasions, and were even invited to participate in a kava drinking ceremony.

Kava, mildly narcotic, is noted for its euphoric effect. It was originally drunk only for special rituals, but now was integrated into the very fabric of Fijian life, used to create a bond between those who drank it. I experienced that same apprehension I had back in the Finjan days, when Cedric had introduced us to cannabis. But this was a special privilege, a welcome to the village and to refuse would have seemed churlish. We sat in a circle, with about ten villagers, the kava bowl, a large coconut shell passing from person to person, everyone taking a sip. I needn't have worried, the only effect the kava had on me was a numbed tongue. It was definitely an acquired taste which I had no intention of acquiring.

Fiji had a large Indian population. Most of the shops and market stalls were owned by Indians and filled with Indian imports. Indians had came to Fiji in the late eighteen hundreds, brought there to work on the sugar plantations. At one point, they outnumbered Fijians and had a majority in the democratically elected government. This resulted in a coup by militant Fijians, driving the Indians from government and enacting new laws, one of which prevented Indians from owning land, and, as they saw it, taking over the country. This troubled me but I came to understand, if not to accept the Fijian fear, that a people so unlike themselves, with a different religion, a different work ethic, different cultural and social values, would be in charge of their country. Whereas in Berlin there were two separate cities, in Fiji there were two separate peoples.

There were other benefits to this whirlwind travelling. It enabled me to visit places I had close ties with, like New York, and most important Montreal. It was strange being back in Montreal, the city where I was born, where Ronit was born and where Pistol Pete and Rose were buried; a city filled with Finjan memories, mostly wonderful but some too painful to risk evoking.

I hadn't been to Montreal for more than ten years and now found visiting it far easier than growing up in it. The French/English conflict had affected every aspect of our young lives. As children we had lived in a French speaking neighbourhood and my brother and I were subjected to a constant barrage of harassment – teasing, name calling and outright hostility – because we were English-speaking. This was particularly evident in our early teenage years, when we no longer had our policeman friend. Crossing a small park close to our home was a constant ordeal, as French kids would lay in wait, jumping out from behind trees to frighten us and pull our hair. Sometimes we were even pelted with stones. Pistol Pete was a great believer in not succumbing to aggression. He believed in fighting back and refused to be hounded out of the neighbourhood. I ended up carrying a meat cleaver, held by a loop sewed into my coat lining and once actually used it on my tormenter's head, to Pistol Pete's applause.

During the Finjan years we suffered no such humiliations. The French/English conflict was greatly reduced mainly because we were living in an English part of town; we even had French Finjan regulars. On tour it was great to be back in Montreal and to contact old friends. I could appreciate Montreal in a way I was unable to when I was growing up there and, most important, appreciate the French influence which gave Montreal a special flavour lacking in the blandness typical of many Canadian cities. But my early experiences precluded me from ever wanting to live there again.

Touring had another major advantage: it made it possible to connect with friends and family all over the world, if only briefly – Ronit in Santa Barbara; my cousin Marny in Los Angeles, who ended up travelling with us on the north American lap of the tour, helping with the merchandising; my mother, brother, Gitte and their son Blue, who was so impressed with our tour bus, we had difficulty getting him out of it after allowing him to inspect it. One of the most prized connections was with Dwina and Robin, one of the Bee Gees brothers. Dwina was a very dear friend whom I hadn't seen for some time as she was mainly living in her Miami home.

***

It was in the late eighties, several years after my trip to Tibet that I first met the Bee Gees, or more accurately, Dwina Gibb, who was married to Robin Gibb. By this time, the Bee Gees were listed among the bestselling artists of all time, their music popular around the world. I met Dwina in a rather convoluted way.

Two of my friends, the writer David Wallechinsky, son of the novelist Irving Wallace, and David's wife, Flora, were visiting London, and staying with my friend Richard, who lived in Covent Garden. Since I was working in Covent Garden, I dropped by often to see them. And it was during one of those visits that I met Mani.

Mani was a superb vegetarian chef, who had cooked for Michael Jackson. The popstar was a friend of Robin and Dwina Gibb, who, like Michael, were vegetarians, and had recommended that Mani come to England to cook for a special occasion they were hosting. Flora and David, strict vegetarians, were also friends of Michael Jackson and, back in Los Angeles, had often visited him and partaken in Mani's cooking. They had been more than impressed. When Mani's cooking stint for Dwina and Robin was over, they took advantage of his presence in England to ask him to cook for them at Richard's. Mani moved into Richard's, which was when I met him. We got along famously right from the start. Mani was interested in Tibet and Richard had loaned him my book. He was thrilled to meet someone who had actually been there and was keen to know anything I could tell him.

At the time, I was manning a stall in Covent Garden Market, down the street from Richard's, and Mani would often stop by for a chat, always bringing some special goodie he had prepared. We developed a great fondness for each other. At one point,

Mani decided he wanted to cook dinner for me. He thought it would be more of a treat if he hosted the dinner at the Prebendal, the twelfth-century former monastery where Dwina and Robin now lived, and where he had carte blanche to visit and cook whenever he liked. Mani particularly wanted me to meet Dwina, saying we were meant for each other, and he also wanted me to see her magnificent home, with its beautiful gardens, stream, gatehouse and its own stone circle.

I was thrilled. Mani said I could bring a friend and I invited my closest friend, Rosy, a spirit-of-adventure lady whom I had originally met at the Yeats Summer School. Rosy was as thrilled as I was.

We set off in Rosy's car, hardly believing our good luck. Our arrival, however, was a near disaster. We drove through the splendid arched entranceway, guarded by its ancient gatehouse, with the silhouette of a castle in the distance, and were both captivated by the medieval romance of the setting, when I suddenly had an urgent desire to urinate. By that stage, we were halfway up the long driveway, and the urgency increased, spurred on by excitement and anticipation, until I could hardly contain it. Rosy stopped the car before we got to the main building. It would have been too embarrassing to introduce myself with the words: 'I'm Niema. Where's your loo?' The driveway was edged with flowering bushes and Rosy insisted I do the deed hidden behind them, where it was dark and secluded. I squatted, concealed from view, or so I thought.

Suddenly the entire area was flooded with light so bright it was almost daylight. I had probably tripped a security wire. Pants down, bathed in daylight and with Rosy mischievously chanting, 'Everyone can see you pee. Everyone is looking,' I nevertheless had to conclude the business in hand or arrive with wet trousers. These matters, once started, are hard to stop. Then I jumped up, fumbling with my zipper and froze, like a rabbit caught in headlights. Perhaps at that very moment TV cameras were filming me; perhaps I had set off an alarm and security guards, instructed to shoot intruders, would accost us? What a way to begin a visit. I was humiliated, crushed, unable to move. But nothing happened. So, with an emptied bladder and damp knickers, struggling to regain my composure, I slunk into the car. After we'd parked, I took Rosy's arm for reassurance, and we made a less than grand entrance.

Mani was right. There was an immediate connection between Dwina and me. It was as though we had always known each other. After a state-of-the-art dinner, Rosy entertained Dwina's young son, Robin-John, by magically transforming balloons into comic animals; Robin returned to his studio to work; Mani busied himself with the aftermath of the excellent dinner; and Dwina and I talked, sitting cross-legged before the open fire.

Dwina was originally from Ireland and very interested in all things Celtic. She told me she was in the process of publishing *Celtic Dawn*, a literary journal, and was intrigued by my interest in Yeats and by the fact that I had attended the Yeats Summer School in Sligo for several years running.

'Really? I know Sligo well,' she said excitedly, 'and Yeats is one of my passions.'

We were delighted to discover a mutual devotion to Yeats. It was as though we had discovered we were children of the same parents. She was fascinated when I told her I had helped direct and choreograph several of Yeats's 'Plays for Dancers' in Montreal and in London.

Suddenly she had an inspiration: 'Would you write an article for *Celtic Dawn*? she asked enthusiastically.

'I'll not only write an article,' I said, moved by her enthusiasm, by the wonderful dinner, by the Prebendal, by her blonde hair which fell like a shawl over her shoulders, 'I'll give you photographs of our Yeats productions. I have some great photographs, even one of Ninette de Valois watching me demonstrate some dance movements.' That promise was like the exchange of rings promising eternal friendship.

From Yeats we moved easily to things more personal. Dwina showed me the beautiful illustrations she was working on for *Celtic Dawn* and read me some of the poetry she had written for the first issue. After the others had gone to bed, we sat by the fire long into the night, exchanging ideas, inspired by the glow of the flames, the candlelight and each other. Although the externals of our lives were vastly different, there was an affinity, an internal similarity.

After that first encounter we were fast friends. When Dwina and Robin were in England, I visited them often and I brought various friends to meet them as well. When I introduced them to Cedric, who had performed in the Yeats plays and whose photograph, as the blind beggar, was later published in *Celtic Dawn*, Dwina was delighted to meet him and insisted that we sleep over to prolong the visit. At a later date, I attended the launch of Dwina's book, *Cormac*, a riveting tale set in Ireland's Celtic past, and brought Richard to the book launch to meet her. I stayed with Dwina and Robin in their Miami home – the very place, it was rumoured, in which President Kennedy and Marilyn Monroe had their secret trysts. (It even looked like the White House.) They met my mother, when she was spending the winter in Miami, as many Montrealers did to escape the cold winters. They met my brother, Gitte, my niece Diane, my nephew Blue and, of course, Ronit, when we were all visiting Rose in Miami. And I met their relatives. I always felt welcome at the Prebendal and had some memorable times there, especially at their New Year celebrations.

For some years, Robin and Dwina began the New Year with a special Hogmanay party, the Scottish welcome to the New Year.

Aside from their fascinating guests, like Andrew Lloyd Webber's collaborator, Tim Rice, and George Harrison of the Beatles, and the exceptional food, there were the fascinating Scottish rituals. This included the initial ceremony, in which a tall, dark stranger enters the house with a lump of coal so that the New Year begins with a gift, and the special Scottish dancing, and, of course, the playing of the bag pipes. A Scottish group, The Clan, dressed in authentic finery, played music and taught everyone Scottish reels. I loved it and never missed a single celebration.

One Christmas, however, Cedric was visiting and, together with several of our friends, we rented a country cottage for two weeks as a New Year's treat. I told Dwina I wouldn't be able to attend the party that year because I had friends staying and didn't want to leave them.

Her immediate response was, 'Don't leave them, bring them!'

'Impossible,' I said. 'There are at least ten of us.'

Dwina, ever generous, ever gracious, simply said, 'Bring them all.' And so I did. It was a great evening, a New Year's party to remember.

Dwina's generosity hailed from way back. When she first came to England from Ireland, as a young penniless artist, she lived in a squat with several friends. They were all so poor that their dinner was often a shared tin of baked beans. When Dwina's fortunes changed dramatically after marrying Robin Gibb (a quirk-of-fate marriage that nobody could have predicted, much like the marriage of Victoria to Alan Bates), she made sure to share her good luck with those friends and was still supporting several of them financially when I met her.

Sadly, I haven't seen Dwina for some time. After Robin died in 2012, she became reclusive. The Bee Bees are no more. At the time of writing, only one of the brothers, Barry, is alive. But the impact they made on the world will live forever, just as the impact Dwina made on me will last forever. She will always be my sister. My heart hurts for the loss she is suffering, but I must leave her to grieve in her own way. However, I know that one day we will be reunited, and I celebrate that day.

29

Diana Dors and Jason

<hr>

IT WAS NOT LONG after I met Dwina that I left London. I needed
an oasis that was closer to nature and I had a yen for the sea.
Oceans fascinated me. When travelling anywhere close to an ocean,
I always tried to get a room with a sea view. For me, the ocean, like
the desert, was a source of nourishment. I drew both energy and
comfort from its vastness and power. It was a restorative force in my
life. So, after living in London for over twenty years, I was fortunate
to move to a seaside village on the Kent coast, about an hour and
a half from London, in a flat that I loved. It was in an old customs
house, where, in bygone days people coming from France would
have had to register. The customs house had been converted into
twelve flats and I had the only one with a garden. The building was
right on the beach, directly on the sand and all my windows faced
the sea. It was like living on a boat which, although standing still,
was connected to the sea, much like the bure in Fiji.

Most of the other flats were holiday homes, and the only other fulltime resident was Jason, who lived in the flat below mine with his girlfriend, Nicole. I soon discovered Jason was the son of the famous actress, Diana Dors, known as the Marilyn Monroe of England – although it was Jason's contention that Marilyn Monroe was the Diana Dors of the US.

It didn't take long for Jason and me to find each other; it was like the inevitable drawing of the waves to the shore outside our windows. Jason was in his mid-thirties, tall, lean, with mischievous eyes that were mostly blue, but which changed colour like the sea. He had soft, curly, light-brown hair and a smile that could light up the darkest cloud. He was a veritable lady killer. Women adored him and he adored women. He warranted the 'lady killer' accolade not only because of his good looks, but because he had a special affinity with females; he truly liked them, and had that rare gift of bringing a sparkle to their eyes and a moment of joy to their hearts, be they young, old, or somewhere in between. I'd seen Jason stop an elderly woman in the street to complement her hair do, or a teenager to tell her how her dress complemented her eyes. Jason really noticed. And although Jason wasn't from the Timothy Leary generation of 'turn on, tune in, drop out', he was there anyway.

Less than a month after we met, Jason said to me: 'Niema, I'd like you to write a book about my mother, my father and about me. I have an interesting story to tell and I want to tell it while I still remember it. And you will be able to meet many of my mother's friends who are still alive. They always refuse interviews, but I'm still in touch with some of them, and if I ask, they'll give an interview to you.'

'Hold on, Jason,' I said. 'Remember I'm from Montreal, and when I was growing up, we weren't allowed to go to the cinema until we were fifteen. I hardly saw any films and I had no idea who your mother was until I met you. I still know very little about her.'

'That's no problem. I'll tell you everything,' he said enthusiastically. 'My mother was a legend in her own time, everyone knows about her. She was a class A actress. You know she played Ruth Ellis, the last woman to be hanged in England, in the film *Yield to The Night*? She got rave reviews. I promise you, I have things to tell about the Dors story that no one has heard and that everyone will be interested in hearing.'

To prove this to me, Jason began telling me intriguing snippets to spike my interest. It worked. I began to ask questions about Diana Dors and was fascinated by the answers. Jason was right. It seemed everyone above a certain age not only knew about Diana Dors, but talked about her with great affection. She was a household name. She had appeared in films and on television, and had also performed throughout the UK, singing, dancing and in cabaret. She'd had her own newspaper column and had been an agony aunt. Praise was heaped upon her not only for her acting but for her generosity, compassion, wit and intelligence, and especially because of her lack of airs and graces. She had a 'one of us' persona but with celebrity status.

I was most impressed. I started doing some research and discovered something that I found especially interesting. She had been into 'visualization' before the term was even coined, and she practically invented today's popular edict of 'follow your dreams'. She was a shining example of the advice attributed to the German writer Goethe: 'Whatever you can do, or dream you can do, begin it, boldness has genius power and magic in it.' She was 'New Age' before the New Age had arrived. I decided to write the book.

I started by researching her childhood and was surprised to discover that there was nothing extraordinary in her early childhood to foreshadow her extraordinary success. She had been an ordinary little girl, with ordinary parents who lived in an ordinary town. She was not especially pretty, with mousey brown hair and a patch over one eye to correct an eye problem. Yet, at age eight, when the teacher asked the children what they wanted to be when they grew up, she rose from her seat and announced, 'I am going to be a famous, rich, movie star, and have a big swimming pool, a mansion and a white telephone.' To make that happen, she would sit cross-legged in her garden, her eyes closed, and visualize what she wanted. And that's exactly what she got.

I was intrigued to know how she had surmounted her humble beginnings to become, at the age of twenty-nine, the highest paid and most popular English actress. How at age twenty-five she had performed opposite Rod Steiger in the film 'The Unholy Wife', and had signed a three film contract with RKO pictures. I embarked on further research. After listening to Jason talk about his mother, I became even more fascinated, not only by her story, but by his. Jason's story was compelling. It highlighted the problems faced by children born to celebrity parents; embodying both the glories and pitfalls they had to live with.

Jason was the much-loved child of Diana Dors and Alan Lake, who was also a well-known actor. Jason's early life was riddled with indulgences. He didn't have a play *room*, he had a play *house*; if he didn't want to go to school, he had a private tutor; when he went to the circus he was allowed to cavort with the animals because his mother knew Billy Smart, the owner of the circus; and, if he wanted to act in a film, no problem, his mother could arrange that too. He began acting when he was only seven, in the film *Just William*. He grew up under the focus of television and film cameras busy filming his mother, his father, even himself, and with the public's wild adoration for his mother, some of which rubbed off on him. The mansion he lived in – Orchard Manor – had an indoor Olympic-sized swimming pool as part of the living room, which was lit by underwater coloured lights and had stained-glass windows; and every room had a white telephone. But, best of all, he had love.

However, a massive calamity befell Jason when he was just fourteen years old, demolishing those early glories. Diana Dors died of cancer. He had no idea that his mother was even ill, let alone dying. Diana and Alan had never let on that she had cancer, to spare him the pain of knowing. He thought his mother had gone to the hospital for a check-up. Alan had spent Diana's final days with her in the hospital and Jason was left at home with the house boy. He learned of his mother's death via the media, live broadcasts of her dying hours were aired on both radio and television

Although his world had fallen apart, he did his best to put on a brave face. He refused to give the television cameramen, who filmed his mother's funeral, the satisfaction of seeing him cry. He held back the tears as he followed the hearse to the cemetery and even when he put a white rose into his mother's grave. He maintained a brave face for his father's sake as well, not wanting to cause him further suffering.

Alan was devastated by Diana's death and was unable to continue living without her. A month after Jason's fifteenth birthday, Alan committed suicide in Jason's room by shooting himself in the head. Later, when Jason returned home to retrieve some of his belongings, he found bits of his father's brain among his records, books and CDs. But this time Jason didn't have to supress his tears for there were none. The shock was too great for tears.

Suddenly Jason had no mother, no father, no home – Orchard Manor was quickly sold – and no money. His half-brother, Gary, who was in his early twenties and who lived in Los Angeles, had power of attorney over Jason and over the money. Jason went to live in California with Gary. Disaster followed. It was no wonder. There wasn't a single mature adult to help Jason through his terrible grief or a single male role model, or even female figure, to set an example for him. He was left to flounder. Jason went from a star-studded life, filled with luxury, admiration and love, to a life where no one knew who he was or cared to know.

Gary regarded him as a nuisance, an interference in his living-in-the-fast-lane life. Still in his early twenties, he was in no way equipped to cope with a traumatised adolescent. Jason stopped going to school and would disappear for days. His slide into a life of drugs and alcohol abuse was inevitable. It was the only way he could cope, the only way he could tolerate being alive. 'What did I know about the real world?' Jason once said to me. 'I never lived there.' Gary couldn't wait to get rid of him. As soon as Jason was eighteen, he was sent back to England with a hundred pounds.

In England, he soon found himself living with a woman and her young son. For a while he had a home and a family. But when he was hardly out of his teens, his partner became pregnant. He had become accustomed to a life without focus or responsibility, and being restricted by a partner and a child was like serving a prison sentence. He was able to endure playing a father role for about two years before he fled.

He turned up in Ibiza and wore himself out, indulging in a lifestyle of sex, drugs and rock and roll, which he was able to sustain only because of his name. Wasted by drugs and alcohol and wanting desperately to sort out his life, he returned to London. But instead of sorting out his life, he became a drug dealer and almost killed himself with an excess of his own merchandise. Eventually, in a last-ditch attempt at survival, he came to live in Broadstairs with Nicole. He loved the sea and felt living by it would restore his health, cure his alcohol addiction and bring him peace and freedom from a tormented life.

I developed a great affection for Jason. We spent hours together, him pouring out episodes of his troubled life; me listening and finding it difficult to hold back the tears. I wanted to give him all the support I could, in his attempt to still the chaos of his life.

Day by day, I watched Jason struggling to construct a new life, making promises, breaking promises, confronting his demons and slowly winning, but very slowly. Often I was furious with him. He would wake me in the middle of the night with his loud music. He was late for appointments. He would disappear without warning for days on end. Jason was hard work, and relying on him to help me write the book was frustrating to the point of wanting to give up. But I didn't give up. Incidents, like the following, redeemed him, made my heart ache and impelled me to finish writing the book.

One day, I opened my door to a beaming Jason. In the palm of his hand was the tiniest bird I had ever seen, no more than two inches long. He told me a bird's nest had fallen three floors from the roof of our building onto his concrete patio. When he lifted the nest he found a baby dove under it. He was certain it was dead but when he picked it up, to his amazement, it was alive.

'How could a bird survive smashing onto the concrete? That has to be a miracle. I'm calling her Lucky,' Jason said, looking at the small, fluffy ball in his hand, his eyes shining with unadulterated love. 'I'm going to raise her to be my pet love bird.' Of course, for Jason, if 'love' was involved, the dove had to be a 'her'.

'You know, doves are different from seagulls,' he explained. 'Seagulls are wild, you can't really tame them, but you can teach doves, you can train them. Remember that ungrateful Gregory Peck?' he said, recalling an injured seagull he had devotedly nursed back to health. 'He went back to the wild as soon as he was better, even with part of his leg missing. And he never comes to visit me, he never writes, he never phones,' he added, jokingly. 'But Lucky will be different.'

'She's so small,' I said. 'Doesn't she need her parents to feed her?'

'I'll be her parents. I'll feed her with a syringe. I'll take good care of her.'

And he did. He made special baby bird food for her. He fed her every hour or so, day and night, with a mush of porridge and vitamins. Jason, who hated leaving his bed before noon unless it was to sunbathe or go to his AA meeting, set his alarm to wake him throughout the hours of darkness. In the evening, he would put Lucky in her nest with a hot water bottle, wrapping the bottle in layers of towelling until it was just the right temperature and changing it in in the morning. He lined her nest with feathers he found on the beach so she would feel at home, and he covered the box with a blanket and a pillow on top of the blanket to keep the warmth in.

'It's important to keep her warm,' he explained.

Against the odds, Lucky survived. At first she had refused food, and Jason had to force her beak open. But soon she began to open her beak, demanding food with loud chirps as soon as Jason was in sight. And when she was fed, calm and content, she sat in the palm of Jason's hand, watching television with him while he stroked her.

She grew amazingly quickly and soon Jason was able to feed her every three or even four hours, instead of hourly. She'd hop about skittishly, making 'feed me' noises, but not remaining still long enough for Jason to get the syringe into her beak. At first some of the food would miss her beak and smudge her with sticky goo. But after a few days Jason perfected the technique, holding her wings down with one hand and popping the syringe into her beak with the other. He had infinite patience with Lucky and didn't mind how long he spent getting things right:

the syringe washed, the food mixed in proper proportions and at the right temperature, her box and especially her nest cleaned. Jason adored Lucky and was as proud of her as any parent with a precocious child.

'Look how she hops into my hand when it's feeding time... Check out her new feathers. She's growing up, that baby fluff is disappearing... Doesn't she look sweet sitting in her nest? She knows me now, look how she sits on my finger... I'm taking her for walks and she loves it.' With Jason's devoted, totally committed care, Lucky was indeed becoming a lovely, plump baby with real feathers. Jason had pulled it off. He had done pretty much the impossible. Lucky was the ultimate love bird.

When Lucky was several weeks old and had grown to a mighty four inches, complete with grown up feathers, Jason felt it was okay for him to have a break from the twenty-four-hour caring routine. He asked me if I would look after Lucky for one night while he, and Nicole went to a prestigious music festival. Music was his ultimate joy and Adamski, a well-known musician with whom he played music, was not only performing at the festival but had been instrumental in organizing it, and could get him free tickets and backstage passes, which meant free everything. How could he resist?

The idea of looking after Lucky did not appeal to me at all; actually, it frightened me. I had held her in my hand several times, stroked her, marvelled at her progress, but I had never taken care of a bird, and caring for Lucky, who still needed to be fed with a syringe and who was Jason's precious treasure, was especially scary. It was like being asked to look after the Crown Jewels.

'I don't really want to do it, Jason,' I said. 'And I'm going to a cherry festival on Saturday – I'll be away all afternoon. Besides, I don't know how to feed her. I've watched you do it and it looks like I'd need a doctorate in zoology '

'That's no problem, I'll show you how,' he assured me. 'By now she can go for four hours without feeding, so the cherry festival is no problem. We'll practise until you get the knack. I'll prepare her food and give you all the instructions you need. It's only for one night.'

In the end I agreed, as I usually did. 'But Jason, remember, it's only for Saturday night. You'll be sure to be back early Sunday?'

'Positive.'

After my reluctant agreement I underwent an intensive bird-caring course. I took notes. Hot water bottle at night, a fresh one in the morning. Feeding every three hours, with an extra hour's dispensation for the cherry festival. And when I had finished the written part of the course, I graduated to the practical part: the feeding lessons. The first time I fed Lucky, I got porridge all over her face and wings, and one of her eyes was stuck shut, glued by the porridge. I felt awful. The poor little bird looked pathetic, her feathers all sticky, and I looked like I had been in a porridge slinging competition.

'You see, Jason, I'm no good at it, look at what I've done.'

'You just need a few more lessons. It's no problem, now I can give Lucky her first bath,' Jason said cheerfully, anxious to put a positive spin on the situation.

'No, I can't do it,' I protested.

'Of course you can, you'll get the hang of it; you just need practice.'

So I practised and finally managed to get the porridge down Lucky's beak instead of in her eyes and on my clothes. Jason arrived that festival Saturday with Lucky's paraphernalia: her box, a blanket to cover the box, a pillow to cover the blanket, her nest, a hot water bottle, miscellaneous cloths, a syringe, her porridge, her vitamins, and Lucky herself. And so Lucky took up residence in my living room.

I took my duties seriously. Although I was having a great time at the cherry festival, I made sure to be back in time for Lucky's feeding and I was pleased it went relatively well. I didn't go out that night for fear I wouldn't be back in time for Lucky's next feed. Instead, I washed her cloths to be ready for the following day, cleaned her box and put Lucky to bed, following all Jason's instructions to the letter. I even sang her the little song I used to sing to Ronit at bedtime.

I woke early Sunday morning after a restless night and, with fear in my heart, I removed the pillow, then the blanket and peered anxiously into the box. What if I had done something wrong? Lucky was so fragile. I breathed a sigh of relief to find her sitting happily in her nest, her beak wide open, chirping for food. I fed her, put her back in her nest, folded her clean clothes and her blanket, washed her feeding utensils, and waited for Jason, and Nicole hoping they would return before the next feeding.

By late afternoon they were still not back. Instead Jason phoned. 'Would you mind if we stayed another night? We're having such a great time.'

'I absolutely mind,' I said, with more than a little annoyance. 'I don't want you to stay another minute, let alone another night. I can't cope with the responsibility. You must come back now.' I was adamant.

'Okay,' Jason reluctantly agreed. 'We'll be back as soon as we can.'

'Not as soon as you can. Now!'

'Okay. Now.'

I was greatly relieved. Lucky was relatively clean, her box was tidy, her cloths were washed and folded and her feeding apparatus ready and waiting. I had done well. Jason would return to a well looked after Lucky.

But Jason did not return, not now and not later. And I couldn't contact him because he had lost his phone, and Nicole didn't own one. Annoyed and frustrated, I went through the rituals of the feeding and bedding. After another anxious night, I woke early unable to sleep, went straight to Lucky's box and removed the covers. Lucky was squeezed into a corner of the box. Dead. She looked so small, so fragile, so pitiful. I burst into tears and sat on the sofa, crying. At the recollection of that moment, my eyes still fill with tears. That poor little bird, so alive, so active last night and now dead.

When Jason phoned later that morning, apologizing profusely, I interrupted his excuses and burst into tears. 'Lucky is dead. I found her dead this morning in her box. I don't know why, she just died. I did everything right.'

There was a heavy silence and then Jason said, 'I'm coming right back.'

'Please come back soon. I don't know what to do.'

Several hours later, Jason knocked on my door. We fell into each other's arms.

'I'm sorry, Jase. I know how much Lucky meant to you. I'm so sorry.'

'I know. It's not your fault,' Jason muttered.

Jason and Nicole buried Lucky in a small patch of land outside their door. What happened after that burial was more than a revelation, it was an epiphany. We sat in my garden, silent. All at once Jason's face contorted with pain and he began to cry. But he didn't just cry, he wept, he sobbed, he wailed, he howled, he cried as though there was no end to his pain, no end to his tears; his body was racked with sobs, his eyes became swollen, his face grew puffy. He cried. Nicole cried. I cried. We hugged him, we held him, we stroked him, but he was inconsolable; nothing could stop the weeping, nothing could comfort him.

At one point, Jason spluttered and gasped, 'Everything dies on me. Everything leaves me. My mother died, my father died, and now my baby bird died.' And suddenly I understood. Jason had never been able to cry for his mother, for his father, for all the sadness in his life, for being wrenched from loving parents, from a life filled with promises, and sent to a place, to a life, where there was no love, no promises.

Jason sobbed, 'It's my fault Lucky is dead. I'm to blame. I let her down. I was her parents and I let her down. She missed me so much that she died.' He kept talking, choking, weeping. 'This is sent to teach me a lesson. I have to learn from this. I must stop crying and do something to make things better.' But he couldn't stop.

'Jason, it's alright to cry,' I said. 'You're crying for all the times you didn't cry. It's alright to cry now.'

We sat in the garden, holding each other, crying with each other. We were crying for Lucky, for Jason, for ourselves. Was I crying because I remembered another insistence on party going, another box, another baby, small, innocent, fragile, all those years ago. I had been fortunate, my baby had survived, had been my companion, had travelled with me, had shared my adventures, my desert, my friends – Cedric, Brian, Leonard, Irving, Aviva, Joss, Victoria, Dwina, and especially, Shimon – had given me precious moments of joy, had prevented me from becoming an aging girl but instead a woman, a mother; had taught me unconditional love. I had been spared. Jason had not been so lucky, his baby bird had died. His love for it had been thwarted, just as his love for his parents had been thwarted. Finally Nicole and I were all cried out, but Jason continued to cry. Maybe he cried a river, maybe he cried a sea; he cried until he was unable to stop crying. Hours went by, maybe days, maybe weeks.

And then, all at once, Jason stood up, looked out to the sea he loved so much, and said quietly, 'It's okay. I've stopped crying now.'

30

Addy and the Desert

I T WAS JANUARY 2018, the coldest, most miserable, greyest month on record. England was dreary; I was dreary, surrounded by death and loss. Shimon, with whom I had remained close friends, and who was very dear to me, had recently died and with him my Finjan times. I remained deeply affected by Leonard's death, a grief intensified by not seeing him before he died. I was still mourning the death of my darling brother, some years earlier. And my partner for over twenty years had suddenly abandoned me, a blow that left me reeling. I was bereft, wrung out, wounded, and worse of all, I was drained of love.

And if my spirit was bleak, lacking inner sunshine, my body had acquired a cold numbness, deprived of outer sunshine. I was engulfed in a blandness that was foreign to me. I no longer savoured anything. The music had run out of life.

It wasn't real music I lacked. I had a great collection of recorded music and an abundance of live music. Cedric still visited me regularly and made wonderful music, either playing alone or with Ivan, a mutual friend and a brilliant cellist whose music had kept me dancing all night. And the local pubs, concert halls and dance venues were full of music. No, it was another kind of music. It was music I had always been able to tune into because it lived within me. It was a music of the spheres, of the flow of rivers, of the shifting of sands. I could no longer hear that music. My oasis had dried up. I felt myself withdrawing from the now, retreating into the past, into memories of the good times.

One of the very best times had been in the Moroccan desert with Tanya and Chris. Ironically, then the desert itself had been my oasis. The peace, the revitalization of being, the energy I had found there had been a sustaining force and could always be called upon for instant wellbeing. Like in the hymn, the desert was my 'balm of Gilead, that makes the wounded whole'. But now I could not call upon the memory to sustain me. I needed to be held by the desert. I needed to absorb the stillness, to listen to the silence, to inhale the solitude, to connect with the rhythms of creation. I needed to hear that music once more. Morocco not only beckoned, it offered salvation.

As soon as I made the decision to go, the apathy, the heaviness, began to lift. A brief Internet search, a phone call, a credit card were all it took to bring a sparkle into the gloom.

My sister-in-law and close friend, Gitte, my soul sister Irina – the wild Russian who had defied both the belly dancers and the police at the Belgian Bar, and had landed herself in jail as a result – and my dear friend Gerhard decided to come with me. The plan was simple. I knew it by heart. We would fly to Marrakesh, spend several days there, rent a car and drive to Merzouga, in the heart of the desert.

***

Arriving in Marrakesh was like coming home. As soon as I stepped into the sunshine, my senses began to glow. Even though I had been to Morocco many times before, including those nine months with Ronit, the thrill of arriving never lessened. The magic of my times there had created deep grooves of memory that seemed to surface as soon as I touched Moroccan soil. Suddenly I was smiling.

From the airport we headed straight to the CTM hotel in the heart of the medina, the old quarter, where I always stayed. As soon as we settled in our rooms – Gitte, Irina and me in one, Gerhard in another – I made a beeline for the roof terrace, which overlooked the main square, the Place Djemaa el Fna. I wanted to be within the energy of the square; I wanted to see the dancers, the snake charmers, the acrobats, the fortune-tellers; I wanted to hear the music; I wanted to feel Morocco. Over the years, I had spent many hours sitting on that terrace in the sunshine with various friends, among them Irving and Aviva, and Cedric, listening to the strange assortment of pipes, drums and string instruments, nibbling Moroccan cakes, sipping mint tea and basking in the adventure. Even thinking about those times filled me with pleasure; they were my uppers, my tonic.

I sat gazing into the square, allowing the breath of Morocco to fill my lungs, surrendering to the breeze caressing my face, to the sun, coaxing the cold from my bones, and slowly, gradually, I felt myself submitting to a sensuality that had lay dormant for so long. If Tibet had been my spiritual home, my spiritual oasis, Morocco was my sensual home, my sensual oasis. Morocco was the kiss that changed me from a frog into a princess. If my senses had undergone a battering, now, as I sat on the terrace in the warm sunshine, absorbed in the panorama of the square, I felt an awakening and I opened my arms to the embrace of Morocco.

The day had been a difficult one. I had been showered and dressed by five in the morning, the drive to the airport had taken over two hours, much of it in heavy morning traffic; then the usual airport anxieties, the long queues, the crying babies, the multiple checks, the fumbling with passports, with boarding passes. I suddenly felt both emotionally and physically exhausted and, lulled by the sun, I closed my eyes, allowing Morocco to wash over me.

I must have drifted into one of those surreal dreams where the reality of the moment becomes entwined in the illusion of the dream. I dreamed I was suddenly lifted by a swirl of colour and found myself floating in the vast blue expanse of sky above Marrakesh. I was in a trance-like state, a kind of reverie, but my senses were acutely alive. I could see the colours blazing in the souks; feel the loops of soft, brilliantly coloured wool caressing my face; smell the incense in the air, hear the throb of drums, the music of pipes twisting, coiling, undulating through the alleyways, the food stalls, the mosques.

Beneath me was a landscape drenched in golds. A great golden flood of desert rippling with darker gold shadows was spread out under me; the dunes were like pyramids of spices – tangerine gold, saffron gold, lemon gold, cinnamon gold, and the ebony gold of smooth Moroccan skin. A group of young women were fingering the spices, their bodies fully covered in long, richly embroidered kaftans, their faces, except for their eyes, veiled by yashmaks. But as I drifted closer I could see flashes of those dark eyes defying the veil, winking at a parade of young men who approached from the opposite direction, walking arm in arm, hand in hand, graceful, smiling, the effortless flow of their bodies like saplings in a breeze. As they came closer to the girls, I could see their smiles widening as they winked back and mouthed kisses; the girls lifted their yashmaks and returned their kisses. And I felt an exquisite joy.

I woke exhilarated, excited. I wanted to rush into the streets, to hear, to smell, to taste, to feel. It was all there, right outside my door. I was in Marrakesh. And if Morocco was my sensual Mecca, Marrakesh was its heartbeat, its essence. In Marrakesh everything was heightened: the physical sensations, that erotic edge. The colours, textures, and sounds were squeezed together so tight, they could explode like brilliant fireworks. And I thought how right it was for me to have come here now when I was depleted, when the colour had leached out of my life, when I could not feel love. And suddenly, I was overwhelmed by a feeling of love for Morocco. And best of all a feeling that Morocco loved me.

That love was proved to me again and again in the four days we spent in Marrakesh. Love followed me wherever I went. It wanted nothing except to be said, to be given. The man in whose market stall I bought a kaftan, leapt out of his stall when we passed several days later and, flinging open his arms, shouted 'I love you'; the woman in whose restaurant we ate twice, presented me with a gift when we came a third time; the young man at the reception desk called me, Princess, and glowed each time he saw me; the man baking bread in the large wood oven kissed me on the head when I stopped to watch; the hooker girls at the fashionable nightclub, Wine Wine, where I went one night to hear my friend Jaouad sing, kissed me on both cheeks when we passed in the corridor. The hotel manager, Mohamed, hugged me and said a heartfelt 'I love you', when we parted at the bus station in Marrakesh. I was showered with love. I treasured the love and I loved back in some way I didn't understand. But I felt blessed.

After four wonderfully indulgent days in Marrakesh, eating Moroccan pancakes drenched in honey for breakfast, tagine with prunes and almonds for dinner, and in between, drinking freshly-squeezed juices from the rows of stalls lining the square – orange, pineapple, mango and our favourite, pomegranate juice;

lingering over endless cups of mint tea in the cafes; wandering through the souks and alleyways, buying, bargaining, talking, singing, laughing, and in the evening Irina and me dancing to the music in the square, we collected the car we had rented, and headed for the desert.

Driving to the small desert town of Merzouga was an adventure all of its own. Morocco had been undergoing an unusually cold spell, the likes of which hadn't been seen for almost fifty years. The last of it was still evident as soon as we left Marrakesh. The high Atlas Mountains, always covered in snow, were blanketed so deep, some of the passes were closed and we had to wait until they were cleared to continue our journey. Incredibly, it had even snowed in the desert, an event never witnessed by anyone under the age of fifty. (It was strange to think that anyone under fifty had never seen snow, especially for someone born in Canada.)

The roads were clear but the roadsides and adjacent fields were still covered in patches of melting snow. In the towns and villages where we stopped to eat, the menu was irrelevant, so long as the doors could close against the cold. Most cafes and restaurants were open to the elements, since the prevailing problem in Morocco was keeping cool, not warm. We chose where to spend the night, according to which places had some pretence at heating. But even with the heating at full blast we were so cold we slept fully clothed. Irina even wore an embroidered hat with rabbit ears and Gitte, who did computer work each day, typed with fingers so cold she had to sit on them to thaw them out. But we endured stoically, knowing it was all temporary. The cold would vanish once we hit the desert, at least during the day.

We arrived in Merzouga early in the afternoon and headed for Kasbah Panorama, a walled hotel set on a hill with a spectacular view of the dunes. The hotel was everything we could have wished for. The architecture and the décor were traditional Moroccan, decorated with carved archways, curtained doorways, mosaics, Berber carpets and cushion coverings and Moroccan lanterns with inserts like tiny jewels. The rooms were lovely, the walls painted with Moroccan scenes – camels, mosques, minarets, the curtains and bedspreads made of woven Berber material. The rich colours, and the woven fabrics throughout the hotel, plus the low seating strewn with cushions in the main room, created an instant welcome. And the welcoming atmosphere was enhanced by a touch of opulence.

Best of all were the boys who ran the hotel, Mohamed, Hassan and Addy. They were Berbers born and raised in the desert, all from the same extended family. They weren't only relatives but close friends and the warmth and good humour between them created an easy-going ambiance, adding to the hotel's welcome. Being the only guests helped. We had everything all to ourselves. By the second day the hotel felt like home, and the boys like long-term friends.

Breakfast was served on the terrace in the sunshine, facing the dunes. The table was set beautifully with Moroccan pancakes, eggs, flat Moroccan breads, butter, honey, fig jam, dates and mint tea in silver teapots. Dinner was served in the dining room, with candles and napkins made from woven material so beautiful, it seemed a pity to soil them. First came Moroccan soup, then tagine with local vegetables and lamb or beef and a special vegetarian tagine for Irina, all prepared with Moroccan spices and herbs. For dessert, there were Moroccan cakes and oranges, divided into segments and sprinkled with cinnamon and, of course, mint tea. The boys were great cooks.

In the evenings they lit the huge fireplace in the living room and we sat close to the flames, drinking mint tea, chatting and waiting for the drumming. Every Berber boy begins to drum as soon as he can walk. For them drumming is as natural as breathing. The boys had a collection of Moroccan drums, small drums, large drums and one huge drum, as well as metal clappers and other percussion instruments. Before they began playing, they warmed the drums by the fire to stretch the skins, testing the different tones as the skins grew increasingly taut, in a kind of drum tuning. Then they began to play. They passed the different drums from one to another, playing to each other, playing to us, combining the different drum tones into a rhythmic symphony of sounds. As the rhythms grew, sitting still became impossible. Unlike the Gnaoua drumming which filled my head, this drumming took over my body. Irina was already moving. We were impelled to dance.

And the dancing. Oh, the dancing. On our last night the boys abandoned their drums and danced with us. Their friend, Hicham, a tour guide, who lived in Marrakesh was visiting and he joined us. Someone put on a recording of Arabic dance music and Irina and I went feral, the boys not far behind us. The dance had no name, no pattern, no style, no grace. It was just anything-goes dance, raw, unadorned movement. Circles and squares, trios and couples and all of us together. Twirls and stamps and glides and jumps and embraces. And laughing, laughing, laughing. We danced until nothing else existed, until we were drunk with the dancing, the music, the laughing and each other. At one point Addy took me under his *jelaba* and I could feel his heart beat as we stomped backwards and forwards, until I stomped away with long low strides, arms hanging loose, head bowed, like a demented animal. I danced until the sorrow, the bereft, the wounds were exorcised. I danced until the dancing filled all the spaces, until there was no room for sadness. I danced until I could feel the love.

At one point, Hassan, who was the best drummer, left the dance and began to drum. Wild abandoned drumming. He drummed until he couldn't stop. He drummed on his hands and knees. He drummed crawling on the floor, standing, sitting.

His drumming coaxed Gitte and Gerhard into joining us. We all danced, in a line, in a circle, arms raised, arms lowered, the drumming urging us on and on and on. There was no faltering, no pausing, only dancing until we could hardly breathe, our bodies pulsating with dance.

Then suddenly we stopped. No one spoke. And with wordless embraces we disappeared into our rooms. The drumming, the dancing, the music, the boys; it was all fabulous. And we were all fabulous together.

***

Almost as soon as we had arrived at the Hotel, even before we had unpacked, Addy, who spoke the best English, took us to the foot of the dunes, which were within walking distance. We climbed one of the highest dunes. Even though the sand was unusually firm, due to the snowfall, climbing was slow and difficult. We arrived at the summit panting and breathless. But in an instant the tiredness disappeared. Irina leapt into the air, her arms spread wide. The view was so stunning; it took several minutes before anyone spoke. We stood there in awe. Even though I had been in the dunes before, it took a while to assimilate the magnificence. The experience was so far from anything we knew, it took time to grasp it. It evoked an awesomeness that was overpowering. When I looked around, Irina had disappeared. Gitte and Gerhard were sitting silently. What could one say? We needed time to restore balance, to regain composure.

We sat, we walked, we lay in the sand gazing at the heavens, we took photos and we just stood still, overwhelmed by wonder. It was difficult to leave, but Addy was waiting at the bottom of the dunes and the desire not to keep him waiting finally forced our departure. It wasn't exactly that connection with the stillness and solitude I desired. But I was in the desert. I was among the dunes. And for the moment, that was enough.

On the day before we left the desert, I stayed in the hotel while the others went to visit an oasis that housed a kasbah where a Moroccan queen had been exiled. I wanted to remain behind to absorb the last hours of desert, to imprint them on my mind, on my senses; to drink in the stillness, the energy; to connect with the wellbeing. I needed to fortify myself for the long, lean desertless times ahead. And I also wanted to evoke the memory of a place in the desert I had been over twenty years before, in that desert trip with Tanya and Chris the time when we had been *in* the dunes, instead of observing them, when I had disappeared into the landscape; when I could hear the music of the universe. I had brought the diary with me in which I had written about that time. And now, I sat on the terrace facing the dunes, drawn into them, evoking that previous experience, living it again as I opened the diary and read. And as I read, and as I remembered, I added another dimension to the profound desert impact:

Our pension is at the foot of Erg Chebbi, the field of sand dunes containing the highest dunes in Morocco. Before going to sleep, I step from the front door into the sand. Absolute stillness. I get caught up in the stars and the dark outline of dunes, so vivid in the stillness.

We wake at six. The sun not yet up but the sky is light and clear. I step into the stillness of desert with soundless steps. The sand is buff-coloured ripples, splashed with shadows. My shoes leave a 'Kikers' stamp in the sand. We don't speak, even a whisper would be an intrusion. The sky, the dunes, the space, the stillness are intimations of an eternity untouched. We are on the edge of the universe, on the edge of time.

We climb the tallest dune. Camels are still asleep in small huddles between the dunes. I am mesmerized as a great orange ball of sun nuzzles the horizon, turning the dunes pink and pale gold. I sit alone on the crest of the dune and watch the sun climb into the sky, turning everything into magic. A rooster crows. Song in the stillness intensifies the stillness. The French couple appear and sit with me. We nod in greeting. It doesn't seem right or even possible to speak. The silence is overwhelming, blissful. Easy to melt into the curves of sand, to fade into the blushes of colour. The sun is high in the sky. I take off my jacket, form it into a pillow and stretch out feeling the sand warm and soft as it shapes itself to my body.

Tanya is heading back – Chris following. Suddenly everyone is gone. I am alone with the desert. I am loath to leave, the aloneness connects me to the universe, blends me into it. I feel that 'baptism of solitude' the writer Paul Bowles experienced in the Moroccan desert. It is like a holy sacrament welcoming me into the universe. Perhaps this is the closest I will ever come to religion. Hours pass. Finally I rise to go. Difficult to walk in the sand – each step an effort, but the slowness, the effort, prolongs the desert.

And now, back in Marrakesh, the perfect silence is no more; the desert is no more. But that 'baptism of solitude' remains, a solitude that will be remembered in my blood stream, a solitude I can withdraw into forevermore. For once having been there, it will always be there. My imagination will guard it forever – because the imagination knows things, keeps things safe.

I paused a while before I shut the diary, allowing my spirit to follow my gaze deep into the dunes. I was lost in the desert; in the then, in the now. I was back in the dunes, back in the memories, living in this time enhanced by that time, by those times. Remembering Jimi Hendrix's grandmother's dress, orange like the setting sun; Bashir Tazi singing Leonard's *Suzanne* in the palace; the disappearing tent and sleeping in the sand. And suddenly I recalled Tibet and the wonder of Tashi and the mani stone – and especially of the Dalai Lama. I was at perfect peace. Slowly, I closed my eyes.

I must have dozed off because I didn't hear Addy come onto the terrace. When I opened my eyes he was sitting beside me; his presence seemed natural, part of the desert. There was no greeting, no words. The silence was the communication.

After minutes or maybe hours, Addy said: 'Nyeema,' pronouncing my name the Moroccan way, 'I would very much like you to write my story.' His voice was soft and did not intrude upon the stillness. 'It is a special story, you will like it very much.' He paused for a moment. 'It is the story of the nomad boy.' He seemed suddenly animated and looked at me intently, his eyes glowing.

The story of the nomad boy. His story. My story. Our story.

There was too much to say, so I said nothing. I was unravelling time.

But I sensed Addy waiting for an answer. Finally I said: 'Tell me a little about your story, Addy. I would like to hear more about the nomad boy.'

'No. I cannot tell you small pieces of the story. I must tell you the whole story from the start until now. It takes long time.'

'But I am leaving tomorrow, Addy.'

'But you must stay. If you stay I will tell you all the story, then you can write it.'

'I would love to stay. I love it here, you know that, but I cannot stay.'

'Why you cannot stay?'

'My friends are leaving tomorrow.'

'Why you cannot stay without your friends?'

'I must go with them, we are travelling together. We made a promise to each other. I cannot break my promise.'

Addy lowered his head, his face darkening. He was no longer animated. But Addy is a Berber. He understands about promises, about honour. I felt his disappointment. It sat heavy in the silence and refused to be swallowed by it.

I gazed into the dunes, into the folds of sand, the ripples, the cradles; oh, how I wanted to stay. And I said: 'Addy, I cannot stay now. But I promise you that one day soon I will return and nomad girl will write the story of nomad boy.'

Addy raised his head, his face like sunshine. I had promised. '*Inshalla*', he said, his voice sweet like honey.

God willing.

'*Inshalla*,' I repeated and reached for his hand.

God willing.

We embraced to seal the promise and the desert and the story.

Acknowledgements

I want to thank my dear friends Peter Batt and Mark Hoser from saving me from my rubbish computer skills. Special thanks to Peter who patiently quelled my panic and resurrected my manuscript each time it was swallowed by outer space. Thanks to my excellent editors, the lovely Sue Lascelles and the very busy Craig Taylor. Heartfelt thanks to my sister Gitte and friends Irina and Gerhard for being part of my story and my life. I also want to thank David Gwyther, I'm not sure why. And lastly, very special thanks to Addy, Nomad Boy.

 **Matador**

For exclusive discounts on Matador titles,
sign up to our occasional newsletter at
troubador.co.uk/bookshop